The Louisiana Purchase

In 1803, the United States purchased 828,000 square miles of land from France at a price of approximately three cents per acre, dramatically altering the young nation's geography and its political future. President Thomas Jefferson had struggled for three years over the purchase, which many believed to be unconstitutional, during which time the land changed hands between the French and the Spanish. In perhaps the nation's most formative development since the Revolutionary War, the deal secured the U.S. territory that would become fifteen new states, sparked intense public arguments about the American Frontier, and ensured Jefferson a complicated legacy in American history.

With special attention to the diplomatic and constitutional background of the purchase, *The Louisiana Purchase* examines the event in the context of the Atlantic world, including the impact of the French Revolution and Napoleonic wars in Europe, colonial revolutions in the Caribbean, and the westward expansion of the U.S. population. In five concise chapters bolstered by a selection of primary documents including treaties, letters, and first-hand observations, Robert D. Bush introduces students to the political history of this momentous land acquisition.

Robert D. Bush is an Instructor of History at Front Range Community College.

Critical Moments in American History

Edited by William Thomas Allison, Georgia Southern University

The Assassination of John F. Kennedy
Political Trauma and American Memory
Alice L. George

The Battle of the Greasy Grass/Little Bighorn
Custer's Last Stand in Memory, History, and Popular Culture
Debra Buchholtz

Freedom to Serve
Truman, Civil Rights, and Executive Order 9981
Jon E. Taylor

The Battles of Kings Mountain and Cowpens
The American Revolution in the Southern Backcountry
Melissa Walker

The Cuban Missile Crisis
The Threshold of Nuclear War
Alice L. George

The Nativist Movement in America
Religious Conflict in the 19th Century
Katie Oxx

The 1980 Presidential Election
Ronald Reagan and the Shaping of the American Conservative Movement
Jeffrey D. Howison

The Fort Pillow Massacre
North, South, and the Status of African-Americans in the Civil War Era
Bruce Tap

The Louisiana Purchase
A Global Context
Robert D. Bush

The Louisiana Purchase

A Global Context

Robert D. Bush

Routledge
Taylor & Francis Group

NEW YORK AND LONDON

First published 2014
by Routledge
711 Third Avenue, New York, NY 10017

and by Routledge
2 Park Square, Milton Park, Abingdon, Oxon OX14 4RN

Routledge is an imprint of the Taylor & Francis Group, an informa business

Library of Congress Cataloging in Publication Data
Bush, Robert D.
    The Louisiana Purchase: a global context/Robert D. Bush.
    pages cm.—(Critical moments in American history)
    Includes bibliographical references and index.
    1. Louisiana Purchase.   2. United States—Foreign relations—
    1801–1809.   3. France—Foreign relations—1792–1815.
    4. Spain—Foreign relations—18th century.   I. Title.
    E333.B875 2013
    973.4′6—dc23
    2013016469

ISBN: 978-0-415-81435-5 (hbk)
ISBN: 978-0-415-81457-7 (pbk)
ISBN: 978-0-203-06705-5 (ebk)

Typeset in Bembo and Helvetica Neue
by Florence Production Ltd, Stoodleigh, Devon, UK

Printed and bound in the United States of America by Publishers Graphics,
LLC on sustainably sourced paper.

Contents

Series Introduction

Welcome to the Routledge *Critical Moments in American History* series. The purpose of this new series is to give students a window into the historian's craft through concise, readable books by leading scholars, who bring together the best scholarship and engaging primary sources to explore a critical moment in the American past. In discovering the principal points of the story in these books, gaining a sense of historiography, following a fresh trail of primary documents, and exploring suggested readings, students can then set out on their own journey, to debate the ideas presented, interpret primary sources, and reach their own conclusions—just like the historian.

A critical moment in history can be a range of things—a pivotal year, the pinnacle of a movement or trend, or an important event such as the passage of a piece of legislation, an election, a court decision, a battle. It can be social, cultural, political, or economic. It can be heroic or tragic. Whatever they are, such moments are by definition "game changers," momentous changes in the pattern of the American fabric, paradigm shifts in the American experience. Many of the critical moments explored in this series are familiar; some less so.

There is no ultimate list of critical moments in American history— any group of students, historians, or other scholars may come up with a different catalog of topics. These differences of view, however, are what make history itself and the study of history so important and so fascinating. Therein can be found the utility of historical inquiry—to explore, to challenge, to understand, and to realize the legacy of the past through its influence of the present. It is the hope of this series to help students realize this intrinsic value of our past and of studying our past.

William Thomas Allison
Georgia Southern University

Figures

Acknowledgments

Prepared as a supplement to accompany any core texts for a History of the United States undergraduate course, this volume examines more than just square miles and acres acquired with "the greatest land deal in history." The focus rather is on the people and events that made this history happen, the "who? why? when?" and "where?" in history. The story involves both an introduction to primary documents and historical analysis. It incorporates a brief overview of the historiography of the Louisiana Purchase in global history. This volume therefore looks at what was happening in Europe, the West Indies, especially in Haiti, and how these events are reflected in both the domestic and foreign affairs of the United States. The study examines the positions of Britain, Spain and France regarding the Colony of Louisiana within their respective national and international interests during the years between 1800–1803, and their ever changing global priorities due to wartime conditions in Europe. Then, there was the momentous revolutionary events in the West Indies, which ultimately resulted in the independence of Haiti from France in 1804, and the impact of those events upon the future of Louisiana and the United States.

Among those who provided assistance and advice in the preparation of this volume, I want to recognize and thank several of my colleagues at Front Range Community College, Westminster, Colorado. Melissa Izzo, Reference/Instruction Librarian, College Hill Library provided excellent research tips and the use of the interlibrary loan services; Professor Bruce Nye, Lead Faculty, history, was supportive of the project, and along with several of my departmental colleagues, offered their advice; Professor Laurie Miller, Dean of Instruction assisted with the commitment to provide divisional support. Mike Hogan and the staff of Information Technology Center, helped a computer novice to apply the technology needed; and, the staff of the Faculty Support Center, whose daily assistance to those of us in the classroom makes the educational system work. The staff of The Historic New Orleans Collection were most helpful in providing research materials from their manuscript collections. Without the assistance of colleagues such as this, it would not have been possible to accomplish the task. I also wish to thank those colleagues who read the original proposal draft and offered their comments and suggestions. I would be remiss if I did not acknowledge Professor Noble E. Cunningham, Jr., who first introduced me as a young graduate student to the era of Mr. Jefferson. Finally, I want to thank my wife and family for their encouragement and support.

Robert D. Bush

Timeline

1762

Treaty of Fontainebleau. France cedes New Orleans and her colony of Louisiana, west of the Mississippi River, to Spain, her ally in the recent Seven Years' War, against Britain, and which ended the hostilities the following year in the Treaty of Paris.

1769

Spain takes control of Louisiana and New Orleans.

1783

Treaty of Paris. Britain recognized the independence of the United States, which included American's right of navigation on the Mississippi River.

1784

Spain sees the expansion of the United States as an imminent threat to her properties in Louisiana, and closes the Mississippi River to navigation and the right of deposit in New Orleans. This action produces outrage among the Americans in the western settlements, and results in numerous confrontations on the Mississippi River between American frontiersmen and Spanish officials.

1789

The French Revolution begins.

1793

The French Revolution turns bloody with the execution of King Louis XVI by the revolutionaries, and those loyal to monarchy; and then to war, when France declares war on England on February 1 and Spain on March 7 in Europe, prompting the United States to declare its neutrality on April 23.

1795

Because of European entanglements and war, again with Britain, Spain, which changed allies by deserting Britain in favor of France, is receptive to negotiations by Thomas Pinckney, the American Minister, and concedes free navigation of the Mississippi River, the right of Deposit in New Orleans and settlement of the northern border of the Floridas in the Pinckney Treaty in order to avoid potential hostilities with the United States. In the Treaty of Basel (July 22, 1795) Spain becomes an ally of France, and cedes her remaining two-thirds of the Island of Hispaniola (Santo Domingo) to France.

1797–1800

The United States and France enter a period of "quasi war" over American neutrality rights.

1799

On November 9–10, Napoleon Bonaparte seizes power in France.

1800

Napoleon's military victories in Italy against Austria (June) results in the redrawing of the political map; Spain is willing to trade—in return for her dynastic interests in Italy now occupied by France—she will retrocede her colony of Louisiana to France. The result is the secret Treaty of San Ildefonso (October 1, 1800).

1801	President Thomas Jefferson names Robert Livingston as United States Minister to France.
1802: April 18	Jefferson wrote to Livingston in Paris expressing his concern that "the day that France takes possession of New Orleans . . . From that moment, we must marry ourselves to the British fleet and nation."
1802: October 15	Spanish King Charles IV retrocedes Louisiana, per the Treaty of San Ildefonso, to France; Spanish Intendant Juan Ventura Morales in New Orleans closes the Mississippi River to Americans on October 16, and their right of deposit in New Orleans in violation of Article XXII of the Pinckney Treaty. This action produces an outcry in the United States, and even talk of secession or hostilities from frontiersmen in Kentucky, Tennessee and Ohio. Following peace with Britain in March, 1802, France plans for its Louisiana Expedition with funds, troops and colonial administration. But, the failure of French forces to pacify and suppress the slave revolt in Saint-Domingue (Haiti) results in reconsideration of the West Indies enterprise that included Louisiana.
1803	In January, Jefferson nominated James Monroe to join Robert Livingston in Paris with instructions to seek a solution from France on behalf of American interests, including purchase of New Orleans, and lands to the east. French Prefect Laussat departs France, as head of the advance party, to Louisiana in order to prepare for the arrival of the Louisiana Expedition's military forces.
1803: March–May	Britain mobilizes and prepares for war with France because of the latter's noncompliance with the terms of the Peace of Amiens signed in 1802.
1803	In March, Napoleon cancels the Louisiana Expedition; and, on April 10, he decided to sell Louisiana, and the next day, he instructs Foreign Minister Charles Maurice de Talleyrand-Perigord, and Minister of the Public Treasury, François Barbé-Marbois, to inform Livingston and Monroe that he is willing to sell all of Louisiana.
1803: March 26	French Prefect Laussat, his family, and staff arrive in New Orleans to prepare for the anticipated arrival of the French Expedition.
1803: April 30	The United States and France agree on a Louisiana Purchase price total of $15,000,000, which included two conventions to the treaty that settled monetary disputes between U.S. citizens and France stemming from the recent "quasi-war." The documents were formally signed on May 2, 1803.
1803: July 4	The Louisiana Purchase is officially announced in the United States, and President Jefferson calls for a special session of Congress to convene on October 17, 1803.
1803: August 18	Official dispatches from France inform Prefect Laussat in New Orleans of the Louisiana Purchase, and provide instructions on how he was to proceed.
1803: October 20	The Senate ratifies and the President signs the Treaty and two Conventions with France of April 30; then on October 28 and 29, the House of Representatives votes the appropriations with which to carry the Treaty and Conventions into effect. Legislation completed, with amendments, and signed by President Jefferson on November 10, 1803.
1803: November 30	French Prefect Laussat officially accepts Louisiana from Spain in New Orleans' ceremonies.
1803: December 20	American Commissioners William C.C. Claiborne and General James Wilkinson officially receive Louisiana on behalf of the United States from French Prefect Laussat in New Orleans.

1804: January 1	Haiti declares its independence from France.
1804: January 16	President Jefferson sends a message to Congress regarding the formal transfer of the Louisiana Territory to the United States from France, which includes a letter from William C.C. Claiborne and General James Wilkinson to Jefferson announcing the official transfer.
1804: March 26	After lengthy debate in the House and Senate, the final law is signed by President Jefferson, "An act erecting Louisiana into two Territories [Territory of Orleans and the District of Louisiana] and providing for the Temporary Government thereof." The Louisiana Purchase was now complete.

Preface

From Jamestown in 1607 to Appomattox Court House in 1865, three historic events defined, expanded and consolidated the nation of the United States of America. They are: the American Revolution, the Louisiana Purchase and the Civil War. The American Revolution established the ideas of liberty and self-determination. The Louisiana Purchase presented the opportunity and means for the expansion of liberty and simultaneously an unbounded national expansion of the United States' frontiers in which it might flourish. And, finally, the Civil War ensured that through preservation of the Union, both the first and the second events would be available for future generations of Americans.

A great deal of discussion regarding the first and the third of these events is found in most American history textbooks, often a chapter on each; but the second, the Louisiana Purchase, seldom receives more than a paragraph or two, and then discussion moves on to Lewis and Clark. This volume places the Louisiana Purchase in the history of the United States in relation to the other two events, as a volume in the *Critical Moments in American History* series. It discusses the events and significance of the Louisiana Purchase, 1800–1803, in American history, and examines the European diplomatic and global background that made it possible. It is important to understand the global connections and interrelationships of events during the early years of the American Republic, and the resulting events taken on both sides of the Atlantic. And, finally, to integrate international and American events against a backdrop of the political and social revolutions in Europe and the West Indies.

In the succeeding chapters, the political changes in possession of Louisiana are examined and the reasons for them: France to Spain in 1762, Spain back to France in 1800, and finally from France to the United States in 1803. Discussion focuses on the global political, economic, and social ramifications that led to such changes, the debates among participants, and the position on the issue of acquiring Louisiana for the United States from the standpoint of the two American political parties, the Federalists and the Democratic Republicans. The major issue for America's future was access or no access to the Gulf of Mexico by the ever expanding United States on its southern and western frontiers, and, the critical issues of local interests for the states and territories in the south and west with regard to navigation rights on the Mississippi River and at New Orleans. The Louisiana Purchase was not simply a land deal. It was about the inter-relationships between America's institutions and the potential for the future of the nation and her people globally.

On April 18, 1802, President Jefferson wrote to Robert Livingston, the American Minister to France: "Every eye in the U.S. is now fixed on this affair of Louisiana. Perhaps nothing since the revolutionary war has produced more uneasy sensations through the body of the nation."[1] A "Critical Moment in American history" had arrived. It was not just a "critical moment" in American history, but also a transforming one. American global diplomacy would evolve from "reactive" to European actions (i.e. Jay's Treaty, and the notorious XYZ Affair) to "proactive" American initiatives (i.e. the Rush-Bagot Convention, the Adams-Onis Treaty, and the Monroe Doctrine). The debates in Congress between the two political parties on constitutional issues either reinforced existing legal precedents or established new ones. When the rumor of an impending transfer of Louisiana from Spain, the current possessor, to France reached the United States in 1801, it set off a flurry of domestic and foreign activity. After the global experiences of 1800–1803, nothing in American domestic and foreign affairs would ever be the same again. At the time Thomas Jefferson assumed the presidency in 1801, America's western boundary was the Mississippi River. When he left office in 1809, her boundary claims ended at the Pacific Ocean. But to understand the magnitude of this event it is necessary to look at what was happening elsewhere.

Spain acquired the colony of Louisiana in 1762, but did not attempt to administer it until 1766, and then did so only halfheartedly, which led to a local uprising by some of the French inhabitants. The Spanish governor fled, but when Spanish officials returned in August, 1769, it was with an occupation force of twenty ships and over two thousand troops. Spain's introduction to the colony of Louisiana was based on her conquest of a foreign property, and it was not pleasant—neither was it for those inhabitants who participated in the revolt. Six Louisiana leaders of the revolt were executed, and others had their property confiscated. The year 1769, the bloody repression of the revolt, and its consequences poisoned Spanish-Louisiana relations for years.

Tensions between Spain and the United States begin to mount in the West when Spain closed New Orleans to all but Spanish inhabitants and vessels in 1784. For Spain, possession of Louisiana had but one purpose: to serve as a buffer zone between the Anglo-American settlements and Mexico. However, the ever-expanding American frontier, with its need for a commercial and communications outlet to the sea, placed the Mississippi River and New Orleans squarely between them as a source of contention. Frequent incidents, between 1785 and 1795, led to a political solution in 1795, which was necessary for Spain because of events in Europe. After 1795, the commercial intercourse between Louisiana and the western states or territories, became a point of national importance to the United States Government. When he became President in 1801, Jefferson believed that Spain's "feeble state" as a world power would ultimately lead to America's advantage in the area. In a letter to Robert R. Livingston (American Minister to France) in April, 1802, regarding Spain's decline, he concluded: "It would not perhaps be very long before some circumstance which might make the cession of it to us the price of something of more worth to her."[2] The story of the Louisiana Purchase therefore begins with Spain's possession of the colony and her policies on: community relations, international affairs, taxes, property management, relations with the Indians, and general administration from 1769–1803. For Spain, a global reassessment of her colonial interests was a necessity; for the United States, it was an unparalleled opportunity.[3] The French Revolution in 1789, and the wars it generated after 1793 changed everything for Spain, France, Britain, the United States, and the West Indies. And, in the process, the colony of Louisiana as well.

The Louisiana Purchase of 1803 is therefore a "critical moment in American history" that transformed the United States. The land mass of Louisiana acquired in 1803 made up in whole or in part of fifteen future states between the Mississippi River and the Rocky Mountains. This volume brings together primary documents for students to see the interests of many different participants, to understand the sequence of events through a discussion of the historiography from contemporaries, and to consider what might have happened if Louisiana had remained in the possession of a European power. By combining a timeline, documents, diplomatic treaties, personal memoires, the debates recorded in the *Annals of Congress*, and interpretations by historians, history will unfold and illustrate why the Louisiana Purchase was a "critical moment in American history." President Jefferson provided the leadership, vision, and confidence to trust in the judgment of others.

CHAPTER 1

The Louisiana Purchase

A Global Context, Background

Prepared as a supplement to accompany any general textbook on a History of the United States undergraduate course, the focus of this volume is on the people and events that made it happen, and it provides in the narrative both an introduction to primary documents and historical analysis. It incorporates a brief overview of the historiography of the Louisiana Purchase in American history. Spain and France's positions regarding the future of Louisiana are contrasted with their European and global priorities. But, what exactly was this colony of Louisiana?

Louisiana was of little importance as a European colonial possession on its own. This was due to the fact that so little was known about it. Maps of Louisiana were mainly drawn based upon geographical, historical and topographical speculations. French cartographers, with information from explorers in the southern areas of the colony, missionaries or fur traders from Canada, and friendly Indians provided little in the way of exact details of the area; oftentimes these details were, however, conflicting. This was particularly the case for the boundaries between Canada and New France, then Spanish, Louisiana. The sheer physical size of the colony inhibited travel and exploration. The first major break-through in knowledge regarding the history of New France, or Louisiana, came in 1744 with the publication of Father Pierre François Xavier de Charlevoix's (1682–1758) *Journal of a Voyage to North America.*[4] Translated into English in 1746, and 1776, the latter edition was a common reference on book shelves in Britain and the American colonies. Thomas Jefferson owned a copy of Charlevoix's *Journal* in his personal library at his home in Monticello. The *Journal* included descriptions of outposts, relations with the Indian tribes, limited travel routes—both overland and by water—and a history of France's explorations from Canada inland, and up and down the Mississippi River from New Orleans. Because he traveled both in

Canada and Louisiana, Father Charlevoix's descriptions were widely considered the most authoritative. Based on such travel accounts, Jacques Nicholas Bellin, an engineer for the French Navy and to the King of France, drew his map: "Carte de la Louisiane cours du Mississippi et Pais voisins" in 1744, and his "Carte Reduite des costes de la Louisiane et de la Floride," in 1764. Bellin's maps were designed to show French possessions that included the Great Lakes and the Ohio Valley and all the land drained by waters flowing into the Mississippi River and therefore the entire valley.

A second French source of information about Louisiana was that by Antoine Simon Le Page du Pratz (c.1695–1775), *The History of Louisiana*, three volumes, published in 1758 in French as a travel account from his personal observations (1718–1734), and translated into English in 1774.[5] Prophetically, Le Page du Pratz described the Mississippi River and New Orleans:

> It is without reason then, that we say, whoever are possessed of this river, and the vast tracts of fertile lands upon it, must in time command that continent, and the trade of it, as well as all the natives in it, by the supplies which this navigation will enable them to furnish those people.[6]

Le Page du Pratz's work provided descriptions of the topography, fauna and flora, settlements, and Indian tribes—especially the customs, lifestyle, and politics among Natchez Indians, with whom he lived for eight years. After the Natchez massacred several French settlers in 1729, he returned to France in 1731. But despite these travel accounts and others from the eighteenth century, no one really knew what existed beyond the immediate areas along and west of the Mississippi; and, more importantly, no one cared when these lands passed from France into the Spanish global empire in 1762. Being uncharted and unexplored, the colony of Louisiana was regarded as a vast wasteland of no value; the only exception was New Orleans as a commercial entrepôt for trade on the Mississippi River.

The events of the French and Indian War (1756–1763) altered western land claims. France's defeat at the Battle of Quebec (1759) ended French control, which now passed to Britain. However, prior to the Treaty of Paris, which ended the war in 1763, France had secretly ceded her colony of Louisiana to her wartime ally Spain. By the terms of the 1763 Treaty Britain retained Canada, plus former claims by France to any of the lands east of the Mississippi River. But, per the secret Treaty of Fontainebleu (1762), Spain received from France possession of all lands west of the Mississippi River, including the "Isle of Orleans." This division of lands, based on the Mississippi River as the dividing line, in 1763 created the geographical and political demarcations for the future as well. The Mississippi River therefore became the focus of European colonial empires between Britain and Spain, both of whom retained navigation rights on the river.

However, British navigation rights were hindered by Spanish control of New Orleans as the only port with an outlet to the sea. In the Treaty of Paris (1783), which granted independence to the American colonies, the United States received from Britain this same right of navigation on the Mississippi, and inherited the same problem—no access to the sea because of Spanish control at the Isle of Orleans. The stage was therefore set for future disagreement between Spain and the United States.

> Per the Treaty of Paris of 1763, Britain originally divided Spanish Florida into East Florida and West Florida in 1764 at the Apalachicola River from which East Florida extended to the Atlantic. West Florida extended from the Apalachicola and Chattahoochee Rivers to the Mississippi, which included Baton Rouge, Mobile, Natchez and Pensacola.

The British had not seen fit to challenge the transfer of New France to Spain at the Paris treaty negotiations; she was content to establish a Proclamation Line in 1763 between the Alleghenies and Mississippi that in theory was to restrict colonists from further intrusions into Indian lands, and reserve them for Indians as one way to maintain peace on the frontier. Further west, beyond the Mississippi River, Spanish Louisiana was seen as a vast wasteland, destitute of settlements, occupied by warring Indians, and for Spain, this was ideal in that no one would want it and therefore not initiate actions to take it. Don Manuel de Godoy (1767–1851), Prime Minister, 1801–1807, to King Carlos IV (1748–1919) of Spain, later concluded regarding Louisiana: "Almost all is yet to be done, just a sprout of life on those unpopulated regions."[7] Such a view of Louisiana dominated official Spanish thinking and planning, and therefore it was an ideal pawn to be traded for something somewhere else.

Spain's global empire stretched from the Viceroyalty of New Spain (Mexico, Texas to California, Cuba as well as the Caribbean and Central America) in the Western Hemisphere and to the Philippines and her other islands in the Pacific. But, Spain's empire was in decline due to the global challenges from Britain, the Netherlands, and for a while, France. For the province of Louisiana, however, it is necessary to examine the forty years (1762–1803) of Spain's possession, and concurrently her continued decline as a global power. In contrast to Spain, France—dominant on the Continent of Europe after 1795—administered Louisiana for only twenty days, November 30–December 20, 1803! And yet, the last two years

(1802–1803) of this Franco-Spanish dealing prior to Louisiana's acquisition by the United States were the most dangerous and global in the potential for hostilities. France, on her part, was caught up in revolution at home after 1789, and in her West Indies colonies after 1791. She faced a coalition of nations against her, including Austria, Britain, and Spain, engaged in a European war in 1793. By 1795, however, France's military power had grown to the point that it forced Spain to switch her alliance from Britain to France, and so too was France's new appetite for global expansion in Syria, Egypt, and the West Indies.[8]

In the United States, President Washington proclaimed America's neutrality from the hostilities in Europe on April 23, 1793. It is therefore on this stage of global interests and events that the fate of Louisiana must be considered within the interrelationships between European and Western Hemisphere affairs.

Once again, events in Europe entered American politics. The catalyst for global events from 1791–1803 was the French Revolution with its national repercussions in Europe, the West Indies and America, and resulting international conflicts spawned by it. The French Revolution in 1789 and European wars after 1793 might have easily led the United States into war with Great Britain. Ultimately American neutrality did lead to a period of quasi-war (1797–1800) between the United States and France on the high seas over the American claim of the rights of neutrals. Within the United States, the impacts of the French Revolution included pro-French clubs, political debates on the events in France as reported in local newspapers, agitation and intrigue by a French emissary in Kentucky, and an increasing political hostility from those conservatives in the United States who saw only chaos in the beheading of the French king in 1793, and its resulting civil and international war attributed to the rule of the mob.

In American political circles, factions who either opposed it, or supported it, became part of the nucleus for two definable political parties by 1796 elections—the old guard conservative (Presidents Washington and then Adams) Federalists, and the new (Jeffersonian) Democratic Republicans. Emerging out of the intense national debate over the new Constitution, and the government it created, two political ideologies emerged and vied for public support. In the first national elections of 1788, those who had supported the Constitution, the original Federalists, as opposed to their opponents—the Anti-Federalists, dominated not only the executive in the persons of President George

> A history of the Louisiana Purchase constitutes an excellent study laboratory for the interrelationships in American domestic politics and global affairs during the critical years between 1800–1803.

Washington and Vice-President John Adams, but also the House of Representatives and the Senate. Their political agenda was predicated upon their clearly perceived need for a new strong national government, which included the idea of the natural right of the county to enlarge its borders, and in the process under the new Constitution to replace the weaknesses of the old Articles of Confederation. The Constitution said nothing about territorial expansion of the nation. In one of their first legislative actions, the Federalists passed the Judiciary Act of 1789, creating a district court in each state along with circuit courts and the Supreme Court of the United States. The Federalist party manager was not, however, President Washington, but his secretary of the treasury, Alexander Hamilton. No one personified the conservative outlook, which would be built into the Federalist camp, better than Hamilton did. His fiscal policies emerged in his reports to Congress on the public credit, the national bank and manufacturing between 1790–1791. Such initiatives outlined his mechanisms for establishing a national program. Hamilton's political and fiscal conservatism looked to English models, especially with his Bank of the United States patterned after that of the Bank of England. The need for credit in order to stimulate trade required confidence on the part of those with wealth to invest, and therefore through implementation of Hamiltonian policies, the Federalists became identified as the political party of the wealthy, bankers, merchants from the east coast cities, and those with international ties to Great Britain. By early 1791, some of those in government, who had originally feared the powers entrusted to a strong national government under the new Constitution, and to those persons with personal interests in government, became more vocal. Among them, was Secretary of State Thomas Jefferson, and, in the House, James Madison. The chartering of Hamilton's National Bank was the test case. Jefferson opposed it on the grounds that it was unconstitutional; Hamilton brilliantly argued that the power to tax and raise revenue, which were stipulated in the Constitution, necessitated a means to manage federal revenues. Therefore, he cited Article 1, Section 8, or the "implied powers" provision, which permitted Congress to make "all laws which shall be necessary and proper" to implement the Constitution. A Bank of the United States was "necessary and proper" in Hamilton's view, and President Washington agreed with him and signed the bill. Slowly, but inevitably, two political factions emerged on the American political scene with divergent views on the role of government under the Constitution, fiscal policy that included taxes along with the national debt, and international affairs. Two events turned these factions into American political parties: (1) the French Revolution after 1793; and (2) Jay's Treaty in 1795.

> "All revolutions since 1800, in Europe, Latin America, Asia, and Africa, have learned from the eighteenth-century [1760–1800] Revolution of Western Civilization. They have been inspired by its successes, echoed its ideals, used its methods."
>
> R.R. Palmer, *The Age of the Democratic Revolution*

The French Revolution began in 1789, and news of the events there were generally seen in the United States as a positive step toward human progress by ending the old corrupt regime built upon privilege. But, by 1790–1791, views changed; and, on April 20, 1792, France declared war on Austria, in August King Louis XVI was placed under house arrest, and in September France abolished the monarchy and declared itself a "republic." In December the King was tried for treason, and executed on January 21, 1793. Shortly thereafter, came French declarations of war against England (February 1), and Spain (March 7). In the United States, these events, along with revolutionary activities among the slaves in the French colony of Haiti after 1791, combined to divide Americans into pro-French or anti-French factions. President Washington, Vice President Adams, and Alexander Hamilton as conservative Federalists could not support the social, political and international chaos that suddenly arrived on American shores due to events in Europe. President Washington responded with the declaration of American neutrality on April 23. The problem with neutrality, however, is you have to have the means with which to enforce it against the combatants. In this regard, the United States was woefully short, since the British navy ruled the seas. As the greatest maritime power in the world, Britain began to stop American vessels at sea in order to search them for cargoes destined for French ports, or coming back to the United States from the French West Indies. Given the choices, President Washington and his Federalist government had no alternative but to seek some sort of accommodation with Britain; and, Secretary Hamilton was already known for his pro-British position. It was amidst this climate, Secretary of State Jefferson resigned from Washington's administration in 1793.[9] President Washington's dilemma was how to remain "neutral" while seeking relief from the Royal Navy, which by 1795 had already impounded over 200 American vessels. From the Federalist point of view, such events were the result of radical French actions. Once again, Secretary Hamilton had a solution. Washington appointed John Jay, Federalist Chief Justice, to go to London with instructions, drawn up by Hamilton, to negotiate a maritime treaty for the relief of American shipping interests.

John Jay was successful. The result of his negotiations with his English counterpart William Grenville was signed as a "Treaty of Amity,

Commerce and Navigation" on November 19, 1794. In its provisions, England agreed to withdraw its remaining troops from the Northwest Territory, which it had originally agreed to do in 1783, and to arbitrate the lingering issue of U.S. Canadian boundaries and war debts owed to British citizens since the American Revolution. The British agreed to compensate American ship owners for their losses, and in return, the United States recognized Britain with "most favored nation" status for trade concessions and the right of its naval vessels to enter U.S. ports. On its part, Britain obtained substantial trade concessions, and, most importantly, the continued neutrality of the United States, which would insure that any pro-French activities would be avoided for the duration of the European war. Jay's Treaty, as it became known in the United States, was submitted to the United States Senate in June, 1795. It immediately encountered opposition from Jefferson, Madison, and their supporters. Quite simply, anything that supported trade concessions to Great Britain was seen as another example of the pro-British foreign policy of the Federalists. By now, the Jeffersonian "republicans" had seen enough of Federalist policies, which they labeled as "aristocratic" and even "monarchical" based upon an overindulgence to moneyed American and British interests. In the American west, the treaty with Britain was seen as coming too late because of English traders and army officers from Canada and their alleged support to Indians in the Northwest Territory. In the southern states, while Jay had secured compensation for shippers in the northeast, he had not gotten similar compensation for those slaves that had been taken away by the British during the American Revolution. For the Jeffersonians, now becoming a distinct political party, Jay's Treaty was the centerpiece of everything they detested among the Federalists' control of government. The treaty was ratified in the Federalist dominated Senate by the two-thirds majority it needed in August, 1795, and President Washington signed it. Jay's Treaty went into effect on February 29, 1796, which was an election year. And, in the election campaigns, it became the Democratic Republican rallying cry for opposition to the Federalist candidates; for the Federalists, it was portrayed as securing peace with Britain, increasing American trade, and resolving the long-standing border issues with Britain in Canada. In addition, the international repercussions of Jay's Treaty in Europe were to profoundly impact the United States. Spain immediately viewed it as the precursor of an Anglo-American alliance, which was to be avoided at all costs, in order to protect Mexico. Jay's Treaty was the immediate cause for Spain to undertake negotiations with the United States over issues in the west, i.e. navigation on the Mississippi River and the Floridas borders. France also regarded it as a clear shift from American "neutrality" to a pro-British foreign policy, and interpreted it as an abandonment of the 1778 Treaty of "Amity and Commerce" between the United States and France.[10] She therefore began to license French privateers, vessels sailing under "letters of marque", to act as warships, which therefore authorized them to seize American ships trading with Britain as a counterbalance to the Royal Navy. American shippers soon paid the price in millions of dollars worth of cargoes lost to French privateers.

In the national elections held in 1796, the Federalists chose John Adams of Massachusetts, and Thomas Pinckney of South Carolina; Thomas Jefferson of Virginia was selected to run for the Democratic Republicans, along with Aaron Burr of New York. In the election, which was one of the most contentious in American history, Adams won 71 electoral votes, Jefferson came in second with 68, Pinckney won 59, and Burr with 30. Now (March, 1797), it was up to President John Adams to deal with both national problems in the west and south, and international affairs under these circumstances.

One of President Adams' diplomatic priorities was to resolve issues with France, which by 1797 had gone from bad to worse. He dispatched an American Commission (Federalists John Marshall, Elbridge Gerry and Charles C. Pinckney) to France in an effort to settle the "quasi-war" at sea. The Americans were informed that in order to have an audience with French Minister of Foreign Affairs Talleyrand, they were expected to pay a diplomatic gift of money to three French agents, who would later be labeled in the report to Congress from President Adams as "X, Y and Z." When President Adams reported on the situation to Congress, Federalists immediately took the opportunity to vent their anger against France, and Secretary of State Timothy Pickering even demanded war. Congress responded in 1798 and authorized American privateers to seize French ships and cargoes, but stopped short of an official declaration of war. By July, Franco-American relations were at the lowest ebb in history. In opposition to France's seizures of American shipping, and with Congressional authorization, President Adams saw the opportunities (1798–1800) to both retaliate against the French for their seizure of American shipping, and extend American commercial activities by trade with the rebels in French Saint-Domingue.[11] Accordingly, the United States signed a commercial treaty with the rebels and supplied them with a variety of supplies, including guns and ammunition. Britain also had a commercial treaty with the rebels, and for the same reason—to undermine French power in the Caribbean since they were already at war.

In domestic affairs, the Federalist-dominated Congress moved to meet the threats of a possible foreign intervention in American affairs and authorized an increase in the regular army; and, it passed in 1798 the Alien and Sedition Acts. This action, particularly the Sedition Act, was regarded by Democratic Republicans as an effort to silence any political opposition; and they responded to it in November, 1798, with the Kentucky Resolutions, authored by Jefferson, and the Virginia Resolutions, authored by Madison, both of which challenged the application of federal laws that were deemed "unconstitutional" by action taken in a state legislature. Fortunately, President Adams, who preferred diplomacy to war, received word in 1799 from France that if the United States were to send another delegation, it would be favorably received. He did so, and to his credit, President Adams ended the "quasi-war" with France by the Convention of 1800, signed on September 30, 1800. France agreed to settle claims for American shipping losses in return for the United States agreement to halt its commercial activities with the rebels in Haiti. France was now under the control of Napoleon Bonaparte, who needed peace to consolidate his power.

In France, which retained some degree of nostalgia for its former colony (1718–1762), during these years between 1795 and 1800, Louisiana became part of a larger dream under its new revolutionary leadership after 1799. Especially with the rise of Napoleon Bonaparte (1769–1821), who, along with several others, such as Charles Maurice de Talleyrand-Perigord (1754–1838), French Minister of Foreign Relations, dreamed of reestablishing a French global empire. The West Indies enterprise, creation of a colonial empire with colonies in Guadalupe, Martinique, and Saint-Domingue (Haiti), required a source of raw materials not existing in the islands. Such raw materials were known to be plentiful in Louisiana—forest products, food supplies, and potential markets for the products of the West Indies in turn. At last, the Colony of Louisiana had some importance, not the least of which was the political prestige it carried with it in the rebuilding of France while enhancing the career of Bonaparte. Finally, how better to put an arrogant Britain in its place than to have a French imperial system in her Atlantic back yard. What made these dreams a possibility were the French military successes from 1795–1800 in Europe. Properties in Europe and the Western Hemisphere became pawns in the game of global politics and the reshuffling of empires.

The rise of Napoleon Bonaparte with his *coup d'état* of 9–10 November, 1799, and his new title of First Consul of the French Republic, along with brilliant military victories over the Austrians in Italy in 1800 changed the life of France as a nation, and also thereby the map of Europe. He had imperialistic designs for France in Syria, Egypt and the Ottoman Empire from 1797–1800, and then the West Indies. Napoleon was an upstart. He was not born in France, but on the Island of Corsica. Certainly his military exploits, or those French successes that were deliberately attributed to him, played a role in his rise to power. But, the one thing he lacked was legitimacy. He needed to keep his political career ball rolling, and therefore exploits in the Middle East, the planning for a resurrection of the French global empire in the Western Hemisphere, and restructuring of political affairs in France and Europe were all part of his plan to keep himself in the public eye. Revolutions have a nasty habit of devouring their young, and emerging from the Reign of Terror in 1794–1795, the new constitution for the French Republic in 1795 promised stability and order at home after elimination of the radicals. Changes again came in 1797 along with French military successes; finally, Napoleon assumed power by his overthrow of the existing power structure, the Directory, 1799. The treaty (Concordat) he concluded with Pope Pius VII (July 16, 1801), restored relations between the Gallican (French Catholic) Church and Rome that added yet another laurel along this path. Among Napoleon's designs for the future was the need to eliminate obstacles, and one of these was the "quasi-war" with the United States, which if it persisted would drive the Americans into the British orbit. These efforts and his military accomplishments led directly to political changes in Europe, the Middle East, North America by 1803 and the West Indies in 1804. It is therefore to the individual participant nations and their global priorities that one must turn. In this process, the colony of Louisiana suddenly had a new life expectancy and role to play.

In 1795, the "Mississippi Question" and access to New Orleans directly involved only Spain and the United States. But with the events of a secret treaty between Spain and France in 1800, the status of Louisiana entered the picture against both a European background, and connections to the West Indies. Spain, which possessed Louisiana from 1762 to 1803, secretly retroceded Louisiana to France in 1800, from whom she had received it in 1762. By 1800, France had the most powerful army in Europe, and dreams of reestablishing a new global empire.

The election of Thomas Jefferson as President in 1800, the contest over the election itself in the House of Representatives between himself and Aaron Burr in 1801, had hardly been completed and domestic issues begun when events in Europe suddenly took precedence. Rumors of the retrocession reached the United States in 1801, and created a host of new and challenging issues. Once Spain retroceded Louisiana to France in return for dynastic interests in Italy, on October 1, 1800, the picture changed immediately for America, and for President Jefferson. The Louisiana Purchase, in retrospect, was a product of revolutionary events that began in Europe, but soon spilled over into the West Indies and the United States.

Whoever controlled the mouth of the Mississippi River controlled the entire valley and lands that drained from it. Global politics arrived on

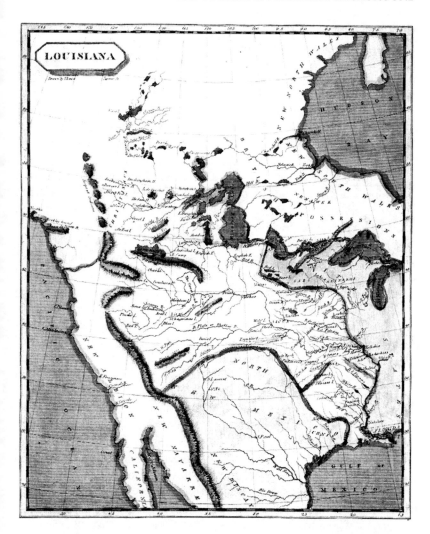

Figure 1.1 Louisiana 1804. Map of the Louisiana Purchase ("Louisiana"), by Samuel Lewis and Aaron Arrowsmith. This map was the formative attempt to portray the Louisiana Purchase prior to publication of Lewis and Clark's maps in 1814, and utilized sketches of the upper Missouri and Mississippi basins, which were originally drawn in 1795 by a French engineer, Pierre Antoine Soulard. It was the first attempt to portray the extent of the area in the decade before Lewis and Clark's map, and originally printed in their *New and Elegant General Atlas*, Philadelphia, 1804. Courtesy of The Historic New Orleans Collection.

America's doorstep with a huge thud![12] The issue of freedom of navigation on the Mississippi and an American right of deposit, whether at New Orleans or some other location (such as Mobile) on the Gulf of Mexico, was debated in the legislatures of several American states and territories, in the press, within the federal administration, and by members of Congress from both Federalist and Democratic Republican political parties. Thus the discussion of this event considers commercial, military, political and social events in a global setting, as well as the interests of Louisiana citizens and Americans.

With some ideological misgivings, and not wishing to be pushed into a possible war with France by boatloads of frontiersmen descending upon New Orleans in 1802, seeking to protect what they regarded as their interests, President Jefferson decided to respond with urgent diplomatic efforts.[13] He had previously appointed Robert E. Livingston of New York as Minister to France. He now added James Monroe, currently the Governor of Virginia, to the diplomatic team to negotiate with the French. These men were added in addition by James Madison in his capacity as Secretary of State. The United States diplomats included President Jefferson, and two future Presidents, Madison and Monroe. Jefferson and Madison, as Secretary of State, met with European representatives posted in Washington, and corresponded with American ministers in France (Robert E. Livingston), Great Britain (Rufus King) and Spain (Charles Pinckney) on the impending retrocession of Louisiana from Spain to France throughout 1802. The problem for the United States was that neither Spain nor France would admit to the existence of their secret treaty of 1800, and denials from both countries left American diplomats in a quandary. President Jefferson was as well-informed on the issues as anyone in those days could have been. He had extensive political experience both in Virginia and then in Congress, where he had been the principal author of the American land ordinances of 1784; and therefore, he had an intimate understanding of western expansionism. Americans who moved into the western territories did so per the provisions of the Northwest Ordinance of 1787, and in a pattern of settlement that would dominate the first half of the nineteenth century.[14] By contrast, Spanish Louisiana operated under an administrative and legal system that essentially began with Hernando Cortez in Mexico and had been modified and extended throughout the Indies. Spain granted royal land grants to individuals because in theory all property belonged to the crown, and such grants were done in accordance with the laws of Spain (Castile) and the Indies.[15] The two systems of property ownership and the rights of their owners could not have been more different. These differences in property ownership, fundamental to the populations in the two areas, along with the form of royal government that administered them, were bound to collide. Jefferson understood the importance of the magnitude of issues facing him as President; the United States must address the needs of Americans moving to the frontier in ever-increasing numbers and negotiate with European powers. His objective was resolution of national, commercial, and political interests on the western and southern frontiers, during an era of continual change and, with it, unrest and even the possibility of war that might involve the United States.[16] By the spring of 1803, because of the possible resumption of hostilities in Europe, it was, therefore, clear to him that it was action now or never.

The issue after October of 1802 was therefore no longer just the revoking of American commercial "rights" in New Orleans by an overzealous and ambitious Spanish Intendant in New Orleans, but rather the bigger problem was American interests and political unrest throughout the west and south. Rumors of unilateral military action by frontiersmen marching on New Orleans were widely circulated in the press and in conversation. Jefferson's most immediate concern, however, by the end of 1802 and into spring, 1803, was the question of French intentions. From December, 1802, to April of 1803, the diplomatic and political crisis in the United States focused on the known planning for a French military expedition that was preparing for departure to New Orleans. It was the combination of these events, and the distinct possibility that if France did send a military expedition to Louisiana, hostilities between the United States and France would be inevitable. Unlike the lingering presence of a "feeble" Spain, as Jefferson called her, on the Mississippi and in New Orleans, France by 1802 possessed the most powerful professional army in the world. Therefore, the very presence of a French military force in North America meant an alliance with Britain would be a necessity. In his letter of April 18, 1802, Jefferson put it bluntly:

> There is on the globe one single spot, the possessor of which is our natural and habitual enemy. It is New Orleans, through which the produce of three-eighths of our territory must pass to market, and from its fertility it will ere long yield more than half of our whole produce, and contain more than half of our inhabitants. France, placing herself in that door, assumes to us the attitude of defiance.[17]

This event would substantiate the arguments by the Federalists, Jefferson's political opposition, that Britain alone was America's only reliable ally. A war with France, and an alliance with Britain, could destroy his Democratic Republican Party, and any chance for Jefferson's reelection as President in 1804. Domestic politics and foreign affairs were intertwined, and President Jefferson took every step with the greatest caution and calculation.

CHAPTER 2

Louisiana in Spanish Global Policy, 1762–1802

On November 5, 1762, France ceded the "island" of New Orleans and all of her colony of Louisiana west of the Mississippi River to Spain, her recent ally against Britain. France's King Louis XV and Spain's King Carlos III were cousins, and France had attempted first to lure Spain into the war against Britain in 1761, which included offering Louisiana as an incentive. But this offer met with no success. However, early in 1762, Britain got word of the "Family Compact" between France and Spain, and declared war on Spain. But it was now too late to save the situation for France. Having lost Canada to British troops in 1759, during the "French and Indian War," and with British forces attacking Spanish colonies almost at will from the Philippines to Cuba, it was time for peace talks before the whole Spanish global empire would be in a shambles. France ceded her Colony of Louisiana in 1762 to her wartime ally Spain in order to prevent the British from claiming it at the peace talks in Paris in 1763. In the Treaty of Fontainebleau (1762) Spain became the new possessor of the lands west of the Mississippi River from the Gulf of Mexico in the south to Canada in the north, and to the Rocky Mountains in the west. In the Treaty of Paris, which ended the war a year later, Britain retained East and West Florida, but returned Manila and Havana to Spain. The huge area of Louisiana west of the Mississippi, which Spain had just acquired from France, she believed, would therefore provide a necessary buffer zone between Mexico, the crown jewel in Spain's empire, and the British colonies east of the Mississippi and Canada to the north. The history of the Louisiana Purchase begins with Spanish acquisition of the colony in 1762, and her administration in the Mississippi Valley after 1769 that placed her squarely in the path of the expanding English colonies and then the United States during a period of the next forty years until 1803.[18]

The real contest for global dominance in the seventeenth and eighteenth centuries was between developing Britain and a declining Spain; this competition stretched from the Caribbean to the far reaches of the Pacific.[19] Only because of the vastness of North America had France been able to enter the global pursuit for colonies, in Canada (Quebec in 1608), and Louisiana (in 1718). The first Spanish governor for Louisiana, Don Antonio de Ulloa (1716–1795) did not arrive in the colony until March, 1766. Since the colony was not regarded as a major acquisition by Spain, Ulloa, a naval officer, was ill-prepared to take control because he lacked the troops, ships and funds necessary to do so.

> Spain reluctantly accepted the colony of Louisiana from France in 1762 because she could ill afford to allow it fall into the hands of the Anglo-Americans which would have placed them on the doorstep of Texas and within striking distance of Mexico.

From the beginning, Spain's administration got bogged down in mismanagement and quarrels with the remaining French officials, and the local population. A group of the population finally rose in revolt in 1768 after it appeared that Ulloa was totally out of his element. Frustrated with the hostility of the local French population, devoid of the necessary instruments of power that had not been provided to him, Ulloa simply left New Orleans and retired to the fort at La Balise, at the mouth of the Mississippi, and from there took refuge aboard a French ship.[20] As a result of these actions, for Louisiana's French inhabitants things went from bad to worse. Spanish authority had been flagrantly disobeyed. The news of Ulloa's plight reached the Captain General of Cuba, under whose

Spanish Governors of Louisiana

Spanish Governors of Louisiana, 1766–1803:
Antonio de Ulloa, 1766–1768
Alexander O'Reilly, 1769
Luis de Unzaga, 1769–1777
Bernardo de Galvez, 1777–1785
Estevan Rodrigues Miro, 1785-1791
Francisco Luis Hector, Baron de Carondelet, 1792–1797
Manuel Luis Gayoso de Lemos, 1797–1799
Sebastian de la Puesta y O'Farrill, Marques de Casa-Calvo, 1799–1801
Juan Manuel de Salcedo, 1801–1803

administration the province of Louisiana was entrusted by the government in Spain. Rebellion anywhere in the Spanish empire was a serious matter. Spain's response was not long in coming in the person of Don Alejandro O'Reilly, Inspector General of the Army.[21] Because of delays in Europe and the local anti-Spanish feelings in New Orleans, Spanish possession of Louisiana did not take place until August 18, 1769. O'Reilly arrived first in Cuba, and with orders from King Carlos III to:

> organize the proper number of soldiers and ammunition and other supplies which you feel are necessary, and that after having taken possession of it [Louisiana] in my Royal Name, you make formal charges and punish according to the law, the instigators and accomplices of the uprising which occurred in New Orleans.[22]

Ultimately, Spanish authority, imposed by O'Reilly with over 2,000 Spanish troops, provided for stability and order among the disgruntled population. Spanish administration of the colony after 1769 followed a familiar pattern in her global empire, where she imposed the laws of Spain and the Indies on her subjects in matters of fiscal, judicial, and regulatory affairs. Six of the Louisiana French rebel leaders were executed, and others had their property confiscated.[23] Spain's military occupation of Louisiana began with her treating the colony as a conquered province. Small garrisons of troops were sent up the Mississippi River to establish forts, conduct relations with the Indians, and to monitor Anglo-American activities. In many cases after 1770, Spanish officials used former French officials, soldiers, traders and even clerics still resident in the colony as hired agents. With the British in Canada after 1759, and Spanish Louisiana's status as a "border" province administered from Cuba, the Mississippi River became a lifeline of forts and outposts that all looked past New Orleans to the Gulf of Mexico. But, Spanish officials soon learned some very hard lessons in dealing with their neighbors. As a result of the lack of Spanish colonists, unlike the English flood in their American colonies to the east, Spain's governors required flexibility in the application of immigration policy of their administration.[24] The population remained French speaking, and the majority of the white population were either French or of French descent. Although Spanish laws and institutions were imposed, the French language continued to be used in the daily working relationships within the colony, and even Governor O'Reilly himself sent orders to his local military commanders in French as well as Spanish. True, O'Reilly had pacified the citizens in New Orleans and adjacent areas, and imposed Spanish laws after 1769, but the further away one got from New Orleans the less those laws could be enforced. The basic problem faced by all of the Spanish governors in Louisiana was lack of a Spanish population; therefore, the necessity of accommodation to diverse nationalities, races, and languages placed a strain on government. Immigration into Louisiana from the American settlements, which were Protestant, added more fuel to the fire. "The emigration from the western part of the United States and the toleration of our government," wrote Catholic Bishop Penalver, "have introduced into this colony a gang of adventurers who have no religion and acknowledge no God." [25] Compounding these issues was the fact that the colony of Louisiana was never self-sufficient in the production of foodstuffs. The need to import food and other essentials required flexibility in the administration of imports, trade regulation and even price controls in New Orleans. In order to encourage settlement, traditional land policy in the Spanish Indies was also modified, so that, although in theory all land belonged to the Crown, inducements such as large allotments could be offered to anyone wishing to settle in Louisiana, and especially if they brought others with them.[26] In Spanish Louisiana, Christian Indians were allowed to own or transfer land in accordance with the same laws as whites. This too would change with the arrival of the Americans after 1803. Spanish domestic policies in Louisiana were therefore a combination of tried efforts in the Indies, combined with the necessity of managing a sizable foreign population and all from a distance of the centers of Spanish power—Cuba and Mexico. Spanish rule in Louisiana had hardly gotten underway when global events would further change things, the war of the American Revolution. The Mississippi Valley would become the scene of bitter fighting between English Loyalists, American patriots, and Indian allies of each. Spain was once again to be caught up in a global war, and in that struggle the Colony of Louisiana would play its part.[27]

In the treaty that ended the French and Indian War in 1763, France had been removed from North America, and Spain lost Florida but was confirmed in her possession of Louisiana. Britain divided Florida into two new properties in 1764—East Florida and West Florida. East Florida extended from east of the Apalachicola River and south of the border with her colony of Georgia to the Atlantic, the Gulf of Mexico, and with its capital at St. Augustine. West Florida extended from the Apalachicola and Chattahoochee Rivers to the Mississippi and with its southern boundary as the Gulf of Mexico. The northern boundary was defined at 32 degrees 28 minutes north latitude. West Florida included Baton Rouge, Pensacola, Mobile, Manchac, and Natchez. Great Britain now controlled territory extending from Canada to the Gulf of Mexico. Immediately, British traders established connections with the population in Spanish Louisiana and a lucrative trade arrangement resulted. Although contrary to Spanish law and regulations, this trade provided significant foodstuffs and other supplies not available from Spain itself or other Spanish colonies. As a result, the governors of Louisiana looked the other way out of necessity.[28] On the other side of the coin, Spanish fishermen operating in the Gulf of Mexico traded with British subjects, engaged in trade and although both governments would occasionally seize one another's cargo ship, the trade continued to the mutual benefit of everyone. What changed everything was the American Revolution after 1776. Almost from the beginning, both France and then Spain provided covert assistance to the American colonists. After some American victories over the British army, especially Saratoga in 1777, France, seeking revenge for her defeat in 1759 and territorial losses in the treaty of 1763, signed a treaty with the United States and declared war on Britain in February, 1778. Spain too had suffered losses at the hands of Britain and wanted revenge, but with her own colonial possessions in the Western Hemisphere, she could not join an alliance with rebels. Convinced by France that this was the time to act, Spain unilaterally declared war on Britain in June, 1779, and with this action the colony of Louisiana became an active partner in that struggle.

Spain's declaration of war in 1779, during the American Revolution, not only added another European enemy in addition to France against Britain, but the military campaigns of Governor Don Bernardo de Galvez (1777–1785), who captured the British posts of Mobile (1780) and Pensacola (1781), added British West and East Florida to Spain's holdings. Don Bernardo de Galvez deserves recognition in American history not just for his military exploits, which contributed to the success of the American Revolution, but also for his tolerance and record of wise administration in Louisiana.[29] He was part of a group of eighteenth-century Spaniards who wanted to encourage enlightened reforms, economic development, political openness, and restore the grandeur of Spain at the expense of her enemies. In his young military career, he fought against Apache Indians in northern Mexico, then he attended a French military academy, and upon returning to Spain he was assigned to a military operation led by General Don Alejandro O'Reilly. It was the former governor who recommended him to the King for appointment as a colonel in command of the Louisiana Regiment. From his military command, he was then promoted to Acting Governor to replace Luis de Unzaga in January, 1777. His enlightened policies in economic development increased agriculture (especially tobacco), allowed for an expansion of trade while at the same time reducing the smuggling, and promoted immigration into the colony. But, it is military accomplishments that won him fame, the gratitude of Americans in the west through covertly supplying weapons and other war materials on boats going up the Mississippi flying the Spanish flag prior to 1779 past British outposts destined for George Rogers Clark (1752–1818) and his American army in the west.

In 1779, after receiving news of Spain's declaration of war, Galvez launched offensive campaigns to clear the British out of Baton Rouge and Natchez. In 1780, he led the military expedition that captured Mobile, and supplied another that stopped a joint British and Indian campaign in the upper Mississippi Valley. His crowning achievement was the successful siege and capture of Pensacola in May, 1781.[30]

The Peace Treaty of Paris (1783) ended the War of the American Revolution and confirmed Spain's dominance in the Gulf of Mexico, which now became a Spanish lake. By 1783, Americans in the trans-Allegheny region had been trading in Spanish Louisiana for years.[31] This commercial and military intercourse led to familiarity by all parties, and now with peace, it was presumed by the Americans that such contacts would continue. This idea seemed to be reinforced in another provision of the peace treaty in 1783, Britain ceded its former navigation rights on the Mississippi River to the United States, thereby setting the stage for a series of future confrontations with Spain. Spain, now in control of the Mississippi Valley, and both East and West Florida became the doorkeeper to the Gulf of Mexico. And, finally, because East and West Florida had been acquired by military conquest, and confirmed in the treaty, the origin of these properties clearly indicated that they were not part of the Colony of Louisiana. It was this distinction as to Spain's acquisition of the Florida properties that bedeviled American negotiators in Paris and Washington. The political status of the Floridas remained a point of contention during the negotiations for access to the Gulf by Americans.

Spain's political objective in Louisiana from 1769 to 1803 therefore was to protect her more valuable Mexican properties from the Anglo-Americans. At first, it was British influence in the Mississippi Valley, then after 1783, the newcomers poured in from the young United States of

Spanish Global Policy

Spanish global policy was dictated by her involvement in the European wars of the French Revolution. From Britain in the west to Russia in the east, the political map of Europe and the Mediterranean was in constant flux, and therein Spain was caught up in war: War of the First Coalition, 1791–1797, against France until she changed sides in 1795; then, the War of the Second Coalition, 1799–1802, as an ally of France against her old nemesis, Britain.

America. Throughout all of these years, however, the colony of Louisiana itself was of secondary importance to Spain because it lacked the mineral resources of Mexico and Peru, did not have a pro-Spanish population, and was devoid of agricultural or merchant activities that could contribute to the treasury. In July, 1784, Spain closed the Mississippi River at New Orleans to all but Spanish citizens and vessels, which restricted, but did not entirely prevent, access by American commercial interests to foreign markets on the docks in New Orleans. But, the tide of American settlers entering West Florida from Kentucky, Tennessee and the region of the future Mississippi Territory, with their increasing demands for access to the Gulf of Mexico, led to confrontations on the Mississippi River and in Louisiana. American frontier settlers descended upon New Orleans in their flatboats with products for trade in ever increasing numbers. And, in a tactic reminiscent of earlier years, trade between the Americans and Louisiana continued because the latter continued to suffer from the same problem, her inability to produce the daily needs in foodstuffs, raw materials, and trade goods. Spanish governors, despite official policy, simply looked the other way out of necessity on some occasions, but then they might confiscate boats and cargoes of "smugglers." This inconsistency, and the growing American population in the region, spelled trouble. The Spanish closure policy remained in effect for 11 years, until the Treaty of San Lorenzo el Real (or Pinckney Treaty) with the United States was negotiated in 1795. The Pinckney Treaty of 1795 opened the door to the south and west for Americans, and its repercussions at home and abroad helped set the stage for the Louisiana Purchase in 1803.

During these years, frontiersmen, particularly those in Kentucky, sought assistance for their commercial interests from the American Government; but, when nothing happened to relieve their distress of not having an outlet to the Gulf, they discussed other remedies. The government of the United States, operating under the Articles of Confederation, was powerless. For the inhabitants in Kentucky, the inability of their government to respond to their needs created frustration and despair. It seemed even worse when word leaked out in 1786 that John Jay, Federalist from New York, had negotiated an agreement for trade concessions in Spain's colonies for merchants in the East by abandoning free navigation on the Mississippi for the Westerners in exchange. Jay's negotiations with Spain failed, but the impact was no less severe for the belief in betrayal from those in the east against those inhabitants in the west. Nowhere, therefore, was there more frontier intrigue than in Kentucky, which had been created from a portion of the lands ceded in 1784 by Virginia from its old colonial land grant to the Federal Government. Kentucky applied for statehood per the provisions in the Northwest Ordinance of 1787 the following year. However, the United States was in transition to a new Constitution that delayed this process, with the result that some settlers and land speculators looked for other solutions.

One of the ideas discussed during the 1780s was to seek incorporation into Spanish Louisiana, which would guarantee Kentucky's inhabitants access to the Gulf of Mexico via New Orleans, or in West Florida through Mobile or Pensacola. Among those who advocated this alternative to joining the American Union was James Wilkinson, former officer in the Continental Army, and at the time a member of the Kentucky legislature.[32] He moved to Kentucky in 1784 and from there went to New Orleans in order to meet with Spanish Governor Estevan Miro (1785–1791) in 1787.

Wilkinson's proposal to the Spanish in July, 1787, was: to promote Americans from Kentucky to immigrate to Louisiana and become citizens of the Spanish Crown; to liberalize Spanish trade policies for Kentucky, and that he be appointed as the Spanish commercial agent to implement such a trade policy. Or, a second part of his plan was to help foment insurrections on the frontier with covert Spanish assistance so that these areas could break away from the United States and then seek admission into the Spanish domains. Governor Miro listened and appreciated the need for increasing the population of Louisiana, which was one Spanish officials had discussed for some time.[33] Governor Galvez had led the way with some liberalization of Spanish policies, and encouragement to immigrants. Wilkinson's plan was to admit settlers from Kentucky on the condition that they took an oath of allegiance to Spain; and, in religion, recognize that Catholicism was the only public practice allowed. Of course, these proposals required money, and Wilkinson was prepared to accomplish the task for payment. For Governor Miro, securing settlers in Louisiana and West Florida who would be loyal to Spain strengthened the colony against encroachments from the north. Miro endorsed the plan, and believed that the religious issue of Protestants from Kentucky could be solved by using Irish priests to convert them to Catholicism over time. In West Florida, for example, when it transferred from British oversight to Spanish, several English families wished to remain and became, or already were, Catholics. But Spanish official policy required immigrants and residents to be Catholic. Miro's idea of retaining the British inhabitants who wanted to stay but were Protestants and converting them *ex post facto* to Catholicism and loyalty to Spain

Among those Americans involved with Spanish plots on the American frontier after 1787 was their secret "Spy #13," James Wilkinson, who was later appointed by President Jefferson as one of the American Commissioners to receive Louisiana from France in 1803.

was accepted. Would this same concept not work for settlers arriving from Kentucky? One of the inducements added to the proposal was the very thing that had brought Americans to the Kentucky frontier in the first place, cheap land prices. In the United States, by comparison, the Northwest Ordinance of 1787 had fixed prices for the sale of lands based upon measured units at a dollar an acre, and payable in specie. For those immigrants who brought others with them to Spanish possessions, the offer included free land allotments. Non-Spanish inhabitants in the Natchez district, for example, were accorded the same religious and trading terms as Spaniards. Spain was confronted with increasing pressure to relax its restrictions, and the need for immigrants to settle in Louisiana was seen as another step in providing for the protection of the colony. In August, 1787, a royal order allowed for Protestants to enter the colony of Louisiana, but Catholicism remained as the only public religion to be practiced, and trade issues were also relaxed upon payment of a lower fixed duty for imports. All of these terms were predicated on attracting settlers from Kentucky. A few settlers did take advantage of the offers, but not enough to make a difference.

The political part of Wilkinson's plan was more dangerous because it involved Spanish involvement in fomenting rebellion in Kentucky. According to the plan, when a Kentucky revolution was achieved, the rebels would seek incorporation into Spain's provinces, or at least diplomatic recognition of their independence and then that in turn would lead to a treaty. Wilkinson's plan was forwarded to Madrid in September, 1787, and discussed by the Spanish Supreme Council of State in 1788, but rejected because of the political repercussions.[34] They decided in December, 1788: (1) to wait until Kentucky became independent on its own initiative before taking any action, such as diplomatic recognition; and, (2) decided in favor of granting a relaxation of immigration laws in order to attract American settlers, and with incentives such as reduction of the Spanish commercial duties, *etc.* For his secret efforts on behalf of Spain, Wilkinson ("Spy #13") received some $7,000 (Spanish currency was the "piaster forte," which was a silver coin minted in Mexico and equal one U.S. dollar) for his services.

In addition, there was a promise of more money for him to provide information regarding American intentions towards Louisiana. But

> Spanish silver coinage was international in value: the minted "silver reales" was the basic unit of currency. The specie used throughout the Western Hemisphere was the Mexican "peso" and the "piastre" both of which were generally equivalent to the American dollar, and equaled eight "silver reales" although the actual value varied from time to time.

Wilkinson still preferred the original plan of detaching Kentucky from the Union, and with it the potential for a large allotment of lands there to be awarded to him, which he could develop and sell. This part of the plan offered much more profit than encouraging settlers to immigrate. By 1790, Wilkinson's plan was no longer accepted by Miro's successors, who saw in any Americans entering their province the potential disaster for Spain's control of Louisiana. Spanish policy turned to encouraging immigration from her other colonies, or from Europe. After his death in 1825 in Mexico, where he was again pursuing plans with the Mexican government for Americans settling Texas, Wilkinson's personal papers revealed the extent of his Spanish activities, including taking an oath of Loyalty to the King of Spain, and shady land speculations. It is therefore one of the ironies of history that he would later, 1803, be designated by President Jefferson as an American Commissioner to take possession of Louisiana on behalf of the United States.

For many in Kentucky, the decision to apply for statehood in 1792 under the new U.S. Constitution was conditional upon the federal government negotiating with Spain to achieve their objectives for navigation on the Mississippi and a right of deposit in New Orleans, or at some other site with access to the Gulf. Of the four new states added to the United States by 1803, three were in the west—Kentucky (1792), Tennessee (1796), Ohio (1803) and one large new Mississippi Territory in 1798. Spain's possession of New Orleans and its closure of navigation on the Mississippi, along with the right of deposit at New Orleans, was a critical issue in the West. From 1784–1795, there were persistent rumors that circulated in the United States of a "Western Conspiracy" among American settlers and land developers, such as that by Colonel William Blount in Tennessee.[35] Rumors of unrest in the trans-Appalachian territories by disgruntled settlers, some even seeking the support of Spanish officials because of the inability of the American government to protect and promote their interests, were common. Spanish officials in Louisiana, including Governor Miro, were well aware of the dissatisfaction among the frontiersmen with their own government. But the Americans were also dissatisfied with Spain. The real question, therefore, was which one might ignite first? While en route to New Orleans to establish his business in 1796, James Pitot, French naturalized citizen of the United States, wrote from Natchez: "In the western states, and especially in Kentucky, I heard discussed a hundred times the issue of the conquest of Louisiana, against which there was a majority in Kentucky, who, by preventing recruitments, made themselves suspect to the others."[36]

Simultaneously, political intrigue, even monetary support to American spies, by some Spanish officials continued to stir up unrest. And others believed in taking their own action by descending upon New Orleans in force. Restricted use of the Mississippi River and a right of deposit in New Orleans, during this period of American population immigration into the south and west, and spontaneous local Spanish intrigue, combined to create a catalyst for conspiracy. There was even talk in Kentucky of secession from the United States if that were the only remedy for their future livelihood. The fear among the Spanish officials in Louisiana, however, was of an American invasion by frontiersmen coming down the Mississippi River. George Rogers Clark, for example, began to recruit men and donations for a French Revolutionary Legion in 1793 with which he proposed to capture Spanish settlements along the Mississippi.[37] The extreme distances, and lack of timely communications within the Spanish global empire, heightened Spanish concerns and led to several efforts to improve Louisiana's defenses. The Spanish administrative system itself contributed to this nervousness. The King, Carlos IV, communicated only with Marquis de Someruelos, who was Captain-general of Cuba and adjacent territories, of which Louisiana was one. The resident governor in Louisiana in 1803 was Brigadier General Don Manuel de Salcedo (1801–1803), who, as with his predecessors, was required to get his orders, finances for administration and supplies from Cuba. Money that came for expenses therefore passed through Spanish hands in Cuba. Spanish governors in Louisiana, therefore, were always short on troops, supplies and support from their headquarters in Havana, and consequently they were willing to try anything in order to determine what was happening on their immediate borders, and this included recruiting spies. Hard money was difficult to come by on the American frontier, so that anyone having specie of any kind provided its owner with persuasive powers.

Relief and concessions for the Americans finally came with the Treaty of San Lorenzo el Real, or Pinckney's Treaty as it was known in the United States (October 27, 1795), which was negotiated by Thomas Pinckney on behalf of the United States, and Don Manuel de Godoy, Prime Minister to King Carlos IV, on behalf of Spain. See the treaty text in Primary Document 1 (page 111). The Spanish concessions to the United States in the Pinckney Treaty represented another major step in her retreat from the expense and troubles of global administration. For the United States, it provided the long awaited promise of relief to the West, and wetted appetites for additional opportunities. The treaty concessions included: the right to free navigation of the Mississippi; the right of deposit in New Orleans, for transshipment of goods to ocean going vessels; evacuation of several Spanish forts along the upper Mississippi; acceptance of the American position for the southern boundary line of 31 degrees north near the junction of the Red River with the Mississippi, as opposed to the Spanish claim of 32 degrees, 28 minutes north near the junction of the Yazoo and Mississippi rivers; and, relinquishment of its oversight and treaties with the Indians.[38] As part of their defense for Louisiana, in 1793 the Spanish put together an alliance of the Creeks, Choctaws, Chickasaws, and Cherokees. Spain feared an invasion force from Britain with its Indian allies across the Great Lakes, and down the Mississippi in a manner similar to what they had done in 1780.[39] For Spain, Indian alliances were a cornerstone to their political and military management of the colony. For the Indians, the Spanish offered a European power to protect them from encroachments on their lands by the United States. Spain provided them with gifts, including guns and ammunition; such tribal alliances constituted a formable obstacle to American penetration into Louisiana or West Florida.

The Pinckney Treaty for Spain was a wartime necessity because of events in Europe, where her early alliance of 1793 with Britain had led to a series of military defeats at the hands of France. Spain therefore changed sides in July, 1795, and allied with France. Another factor for Prime Minister Godoy was the immediate threat of an Anglo–American alliance, including the potential for the latter's advances on the frontier by force of arms. Jay's Treaty (November 19, 1794) between the United States and Britain was a source of concern for Spain. The Spanish governor in Natchez, Manuel Gayoso de Lemos, was articulate in his objections to the treaty. He wrote (June 17, 1796) to Daniel Clark, Sr. and outlined his concerns:

> In the time that the treaty was signed the political affairs of Europe determined our court to do anything to keep the U.S. in a perfect neutrality, and thereby destroy a new plan that was forming to renew and continue a destructive war. The treaty with England had a different object; it was to attract the Americans to their interest in such a manner as to have still in her power to keep them dependent; the plan had fallen through, and the British will no longer deliver the posts; our treaty, that was made to counter-balance that, will suffer equal difficulties; for the circumstances being altered will be the conditions on every side. Spain made a treaty with the Union, but if this Union is dissolved, one of the contracting parties exists no longer and the other is absolved from her engagement. It is more than probable that a separation of several states will take place that will alter the political existence of that power that could influence on the balance of that of others; therefore Spain, being deprived of that assistance which could arise from her connection with the Union,

> will alter her views . . . Therefore even when no change should
> happen in the U.S. the treaty will be reduced to the navigation of
> this river.[40]

The debates in the press and Congress over pro-British terms in Jay's treaty delayed its ratification in the U.S. Senate until June, 1795, and its implementation until February, 1796. Although it was a commercial treaty, the Spanish believed it was a precursor for a potential Anglo-American alliance, since Spain had switched her European alliances and joined the war with France against Britain. In the event of hostilities in North America, the British army had only to move from Canada into the Mississippi Valley and then south, while the Americans could come down the Ohio and the Mississippi rivers for a combined land assault on New Orleans. The British fleet could easily blockade the mouth of the Mississippi and control the Gulf. For Spanish officials, the plan was to neutralize the Americans by granting them what they really wanted, a commercial outlet to the Gulf of Mexico. But even prior to the Pinckney Treaty, the need to relax the trade restrictions on the Mississippi, and allow American goods to enter Louisiana had been discussed, and approved as a necessity in Spain. The military reverses by Spanish armies in Europe, the need to accommodate the Americans in order to keep them out of any alliance with Britain, and the continuing pressures exerted along the American-Spanish frontiers in West Florida, all came together to dictate a change in Spanish policy that would be favorable to the United States.

Article I of the treaty set forth the purpose clearly: "There shall be a firm and inviolable peace and sincere friendship between His Catholic Majesty, his successors and subjects, and the United States, and their citizens, without exception of persons or places." Peace, or at least the avoidance of additional hostilities from any source, was a necessity for Spain. Spain could not forget that during the Seven Years War (1756–1763), Britain had successfully captured the Spanish ports of Havana in Cuba, with a combined army (which included militia from the American colonies) and navy operation, and Manila in the Philippines because of her global naval supremacy. In 1763, Spain had lost West and East Florida to Britain in the peace negotiations that ended the Seven Years War (1756–1763), although she recovered both Havana and Manila in the resulting peace negotiations at Paris in 1783. Then, during the first year of European war as a result of the French Revolution, Britain invaded Santo-Domingo in 1793, and French Guadeloupe and Martinique in 1794. British sea power was Spain's greatest fear for her global interests in the Pacific, the Caribbean, and the Mediterranean. For Spain, the message was clear: she must consolidate and prioritize her global interests, and rid herself of her secondary and unprofitable colonial possessions. Santo Domingo (Haiti) was the first to go in 1795; Louisiana would follow in 1800.

Spanish and British imperialism had clashed on many fronts over the years, and Spain had come to see France as a natural ally. In the late seventeenth century, Spain ceded a portion (about one-third) of her Island of Hispaniola to France, and this colony became French Saint-Domingue. The Spanish cession of the remainder of the island to France in 1795 completed one phase of Spain's retreat from its colonial possessions in the West Indies. The entire French island of Saint-Domingue, and with it the Negro slave rebellion that erupted there in 1791, was now exclusively a French problem. The issue of Spain's ceding Louisiana to France in addition to Haiti was discussed at this time as well, but no action was taken in 1795. In 1796, a military alliance between France and Spain led to further losses of Spanish colonies to Britain, and again in 1798, Spain raised the possibility of retroceding her Colony of Louisiana to France. But the offer was not accepted. British sea power on a global level attacked Spanish shipping, and economic problems at home, combined to create an ever-worsening situation. Spain was on the verge of bankruptcy. For now, an agreement with the United States over the Mississippi question would prevent, or at least delay, the prospect of further hostilities.

Issues regarding the northern Florida boundary between the United States and Spain were settled in favor of the American position in the Pinckney Treaty, navigation restrictions on the Mississippi were lifted, and the port of New Orleans opened to all commerce. By the terms of the Pinckney Treaty, the northern boundary of the Spanish Floridas (West Florida and East Florida) with the United States was determined at 31st degree of north latitude due east to the Flint River, and from there to the St. Mary's River and down the channel directly to the Atlantic Ocean. Up until this time, Spain claimed the boundary, which she had received from Britain in 1783, as 32 degrees 28 minutes north latitude. A survey of the agreed upon boundary was to be taken per the Treaty as the final resolution of any boundary dispute. The United States immediately set to the task of the survey. In April, 1796, Andrew Ellicott (1754–1820), Quaker Federalist from Philadelphia, was appointed Boundary Commissioner by President Washington to lead the American effort, a task

During the wars of the French Revolution, Spain signed a Treaty of Basel with France (July 22, 1795) which was directed against Britain, the historic enemy of both powers, and which in addition to the European provisions, included her complete withdrawal from the remaining Spanish two-thirds of the Island of Hispaniola (Spanish, Santo Domingo) which she ceded to France.

that would occupy him for three years. The Federalists were expanding the frontiers of the United States under the Constitution without reservation by means of diplomacy. They had already done so in the Ohio country by warfare against the Indians in 1794–1795. Ellicott, a member of the American Philosophical Society, was an engineer, professor and surveyor with experience in mapping western territories, the boundaries for the District of Columbia, and the city of Washington. The American team included a small military force of thirty soldiers, who were along to protect them from hostile Indians, and to show the flag to the Spanish and others who might be working for their own interests. In this latter regard, it is interesting that Ellicott had been given verbal instructions in Washington from Secretary of State Timothy Pickering prior to his departure to keep an eye on General James Wilkinson, whose Spanish connections were by now known. Ellicott established his base in 1797 near Natchez, in an area that now passed to the United States. However, it was a year before he was able to begin the actual survey, since he had to await his Spanish counterparts. In May, 1797, the Spanish governor at Natchez suspended transfer of the fort to the Americans because of the current hostilities, the quasi-war (1797–1800) with France, who was an ally of Spain. According to Spanish district governor Manuel Gayoso, the delay was necessary also because their engineers were busily engaged in repairing fortifications up and down the river for a possible British invasion. Again, the Spanish fear of an Anglo-American alliance, and joint military operations in the Mississippi Valley contributed to their inaction, and excuses for non-compliance. Confronted with Spanish delays and duplicity in complying with the terms of the treaty, threats of Indian hostilities in the area, and personality clashes, Ellicott nonetheless completed the survey by the spring of 1800. The reports that he sent back to Washington detailed Spanish recalcitrance, and provided additional information that led to an overall impression of Spain's posture.[41] Such reports simply confirmed Jefferson's view, and that of his Cabinet regarding a "feeble" Spain. However, the northern boundary line of 31 degrees north latitude for Spanish West Florida remained as a source of contention for several years among those American settlers and land speculators who had to live with it. There still was no direct access to the Gulf of Mexico without trespassing into Spanish territory. In March, 1798, an agreed-to fixed boundary line opened additional areas from the vacated Spanish lands north of 31 degrees that allowed the United States to designate them as the new Mississippi Territory, and which included the former Spanish town of Natchez. Federalist Presidents Washington and John Adams, and the Federalist Congress, successfully expanded the United States towards the Gulf of Mexico.

As a result of the commercial provisions for the free navigation of the Mississippi and the right of deposit in New Orleans, after 1798, Spanish Louisiana witnessed a vibrant period of prosperity through increases in American trade, and immigration so that it was generally conceded that the "Mississippi Question" had been

> "From the moment his Majesty loses dominion of the Mississippi, an equal fate will be decreed for the Kingdom of Mexico."
> Spanish Governor of Louisiana Manuel Gayoso de Lemos to Don Manuel de Godoy, Prime Minister, April 19, 1798

resolved. But the Pinckney Treaty with the Americans had a negative impact on Spain's military alliances with Indian tribes in the Mississippi Valley. The series of Indian defeats in the Ohio Territory by the Americans in 1794, and loss of their lands in the Treaty of Grenville in 1795, was common knowledge among the southern tribes. The new boundary line placed a portion of the Chickasaw and Choctaw Nations within the United States. For years, both tribes had been provided with trade goods, especially guns, by the Spanish. Now, they faced hostile frontiersmen also with guns, and a United States government that had just pacified (1794) the Ohio country by defeating several of the northern tribes. American troops were now stationed in Natchez, on the doorstep of the southern tribes. There was a persistent rumor in 1798–99, that several of the Indians were planning a sneak attack on the Americans, and it was only by the intervention of the Spanish governor at Natchez that they were dissuaded from doing so. Provoking open warfare between the Indians and Americans, while Spain was still in the area, would have negated the policy directives from Madrid. Such a situation may well have created the very Anglo-American alliance Spanish policymakers were bent on preventing. This potentially dangerous prospect was nonetheless a by-product of Spain's own doing. By means of a series of Indian alliances over the years, Spanish governors had sought to protect their colony from encroachments from the British and, later, Americans. Indian tribes bound by treaties with Spain included: the Sewanee, Talpoose, Alibamons, Choctaws, Cherokees, Creeks, and Chickasaws. As a result of Spain's historical alliances and gifts to the Indians, Governor Don Bernardo de Galvez had made good use of his Indian allies in the capture of Mobile and Pensacola from the British in 1780 and 1781. In addition, unlike American policy in the west, with its constant settlement on Indian lands, Spanish policy had been one of establishing only a series of trading and military posts among the Indians in the Mississippi Valley. Spanish officials told the Indians that these forts were there for their protection as well from the potential encroachment by the English and then the Americans. The policy of Spanish posts and military alliances, rather than settlement on Indian lands, was not therefore seen as a threat by the tribes. As long as the Indian allies remained loyal to Spain, providing intelligence and a military presence, Spain avoided the costs of maintaining her own military garrisons there. Louisiana, for example, cost the Spanish government around $600,000 a year to administer; West Florida cost her about $30,000 a month on average. Without the Indian alliances, these figures would have been even higher.

The Spanish provided the tribes with gifts, guns and other weapons on a regular basis; but, this could be a hazardous policy because of the inter-tribal disputes that often erupted. The Chickasaws and Choctaws were rivals, and, despite Spanish efforts to keep the peace, they frequently raided each other. But, nothing aroused the animosity of American frontiersmen more than European traders providing guns to the Indians. The legacy of bloodshed between whites and Indians in the Ohio Territory and the trans-Appalachian frontier stretched back to the "French and Indian War" (1754–1763). For the frontiersmen, it did not matter whether guns for Indians came from the French, the Spanish, or the British in Canada, the result was bloodshed. For years, giving gifts to the Indians in return for their alliances was a cornerstone of Spanish policy in the Mississippi Valley, which worked and therefore was less expensive than attempting to garrison the vast reaches of the colony with Spanish troops. Because it worked well with the Indian Nations, the Spanish governors simply applied the same principle of giving gifts, money, in their dealing with some Americans. The Pinckney Treaty, however, opened the floodgates to American settlers after 1795, both for purposes of trade and settlement. Resolution of the "Mississippi Question" with Spain offered an incentive for more Americans to move into the west. The Mississippi Territory was officially created by the United States in 1798 with the new southern boundary lines for Florida as stated in the treaty. The Mississippi Territory included the future states of Mississippi and Alabama, and the river systems that drained into the Gulf, but that flowed through the remaining areas of Spanish West Florida and terminated in ports such as Mobile. For American settlers here, New Orleans was not their first choice. In her desire to placate the Americans, and European requirements, Spain abruptly abandoned her Indian allies with the Pinckney Treaty. Per Article V, for example, both Spain and the United States "shall by all the means in their power maintain peace and harmony among the several [Indian] nations who inhabit the country. . ." No more Spanish gifts and guns! The Indians, in turn, having now to seek their own security against American encroachments on their lands from western frontiersmen quickly abandoned her. By 1798, rumors of possible Indian attacks on the Americans in the Mississippi Territory, which Spain was no longer able to control, created a situation in which the United States responded with additional troops. The militia in the adjoining states were put on alert, especially in Georgia, and it looked as though the frontier would once again be in turmoil. From about 1798 on, however, the tide of American commercial and political influence was unstoppable in the lower Mississippi Valley. On the eve of the Louisiana Purchase, New Orleans had been transformed into a bustling port for American commerce. Both contemporaries and later scholars of Spanish Louisiana have agreed that the period from 1798 to 1802 was, despite Spanish policies, one of increased local trade, international commerce, and population growth along with general prosperity.[42] American flatboats carried cargoes of grain, cotton, tobacco, meat, lumber, and wood products that arrived from the Mississippi and Ohio Valleys to New Orleans in flatboats that numbered in the hundreds each year. In addition, New Orleans, with a population estimated at between 8,000–10,000 souls, took on a role as an emerging port for global trade, which was indicated by the increasing number of seagoing vessels at her docks. Spanish immigration and commercial policies, after some turbulence due to changes in governors, finally contributed to the influx of Americans because it became quite liberal—one had only to swear allegiance to the King and indicate a willingness to recognize the Catholic religion in public. Spanish policy and government in Louisiana had to be flexible due to the severe limitations placed on her by an understaffed administration and because of the distance from the seats of Spanish power. The numbers of Americans entering Louisiana and West Florida to settle and trade increased substantially during this period. But there was another problem for the United States, planters in Georgia and the Carolinas complained because of the number of runaway slaves over the years that fled south, and lack of supervision along their porous borders in West Florida by the Spanish administration. Runaway slaves from the United States could find sanctuary among some of the Indian tribes in the Spanish possessions, especially among the Seminoles in Florida. In just about every quarter of the American West, Spain was seen as impotent and a prime target for enterprising individuals.

The role of American settlers and merchants in this economic growth in the old southwest is widely recognized; this new commercial growth was reciprocally beneficial for both Spanish and American interests for a while. Spanish Louisiana was a major market for goods produced in the United States, as well as raw materials and in particular foodstuffs from the west. But, like any colonial administration by a European power, Louisiana presented its fair share of problems. Jack D.L. Holmes has succinctly described some of the problems of the Spanish governors. He wrote:

The economic problems of the Spanish governors of Louisiana were obviously among their most pressing and most frustrating. It was simpler to deal with jealous and mercurial Indian chiefs, crafty British smugglers, and grasping American conspirators than to convince the king to order the viceroy of New Spain to send financial aid in language strong enough to induce him to send such aid and to frighten the captain-general of Havana into resisting the temptation to hold out the bulk of it to use in Cuba.[43]

Spanish administration in Louisiana has been the subject of both later historians, and contemporaries. One of the latter who wrote on the subject was James Pitot (1761–1831), whose *Observations on the Colony of Louisiana from 1796 to 1802* provides extensive insight. Pitot wrote in part:

Louisiana—which Spain surely wanted to possess only so as no longer to see a French colony grow larger at the mouth of a river whose branches lead to the borders of Mexico—has been subjected to an altogether special administration. . . Thus, isolated like a gangrenous growth from the body of the state, but useful for the preservation of one of its members [Mexico], the Louisianians were always Spanish in name, French at heart, and often ran the risk of contraband trade with foreigners.[44]

Pitot, a French citizen, immigrated to the United States from Saint-Domingue, where he had been a sugar merchant. Following the outbreak of the slave rebellion there in 1791, and after returning briefly to France he traveled to the United States in 1793 and became an American citizen in 1796. From Philadelphia he traveled to New Orleans, where he started in business as a merchant. However, he kept his American citizenship a secret from the Spanish, and prepared his "Observations" in 1802 as a report for the anticipated arrival of the French. Like other writers later, he believed that Spanish policy in Louisiana deliberately attempted to keep the colony only as a weak buffer zone with which to protect her more valuable Mexican properties. Upon his arrival in New Orleans (August, 1796), Pitot was quick to assess what he found there. He wrote in part:

The errors of the Spanish government in Louisiana are those that perpetuate the mediocrity of a country, but which individually do not bother its citizens. Such an administration restrains commerce, restricts population, and does not encourage agriculture; and, by this unchanging policy, as well

as the mingling of Spanish families with French ones, it has
hardened an indifference in the colony that scarcely suspects the
possibility of a better existence.[45]

In the Spanish system of administration of her colonies, government
was divided between civilian and military affairs; the intendant was the
chief civilian financial official, who had exclusive control over taxes,
customs, and commercial duties. Military affairs were handled by the
governor. This is why the Spanish Intendant for Louisiana, Juan Ventura
Morales, could revoke the right of deposit for Americans in New Orleans
in 1802–1803 without either prior knowledge of or approval by the
governor, Don Juan Manuel de Salcedo. It was circumstances such as this
that caused American hardliners, such as the American Consul Daniel
Clark, Jr. (1766–1813) and/or pro-French citizens, such as James Pitot,
to look forward to any new administration, either the American or the
French, which would capitalize on Louisiana's economic vitality for the
future.

But, events in Europe once again dominated the local scene. In 1800,
the secret Treaty of San Ildefonso (October 1, 1800) was signed between
Spain and France. See the full treaty text in Primary Document 2 (page
122). The circumstances surrounding this secret treaty reflected European
power politics of the day. Mariano Luis de Urquijo, Foreign Minister,
represented Spain, and Marshal Louis Alexandre Berthier represented
France. The Treaty included transfer of the Duchy of Tuscany to Prince
Luis of Bourbon-Parma, brother-in-law to Carlos IV and nephew of the
Queen; in Tuscany, he would become King with French help. In addition,
Spain agreed to transfer six warships to France; and, within six months of
Parma's receiving Tuscany, King Carlos IV of Spain would retrocede
Louisiana to France. Final terms were concluded in a Treaty of Aranjuez
on March 18, 1801, and signed by Don Manuel de Godoy (1767–1851)
for Spain and Lucien Bonaparte (1778–1846) for France. The deal was
finalized by the signature of Carlos IV on April 11, 1801. Spain's global
policies, in which Louisiana was regarded as a liability, were European in primacy, and dynastic for the royal family regarding the Italian properties. Prime Minister Godoy summed up the advantage of acquiring properties in Europe over that of supporting colonies, such as Louisiana, which provided no returns for Spain:

> "To persons brought up under a form of government to which the English and Americans have been accustomed, the Spanish government must be an intolerable yoke."
>
> Francis Bailey, *Journal* (May 14, 1797), from Natchez

> In Tuscany all is done, cultivation perfect, industry flourishing,
> trade expanded, benign ways, civilization at high level, rich
> country and monuments and prodigies of art, in precious
> antiques, in magnificent libraries and renowned academies; a
> million and a half inhabitants; state revenues of about three
> million *pesos fuertes*, no debts; extension of six thousand five
> hundred square miles.[46]

For Spain, the prospect of France assuming possession of Louisiana meant cutting her financial losses, which "can be deemed a gain" in that it would be garrisoned now by France, with the most powerful army in the world at that time. How better to protect Mexico from the Anglo–Americans than to let the French do it! James Pitot's comments in his *Observations* regarding Spanish interests, or lack thereof in Louisiana, were correct. In his *Memoires*, written in 1836, Godoy summed up the prevailing official Spanish view of Louisiana at that time, and therefore the advantages of its retrocession to France:

> Because of our lack of means to provide it with an increase at the
> same level of the other Spanish dominions of both Americas, not
> yielding much to our treasury, nor to our trade, and generating
> sizable expenses in money and soldiers without profit, and
> receiving other states [Tuscany] in exchange of it, the return of
> the colony [to France] can be deemed as a gain, instead of a
> sacrifice.[47]

Although not written into the Treaty, France pledged that if she ever decided to vacate Louisiana, she would return it to Spain and not to any other nation. This "pledge" later created a serious issue in 1803 because Spain was not consulted regarding the sale of Louisiana by France to the United States during the 1803 negotiations.

The official title of the Treaty set forth its purposes in no uncertain terms: "Preliminary and Secret Treaty between the French Republic and His Catholic Majesty the King of Spain, Concerning the Aggrandizement of His Royal Highness the Infant Duke of Parma in Italy and the Retrocession of Louisiana." In exchange for Spanish dynastic interests in Italy, France would receive her former colony of Louisiana "with the same extent that it now has in the hands of Spain and that it had when France possessed it" (Article 3). This provision therefore raised the question later as to the status of West and East Florida, since they had been acquired by Spanish military conquest in 1780 and 1781 from Britain and had not been part of the original French colony of Louisiana. American diplomats in 1801–1803, assumed that France had also received Florida as part of the deal, and therefore they attempted at first to purchase New Orleans, or a site in Florida that could serve as a staging area for commerce. Events in Europe regarding the Italian properties dictated a slow response from Spain, while problems in Saint-Domingue (Haiti) continued to plague France. It was not until October 15, 1802, therefore, that the Spanish monarchy instructed colonial officials to proceed with the transfer of Louisiana to France. See Governor Salcedo's "Proclamation" to the citizens of Louisiana (May 18, 1803), Primary Document 6 (page 139). By relying on France to protect her interests in Mexico, abandoning her Indian allies, and making huge concessions to the Americans in Pinckney's Treaty, Spain put herself in an untenable position with regard to new advances of American expansionism. Spain would soon pay dearly for her policy of putting her colonial eggs and future in the French basket!

Louisiana in French Global Policy, 1800–1803

The exact details of the Franco-Spanish treaty were not known in the United States, along with any timetable for their execution, until November, 1801, when Rufus King, American Minister in London, forwarded a copy he had obtained from the British on to Secretary of State James Madison. But the retrocession of Louisiana to France was rumored in reports sent home earlier from American diplomats in Britain, France and Spain. Ever since the Pinckney Treaty had reopened the Mississippi and New Orleans to American commerce, the United States continued to expand further to the west and south. Discussions and rumors concerning Louisiana's status circulated widely in the United States, and within diplomatic channels in Europe. Robert Livingston, American Minister to France, wrote Rufus King, American Minister to Great Britain, in December, 1801, on this subject:

> Among the objects that would most naturally engage my attention
> on my arrival [in Paris] was the state of negotiation, between
> France and Spain, regarding Louisiana—with a view if it had not
> been concluded upon, to throw obstacles in the way so far as it
> would be advantageously done, or if it had been effected, to
> make some such arrangements as could lessen the
> inconveniences which might result from it to our western
> territory—I have however reason to think the whole business had
> been settled before my arrival. I took occasion on my first private
> audience of the Minister of Exterior Relations [Talleyrand] to
> press him directly on the subject taking the common reports as a
> foundation for my enquiry; He explicitly denied that any thing had
> been concluded, but admitted that it had been a subject of
> conversation. I know however from a variety of channels, that it is

not a mere matter of conversation, but that the exchange has actually been agreed upon . . . That Spain has made this concession, (which contravenes all her former maxims of Policy) cannot be doubted, but she is no longer a free agent.[48]

Napoleon Buonaparte

Napoleon Buonaparte was born in Corsica on August 15, 1769, as one of eight children. His parents, Carlo Buonaparte and Letizia Romolio, were from Genoese families, but when France acquired the Island of Corsica in 1769, they accepted French administration. Napoleon was admitted to the French Military Academy at Brienne in 1779, and later in 1784 to the Military Academy in Paris, from which he graduated with the rank of second lieutenant and assigned to an artillery regiment in 1785. When the French Revolution began in 1789, he supported it and later that year Corsica was incorporated into metropolitan France to his delight. Throughout 1792–1793, he was involved in the French political upheavals and acquired a distaste for "mob" violence. International affairs now entered the picture with war against Austria, Spain, and Great Britain, who soon occupied Bonaparte's beloved Corsica. Domestic violence during the Reign of Terror and foreign war during 1794–1795 led to his rise in commands so that by October, 1795, he was Commander of the Army of the Interior. French military successes on several fronts, in Spain, which concluded a separate peace with France in 1795, and then in Italy opened the door for the furtherance of his career during 1796 and 1797. In his personal life, Napoleon married Josephine de Beauharnais in 1796, and at this time he shortened his Corsican name spelling to simply "Bonaparte."

It was his military campaigns in Italy, utilizing new offensive tactics that established his reputation, and with it French supremacy so that he was in a position to carry France's dreams of expansion to Egypt in 1798 and Syria in 1799. But, domestic affairs in France and in Europe required his attention as France once again found itself caught up in political unrest, another constitution, and a *coup d'etat* in November, 1799, with the result that he was made First Consul in December. The year 1800 witnessed his continued military victories in Italy against the Austrians, and negotiations with Spain over properties in Italy in return for the retrocession of Louisiana to France by secret treaty. As First Consul of the French Republic, Bonaparte focused his attention not only on military victories, but using his considerable political skills to settle affairs in Europe during 1801 with treaties, a Concordat with the Papacy in Rome, reorganization of French administration and commercial affairs that would benefit France. A pragmatist, Napoleon was unhampered by the past; his objective was to build and use institutions that worked. His only remaining foreign foe in 1801 was Great Britain, and a "Peace" at Amiens in 1802 created a temporary truce. It was against this backdrop of affairs in Europe that permitted him to consider France's long-term effort to reestablish her role as a colonial power, and in particular in the West Indies. Here, however, there was the persistent problem of the slave rebellion in Saint-Domingue, which began in 1791 and required a military solution, and then with suppression of the rebellion, he could concentrate on the big picture of French colonial interests that included the recently acquired colony of Louisiana. The ferocity of the rebellion in Saint-Domingue and huge French losses, and resumption of war with Great Britain in May, 1803, had their affects on political events in France. A serious plot against him was uncovered in 1804, and domestic achievements, such as promulgation of the Code Napoleon and creation of the first French Empire, with Napoleon as Emperor of the French in December completed his rise to power. From 1804 to his military defeat in Europe following the disastrous invasion of Russia in 1812, Napoleon attempted to control all of Europe, but fell to the combined military coalitions that ousted him from power in 1814. Sent into exile on the Island of Elbe, Napoleon escaped in January, 1815, and, after a brief return to France, he was again defeated in June and this time he was imprisoned on the Island of Saint Helena where he died on May 5, 1821.

King's description of Spain as "no longer a free agent" recognized France's new dominant status in Europe under the leadership of Napoleon Bonaparte, and for that reason, Livingston wanted to know what, if anything, Britain might do. France denied the rumors of her impending return to Louisiana. With proof of French intentions after November, 1801, and their repeated French and Spanish denials, the beginning of 1802 witnessed a renewed urgency on the part of the United States to determine the truth and resolve the situation. It also created a chill in Franco–American relations.[49] Meanwhile, the British government, facing domestic troubles over food shortages and a decline in their currency values at home, was concerned over a possible French return to North America. In France, secret plans for a Louisiana Expedition were prepared. On June 4, 1802, Napoleon wrote to Admiral Denise Decrès, Minister of the Navy and Colonies, outlining his plans and needs for taking possession of Louisiana:

> My intention is that we take possession of Louisiana with the shortest possible delay, that this expedition be organized in the greatest secrecy, and that it have the appearance of being directed toward Saint-Domingue. The troops that I intend for it being on the Scheldt, I should like them to depart from Antwerp or Flushing. Finally, I would like for you to let me know the number of men you think should be sent, both infantry and artillery, and for you to present me with a project of organization for this colony—for the army as well as for the civil authority—and

for the fortifications and batteries we should have to construct
there in order to have a roadstead and some men-of-war
sheltered from superior forces. In this regard, I should like you to
have made for me a map of the coast from St. Augustine and
Florida to Mexico and also a geographical description of the
different cantons of Louisiana with the population and resources
of each canton.[50]

Secrecy was crucial for French preparations because of the possible
repercussions in Britain, who, as possessor of Canada that bordered
Louisiana, was bound to see the reappearance of French troops in North
America as a threat. On January 16, 1802, Federalist Rufus King
(1755–1827), Minister from the United States to Great Britain from
1796–1803, responded to the letter from Robert Livingston, in Paris, on
that very subject. King wrote in part:

I conversed again and again with the Prime Minister, and the
Secretary of State for Foreign Affairs, concerning the cession of
Louisiana [i.e. the retrocession by Spain to France] who assured
me that the measure was in their view of much importance, and
one they could not see but with great concern. An opinion gains
strength that a part of the force should the situation of St.
Domingo permit, will be sent to New Orleans.

Whether it can now be prevented is a question of considerable
difficulty: but in whatever concerns the welfare of our country, we
are called upon even in circumstances of despair to perform the
Duties of Hope. My principal reliance would, I confess be placed
upon a plain and explicit representation to the French
Government which should expose without reserve, and if the first
Essay should authorize it, in great detail, the extent of the
mischiefs which we may be made to suffer from the completion
of the cession; accompanying the same by assurances of our
earnest desire to live in friendship and harmony with France, and
to cultivate and extend the commercial intercourse between the
two Countries, and concluding with a direct insinuation that
foreseeing as we do the pernicious influence of the measure upon
our political and social happiness, it will be impossible for us to
see it carried into operation with indifference.[51]

Throughout 1802, French planning for the Louisiana Expedition
continued. Napoleon appointed General Claude Perrin Victor (1764–1841)
as Captain-General of Louisiana in April, 1802. General Victor was an old

Pierre Clement Laussat

Pierre Clement Laussat was born in Pau, France, on November 23, 1756. His family was locally prominent in the Province of Bearn, and like many children of such families, he was to receive a formal education. Originally intended for a career in law, he soon discovered that his real talent was in fiscal management and his first career began as receiver-general of finances at the local level. The French Revolution, which he supported, opened the door to him for further career advances. But like others—including Napoleon Bonaparte—the changing political scene in Paris meant ups and downs on the career ladder between 1789 and 1800. He served as Receiver-General of Finances for the Intendancy of Pau from 1784–1789, Paymaster General for the Army of the Eastern Pyrenees, member of the Council of Five Hundred, 1797, and Tribune. He participated in drafting the Constitution of 1799 that established the Consulate as the new executive leadership, with Napoleon Bonaparte as First Consul. Then in 1800, the administrative system of France was reorganized into a more centralized system under the minister of the interior. The new political and military institutions of France after 1800 stood in glaring contrast to the overlapping judicial districts, mutually exclusive administrative offices, and rival claims to authority of the old order in France. The system of government by prefects replaced the former intendants of the old order, and the prefects were assigned duties in the French colonies as well as in Metropolitan France.

The acquisition of Louisiana from Spain by secret treaty to France, and the need to provide for an administration in the colony therefore presented an opportunity for Laussat. He requested appointment as prefect for Louisiana from Napoleon, and it was given to him on August 20, 1802. He was the highest ranking French civilian authority for Louisiana, and second only to the military officer in charge, the Captain General. Laussat's duties included that of handling the finances for the Colony of Louisiana, including salaries for French officers both military and civilian, administering French law codes, supervising trade and commerce, issuing contracts for maintenance of the French administration, and overseeing all commercial matters. While Napoleon prepared the necessary troop allocations for Louisiana throughout 1802, it was decided to send colonial prefect Laussat on ahead of the military expedition to make the necessary arrangements for their arrival. Laussat, with his staff and family, departed for Louisiana on January 10, 1803, and arrived in New Orleans on March 26. Unbeknown to Laussat, Napoleon decided, on April 10, to rid himself of Louisiana by selling it to the United States, which he did on April 30, 1803. Prefect Laussat had hardly arrived in New Orleans when it was sold out from under him! He would therefore represent the French Republic in Louisiana, but without the necessary military force with which to carry out his instructions. News of the sale did not reach New Orleans until July, and then it was only rumors and news reported in the American press. Official dispatches with instructions did not arrive until August. In France, Napoleon made plans for the transfer of Louisiana to the United States, and he did so by relying on Prefect

Laussat who was appointed on June 6, 1803, to act as the official commissioner of the French Republic to receive Louisiana from Spain, and then to cede it to the United States.

Upon completion of his transfer duties in Louisiana on December 20, 1803. Laussat was then appointed as colonial prefect for Martinique, where he served from 1804 to 1809. His next assignment was as prefect for Antwerp and then Jemmapes between 1810 and 1814. He completed his administrative career under the restored King Louis XVIII as governor of French Guinea, but soon retired to France where he died in 1835.

comrade-in-arms of Napoleon, an artillery officer, who had been with him at the battles of Toulon (1793), Mondovi (1796) and Marengo (1800).[52] For head of the civil authority, Napoleon appointed Pierre Clement Laussat (1756–1835) as colonial prefect in August, 1802.[53] He had experience in government, where he had been Receiver General of Finances for the Intendancy of Pau, 1784–1789. Laussat served also as Paymaster General for the Army of the Eastern Pyrenees, and finally a member of the Council of Five Hundred in 1797. What impressed Napoleon was the fact that Laussat had sought appointment as colonial prefect for Louisiana "at my own request." As part of the continuation of separation from the institutions of the Old Regime, Napoleon created new administrative departments throughout both metropolitan France and the colonies. One of the new administrative tools he established was an official to administer each department, the prefect in 1800, who replaced the pre-revolutionary intendant. The prefectural corps was created by Napoleon in order to establish an overall system of administrative centralization. The civil reorganization of French government, combined with those in the military, established a new and viable organization in both France and her colonies. Ironically, Napoleon, who created these institutions of colonial administration, unleashed at the same time the very force from the French Revolution that would do them in, the doctrine of popular sovereignty among nationalities.

If this French system was transported to Louisiana, in place of the "feeble" Spanish one, Jefferson had every right to fear the consequences. A French military expedition of over 20,000 men arrived in Saint-Domingue, and, after suppression of the rebellion there, a large portion would, no doubt, be reassigned to Louisiana. Without clarification as to France's intentions regarding Louisiana, and silence from Spain, Jefferson could only imagine the worst-case scenario. His concerns prompted the extensive instructions to Robert Livingston, American Minister in France, in the letter of April 18, 1802.

In the administration for Louisiana, the position of captain-general was the highest ranking French officer who commanded colonial troops and militia; the position of colonial prefect was the second highest ranking French official, a civilian, with responsibilities for administration of funds, levying customs duties, and judicial functions.

Funds allocated in 1802 for the expenses of the Louisiana Expedition were 2,686,000 francs, with additional funds the following year; plus 3,739 military personnel were requested (five times the number of Spanish troops in Louisiana at that time); and, orders for the troops to assemble at the Port of Dunkirk in order to be ready for departure to Louisiana in November.[54] On October 15, 1802, the King of Spain, Carlos IV, finally ordered the official transfer of Louisiana to France, since the Italian properties, per the Treaty of 1800, including the Grand Duchy of Tuscany, had been turned over to Spain in 1801.

However, events in the French colony of Saint-Domingue (Haiti), the slave rebellion, which had begun in 1791, led to civil war and foreign intervention after 1793 from Britain, and the United States, along with the onset of an early winter in 1802 altered French plans. One delay after another combined to keep the Louisiana Expedition on hold. Supplies, troop movements, and commissions for officers to join the expedition required time and logistics. Then, the decision was made to change the port of embarkation from Dunkirk to one in Holland. French troops were ordered in December, 1802, to depart from the Dutch port of Helvut-Sluys, south of Rotterdam, for Saint-Domingue.[55] In another last minute change (December 19, 1802), 2,000 of the requested troops for Louisiana were reassigned by Napoleon for deployment as replacements to Saint-Domingue. Such last minute changes in plans not only delayed the operations, but added considerably to both the actual and projected expenses.[56] Captain-General Victor was an artillery officer. Without infantry support in adequate numbers, no general would risk sending the balance of his forces, cavalry and artillery regiments alone, across three thousand miles of hostile ocean into the unknown. Victor's policy was therefore one of calculated delay, which combined with icy conditions in the port during the winter of 1802–1803, internal administrative problems such as bickering over the official issuance of commissions to military and civilian officers, and the arrival of a British fleet off the Dutch coast, kept the Louisiana Expedition in port.

The troops reassigned from the Louisiana Expedition to Saint-Domingue included the 7th and 5th Infantry Regiments, and the 7th Regiment of Dismounted Artillery. The Louisiana Expedition constituted a force of over a dozen ships and over 3,000 men.

This decision to reduce Victor's troop strength by over one half, and then further indecision from conflicting orders to proceed without adequate ships and men by the French naval officers, created an intolerable situation that led to confusion and inaction. Constant changes in the availability of supplies, and the fact that no infantry

> "The French have attempted to form colonies in several parts of the continent of America. Their efforts have everywhere proved abortive."
>
> Francois Barbé-Marbois, Minister of the Public Treasury, to Napoleon, April 10, 1803

replacements were assigned as replacements for General Victor, suggest the first hint of Napoleon's hesitancy to pursue the Louisiana Expedition until all of the prerequisites for success were completed. His final decision to abandon the Louisiana Expedition altogether was later announced in a meeting on April 10, 1803. See the lengthy description of this meeting by François Barbé-Marbois, Minister of the Public Treasury, in Primary Document 11 (page 154).

By this time, Napoleon Bonaparte alone made such decisions. Yet, the French navy and even Captain-General Victor, received conflicting orders all this time, December, 1802 to March, 1803, for new departure dates, etc. The extremely harsh weather in Europe during the winter and spring of 1802–1803, the prospect of renewed hostilities with Britain, simply reinforced the decision by Napoleon to keep the balance of his French troops where they would be needed most in the event of war— Europe. Finally, persistent reports from Saint-Domingue of staggering French military losses to yellow fever, including the death of General LeClerc, his brother-in-law in November of 1802, and ferocious rebel attacks led to caution, and then despair.

In the several stages of French planning, secrecy and deception were important to French global policy; therefore the decision was made on December 7, 1802, to send the colonial prefect on ahead to Louisiana. Bonaparte grew impatient with the slowness of the preparations for the Louisiana Expedition, and feared that sending a large force would arouse suspicion as to its purpose and destination. "The First Consul," Laussat was informed,

> has considered it important for the interest of the expedition which is about to set out from Holland, that you precede it by state vessel in order that, having reach Louisiana before the expedition, you may be able to prepare everything necessary to receive it.[57]

"Damn sugar, damn coffee, damn colonies!"
      Quote attributed to Napoleon upon hearing in 1803 of General LeClerc's death in 1802, and the continued French military disasters in Saint-Domingue.

"All Louisianians are Frenchmen at heart!"
French Prefect Laussat, *Memoires*, March 26, 1803.

On January 10, 1803, French Colonial Prefect Laussat (1756–1835), who was unaware of the changes in military troop movements for the Louisiana Expedition, departed France for Louisiana, along with several staff and his family, in order to make the necessary preparations for the arrival of the military expedition. He arrived in New Orleans on March 26, 1803, and began to make arrangements, such as locating barracks, food supplies, stables, and other raw materials that would be needed.

He also took the opportunity to report on local conditions.[58] With the exception of the Spanish Intendant Morales, for whom he had kind words, Laussat wrote: "what a detestable policy was that of the Spanish government. What dishonest manipulation! What corruption."[59] It is therefore understandable why the Spanish governor, Don Manuel de Salcedo, and other Spanish officers soon formed a dislike and distrust of their French counterpart, and were not averse to causing troubles for him.

In the midst of his preparations for the anticipated arrival of the French Expedition at any time, Laussat confided to his daily *Journal* his observations on Louisiana. Among his more interesting observations, is an extensive commentary regarding Americans, both in New Orleans and his understanding of those on the frontier. He wrote in May, 1803:

Wherever the Anglo-Americans settle, land is fertilized and progress is rapid. There is always a group of them who act as trailblazers, going some fifty leagues into the American wilderness ahead of the settlers. They are the first to migrate to a new area. They clear it, populate it, and then push on again and again without any purpose other than to open the way for new settlers. Those who thus forge ahead into the unknown places are called black settlers [Lausst means backwoodsmen here]. They set up their temporary shanties, fell and burn trees, kill the Indians or are killed by them, and disappear from this land either by death or by soon relinquishing to a more to a more stable farmer the land which they had begun to clear. When a score or so of such new colonists have congregated into one location, two printers arrive—one a federalist, the other an antifederalist—then the doctors, then the lawyers, and then the fortune seekers. They drink toasts, nominate a speaker, set up a town, and raise many children. Finally, they advertise the sale of vast tracts of land attracting and deceiving as many land buyers as possible. They exaggerate the population figures so that they may quickly reach the sixty thousand souls entitled to form an independent state and be represented in Congress. And so another star appears on the flag of the United States . . . Under the Anglo-Americans, a newly born state may thrive with more or less prosperity, but it will never decline; it keeps on growing and strengthening.[60]

While Prefect Laussat was busily preparing for what he believed was the imminent arrival of the French military expedition under Captain-General Victor, events in Europe and the Caribbean during the winter of 1802 and the spring of 1803—the impending resumption of war in Europe and the renewed ferocity of the slave rebellion in Saint-Domingue—would all have their impacts in Louisiana.

The slave rebellion that began in Saint-Domingue in 1791 started among white planters who saw, in the ideas and changes of governments attributed to French Revolution and therein the doctrine of liberty provided them with an opportunity to link their future to these new ideas and shirk the old order of dominance by royal officials. But soon the revolutionary ideas spread to another tier in society, the "free men of color" who sought equality with whites in the life of the colony but whose efforts were repressed, and from these classes, it spread further among the slaves themselves so that by 1793, there was full-scale civil war. The events in Saint-Domingue had a major impact on both the domestic and foreign affairs of the United States. The rebels became familiar with the libertarian principles and examples of the French Revolution as it went through its various phases, including the bloody period known as the "Reign of Terror" from 1793–1794. The fear aroused among slave owners in the United States was that the Haitian revolution

"But if our slaves were so well treated, why did they revolt? One must ask those composers of phrases who have inundated our country with their incendiary writings; those stupid innovators who brought turmoil to France and killed their King; those Whites of Europe who were found at the head of the insurgents; those idiots who thought that the destruction of commerce would usher in a counter-revolution and who needed an army to sustain their new rights."

Memoir by a French sugar planter, c. 1796

would spark a similar outbreak in the United States. This prophecy seemed fulfilled in 1800 with the slave revolt of Gabriel in Virginia, which resulted in twenty-seven slaves being executed. The exodus from the violence in Saint-Domingue by whites, with some of their slaves, and free men of color to the United States spread the revolutionary message in cities such as Charleston, New Orleans or Richmond, and aroused fear among the white population. This fear of a slave rebellion included Louisiana, which at the time was governed by the Spanish "black code" in force throughout the Indies. The revolution in France spread globally with unforeseen results.

On the foreign affairs front, President John Adams (1797–1801) saw the opportunity for American commercial benefits from events in Saint-Domingue and the rest of the West Indies. The United States and Britain both signed secret commercial treaties with Toussaint L'Ouverture (c.1743–1803), the rebel leader, a free man of color. Disregarding American statements of neutrality, and particularly after the U.S. British Treaty of 1795, French privateers in 1797 captured several American vessels engaged in trade between the United States and the West Indies, as well as those American vessels trading in the British ports, thereby initiating the "quasi-war" (1797–1800) with France.[61] In retaliation for French seizures of American ships at sea, the United States commercial interests provided supplies and arms to the rebels. President Adams took the opportunity to seek a ceasefire and in 1799, his overtures were received in France. Bonaparte wanted to eliminate any chance of the United States joining with Britain in an anti-French alliance. The Franco-American Convention of 1800 ended the "quasi-war." As a condition of the Convention (September 30, 1800), the United States agreed to halt its support to the rebels in return for the French agreement to compensate American merchants for their losses. It was this provision that was later included in the Louisiana Purchase treaty and conventions with the United States agreement to assume these losses and reimburse American shippers. By the time he became President, Jefferson, a slave owner himself, therefore faced the dilemma of what to do regarding these global events in the Caribbean. On the one hand, the more France was tied down in Saint-Domingue, the more time he had for resolution of the Louisiana business; on the other side, however, was the fact of American commercial interests in the northeast, the traditional stronghold of the Federalists, supported continued commercial, even smuggling, activity in Saint-Domingue, and thereby support for a slave rebellion through commerce. President Jefferson initially pursued a policy of ambiguity in that he abhorred slave rebellions, but global events soon had a way of interfering. In 1800, the slave rebellion in Virginia, attributed to the influences of slaves from Saint-Domingue, had brought the issue of slavery, and potential rebellion, home.

Although the United States and France signed a Convention ending the "quasi-war" between them, and officially ended American commercial activity in Saint-Domingue, the matter of slave insurrections in the West Indies and their continued physical and psychological impacts on the United

> Jefferson wrote Rufus King in London (July 13, 1802): "The course of things in the neighboring islands of the West Indies appears to have given a considerable impulse to the minds of the slaves in different parts of the U.S."

States, and Jefferson, remained. Prior to learning of the transfer of Louisiana from Spain to France, Jefferson had agreed that American commercial interests might provide supplies to the French forces in Saint-Domingue, thereby avoiding directly aid to the rebels as his predecessor Adams had done, and maintain his ties with France. But during the winter of 1801–1802, with the rumors of the retrocession and with a copy of the secret treaty, his attitude toward France became one of increased distrust and suspicion.[62]

The formal Peace of Amiens (March 25, 1802 to May 18, 1803) between Britain and France was, in reality, only a "cease fire" agreement; and, by late 1802, it was already falling apart. Events in Europe, French refusal to leave the Low Countries, and in the Mediterranean, Britain's occupation of the Island of Malta, created the climate for a war fever. The resumption of hostilities between France and Britain was a common topic of diplomatic conversation in Europe and the United States. In March, 1803, Britain ordered her military forces to readiness status. Britain ultimately declared war on France on May 18, 1803. France, busily engaged with the European realignments among the nations on the Continent, and with no end in sight to the slave rebellion in Saint-Domingue, Napoleon and his advisors considered their political and military priorities and options.

Ever the soldier and politician, Napoleon believed that with stability on the Continent, it would be possible for France to bring Britain to heel through her economic ruin. Economic dislocation, food shortages, falling currency values, and the suspension of military spending due to peace in Britain, all seemed to support his view. However, for France, it was imperative for her foreign trade to continue growing, and within that sphere, peace in the French colonies was considered a necessity. Saint-Domingue was France's most valuable colony in the West Indies; it was of strategic importance, and served as base for resupply of ships in the Caribbean or en route to the Gulf of Mexico. Louisiana, as a producer of raw materials and consumer of French finished products, was considered as a secondary component in France's West Indies enterprise. Restoration of French power in Saint-Domingue was the first priority. With the assistance of her ally Spain, Napoleon considered the Gulf of Mexico as friendly waters. But the situation in the West Indies was anything but friendly, and when the French military expedition under General Charles LeClerc, Napoleon's brother-in-law, arrested Toussaint L'Ouverture, the rebel leader in June, 1802, the Negro rebellion spread. The rebels saw the French effort to reintroduce slavery, which had been abolished earlier (1794), as unacceptable. Slavery was once again reestablished in 1802, with Napoleon's approval; as a result, the slave rebellion widened even further. White plantation owners from the Islands had successfully lobbied Napoleon and convinced him that without the reintroduction of slavery, it would not be possible to bring the West Indies into the French colonial planning and production for dominance of world markets. With General LeClerc's army of 20,000 men, it was assumed that the island would be pacified, order and property restored to white French planters, and that Saint-Domingue would then become the main supply base for the next phase, the occupation of Louisiana. It was with the reinforcements from Holland, the contingent reassigned to Saint-Domingue from Captain-General Victor's Louisiana Expedition in 1802 that the plan was to be consummated.

Everything therefore depended upon the success of the French forces, but they were suffering not only from disease but also having to fight a guerrilla war for which they had neither training nor experience. The most devastating enemy for them however was the mosquito, and the yellow fever it carried. By spring, 1803, the situation of the French army in Saint-Domingue was desperate. On his voyage to Louisiana, Prefect Laussat's vessel stopped briefly at Saint-Domingue on February 24. He described the situation there in his *Memoires*:

> The situation of our army was deplorable. It acknowledged the Negroes as masters, even down to the city gates . . . From the roadstead, the results of the destruction and pillaging could already by observed . . . Last Saturday the blacks attacked here. They failed to enter the town, but they burned its gates, the houses of d'Estaing, the whole compound occupied by General Leclerc. Four or five days ago, the Negroes made a surprise attack on the Isle of La Tortue, where we had our military hospitals. They slaughtered every human being there.[63]

In November, 1802, even General LeClerc himself had died from yellow fever. When France reestablished slavery in Saint-Domingue, and her other West Indies colonies, it fanned the fires of rebellion even further. The pacification of Saint-Domingue was therefore still incomplete in the spring of 1803. All of these factors would enter into Napoleon's decision to rid France of Louisiana, and, in the process, neutralize anti-French feelings in the United States.

Although there was peace in Europe after March, 1802, another political factor entered into the discussion, the ever-increasing pressures from the Americans, whose patience was clearly at the breaking point—especially after the closure of the Mississippi River once again by the unilateral action of Spanish Intendant Morales on October 16, 1802. Morales' action was based on his view that since the provision for the right of deposit, specified in Article XXII of the Pinckney Treaty, had been for only three years, and resulted in flagrant American smuggling, this action was necessary. But, in some circles, the Spanish action was blamed on the French, who —as Livingston wrote were "no longer free agents"—but regarded as pulling the Spanish strings. French intentions for her return to Louisiana remained questionable, but suspicion and rumors abounded, as rumors of French planning surfaced.

> Although unknown in the United States at this time, additional French preparations for the Louisiana Expedition included gifts for the Indians. These included: medals for the chiefs, clothing, tools and weapons—4,000 regular muskets, 1,000 special muskets for the chiefs, 20,000 pounds of powder, 25,000 flints, tomahawks, knives and other supplies. Nothing would have put the American frontiersmen into their flatboats faster in order to meet this challenge than the French intention to arm and use the Indians as allies.
>
> "Report of 27 September 1802," from Prefect Laussat to Admiral Decrès, in *Victor Papers*.

On his part, France's Prefect Laussat in Louisiana after March 26, 1803, faced not only the problem of no military forces with which to have his position respected, but Spanish recalcitrance and increasing American impatience and hostility. Events on a global scale in Europe, in the United States, and the West Indies were now coming to a head over the future of the Mississippi Question and New Orleans.

CHAPTER 4

Louisiana in American
Domestic and Global Policy,
1800–1803

A weak and "feeble" Spain was replaced in 1800 by France, the most powerful military nation in the world, and led by a man with ambitions to extend that power to the very doorstep of the United States. If this were to happen, it would possibly forever close the westward expansion of the American Republic and the extension of liberty it represented. For Jefferson, the fate of New Orleans and American interests in the west and south were critical to the very future of the United States. In November, 1801, Rufus King obtained a copy of the Secret Treaty of San Ildefonso, and forwarded it on to Secretary of State Madison. In May, 1802, Secretary of State Madison instructed Livingston to inquire whether France would be willing to sell West Florida to the United States, in the knowledge that if she still maintained that it was Spain's possession, then in such a case he was to see if France would be willing to act as go-between with Spain. Simultaneously, Charles Pinckney, American Minister to Spain, was instructed to ask the same questions in Madrid. This initiative to gain information and details met with no success. Both Spain and France denied the existence of any deal for the retrocession of Louisiana. The seriousness of the situation, by the spring of 1802, was the subject of a lengthy letter from President Jefferson to Robert Livingston on April, 18, 1802. See the full text of this letter as Primary Document 9 (page 147):

> The cession of Louisiana and the Floridas by Spain to France, works most sorely on the United States. On this subject the Secretary of State has written to you fully, yet I cannot forbear recurring to it personally, so deep is the impression it make on my mind. It completely reverses all the political relations of the United States, and will form a new epoch in our political course . . . There is on the globe one single spot, the possessor of which is our

natural and habitual enemy. It is New Orleans, through which the
produce of three eighths of our territory must pass to market, and
from its fertility it will ere long yield more than half of our whole
produce, and contains more than half of our inhabitants. France,
placing herself in that door, assumes to us the attitude
of defiance . . . The day that France takes possession of New
Orleans, fixes the sentence which is to restrain her forever within
her low-water mark. It seals the union of two nations, who, in
conjunction, can maintain exclusive possession of the ocean.
From that moment, we must marry ourselves to the British fleet
and nation.[64]

As if French intrigues were not enough of a concern to Jefferson, the
sudden suspension of the American right of deposit in New Orleans by
the Spanish Intendant on October 16, 1802, created a firestorm in the
West. A letter from Natchez (April 13, 1803) illustrated the mood: "Public
opinion is here in a state of the greatest excitement . . . There is not a
well-informed man in this territory who does not perceive that our
country is ruined."[65] The Intendant claimed that legally the three-year
Pinckney Treaty guarantee for American deposit had expired, and that
wholesale smuggling by Americans deprived Spain of her legitimate
collection of duties. Per the Treaty, Spain was supposed to designate an
alternative site for American deposit, but Morales failed to do so. Setting
aside the legalities, Jefferson informed Livingston that the method used by
Spain in this instance had only stirred up the westerners further: "A late
suspension by the Intendant of New Orleans of our right of deposit there,
without which the right of navigation is impracticable, has thrown this
country in such a flame of hostile disposition as can scarcely be described."[66]
The hostility to which Jefferson referred is indicated in a "Memorial of
the Legislative Council and House of Representatives of the Mississippi
Territory to the President, Senate, and House of Representatives of the
United States" (January 5, 1803). After outlining the impact of Spain's
action, they concluded with a pledge, and therein their willingness to take
"such measures" as necessary:

> Your Memorialists, conscious of the wisdom, justice, and energy
> of the general government, rest assured that no succor will be
> withholden which existing circumstances may require; and so far
> as may depend on ourselves, we tender to our country our lives
> and fortunes in support of such measures as congress may deem
> necessary to vindicate the honor and protect the interest of the
> United States.[67]

Typical of the overall western response is another petition: "Memorial to the President, Senate and House of Representatives of the United States," dated January, 1803. It described the impacts of the closure:

> Your Memorialists, inhabitants of the states west of the Alleghany Mountains, humbly state that the port of New Orleans is closed to them by a decree of the Spanish intendant; that they owe the United States taxes which have just accrued, as well as large arrearages, and that they have no other means to pay them but the produce of their farms. That, excluded as they are from a market in the east for their produce, it must rot in their granaries, unless the government consents to receive it from them at a reasonable price, or protects them in the enjoyment of a lawful trade; that they humbly conceive that prompt and decisive measures are necessary, the maxim that protection and allegiance are reciprocal being particularly applicable to their situation. In announcing their confidence in the government of the Union, and in giving assurance of their co-operation in all the measures that may adopted to cause the just rights of every portion of the United States to be respected, they declare that they have a right to require, and do require that the government shall either take measures to guaranty the exercise of a legitimate right or release them from every contribution whatever. Without interfering in the measures that have been adopted to bring about the amicable arrangement of a difference, which has grown out of the gratuitous violation of a solemn treaty, they desire that the United States may explicitly understand that their situation is critical; that the delay of only a single season would be ruinous to their country, and that an imperious necessity may consequently oblige them, if they receive no aid, to adopt themselves the measures that may appear to them calculated to protect their commerce, even though those measures should produce consequences unfavorable to the harmony of the confederacy.[68]

Confronted with the possibility of war, from Kentucky to the halls of Congress, where Federalists jumped on the nationalist bandwagon for war, Jefferson responded by formally naming James Monroe (1758–1831) in January, 1803, as Minister Extraordinary to join Livingston in Paris. Monroe was an excellent choice by Jefferson; he possessed, according to Jefferson, "the unlimited confidence of the administration and of the western people." Then he added: "for on the event of this mission depend the future destinies of this republic."[69] Monroe was a Democratic

Republican from Virginia, served in the U.S. Senate from 1790–1794, and governor of Virginia, 1799–1802, where he had consistently advocated the cause of the Westerners against Spanish policies, and was known for his favorable views of France, as U.S. Minister there, 1794–1796. On January 12, 1803, the Senate approved Jefferson's nominations of Robert Livingston, as Minister Plenipotentiary, and James Monroe, as Minister Extraordinary and Plenipotentiary, to negotiate a treaty or convention with France "for the purpose of enlarging, and more effectually securing, our rights and interests on the river Mississippi, and in the territories eastward thereof". After lengthy and heated debate, on February 25, the Senate authorized the President to "organize, arm, and equip according to law, and hold in readiness to march, at a moment's warning, 80,000 effective militia."[70] On March 2, 1803, Secretary of State Madison prepared lengthy instructions for Monroe, to be shared upon his arrival in Paris, with Livingston. The principle object of his mission was clear:

> The object in view, is to procure, by just and satisfactory arrangements, a cession to the United States of New Orleans, and of West and East Florida, or as much thereof as the actual proprietor can be prevailed on to part with.

Madison then stated the current view in Washington that:

> The French republic is understood to have become the proprietor, by a cession from Spain, in the year_____, of New Orleans as part of Louisiana, if not the Floridas also. If the Floridas should not have been then included in the cession, it is not improbable that they have been since added to it.[71]

The American position therefore was that the colony of Louisiana included both West and East Florida. It was this problem that would need clarification and resolution in the negotiations to be conducted in Paris, or if not at that time, then sometime in the future. The specific instructions given to Monroe from Madison in his "Plan of Adjustment" provided the American negotiators with an outline for their deliberations:

> I. France cedes to the United States, forever, the territory east of the river Mississippi; comprehending the two Floridas, the island of New Orleans, and the islands lying to the north and east of the channel of the said river which is commonly called the South Pass, together with all such other islands as appertain to either West or East Florida: France reserving to herself all her territory on the west side of the Mississippi.

II. The boundary between the territory ceded and reserved by France, shall be a continuation of that already defined above the 31st degree of north latitude, namely the middle of the channel or bed of the river, through the said South Pass to the sea. The navigation of the river Mississippi, in its whole breadth from its source to the ocean, and in all its passages to and from the same, shall be equally free and common to citizens of the United States and of the French Republic.

III. The vessels and citizens of the French republic may exercise commerce to and at such places on their respective shores below the said thirty-first degree of north latitude as may be allowed for that use by the parties to their respective citizens and vessels. And it is agreed that no other nation shall be allowed to exercise commerce to or at the same or any other place on either shore, below the said thirty-first degree of latitude, for the term of ten years, to be computed from the exchange of the ratifications hereof. The citizens, vessels, and merchandises of the United States and France, shall be subject to no other duties on their respective shores below the said thirty-first degree of latitude than are imposed on their own citizens, vessels, and merchandises. No duty whatever shall, after the expiration of ten year, be laid on articles the growth or manufacture of the United States, or of the ceded territories, exported through the Mississippi in French vessels; so long as such articles so exported in vessels of the United States shall be exempt from duty: nor shall French vessels, exporting such articles, ever afterwards be subject to pay a higher duty than vessels of the United States.

IV. The citizens of France may, for the term of ten years, deposit their effects at New Orleans, and at such other places on the ceded shore of the Mississippi as are allowed for the commerce of the United States, without paying any other duty than a fair price for the hire of stores.

V. In the ports and commerce of West and East Florida, France shall never be on a worse footing than the most favored nation; and for the term of ten years her vessels and merchandise shall be subject there in to no higher duties than are paid by those of the United States. Articles of the growth and manufacture of the United States, and of the ceded territory, exported in French vessels from any port in West or East Florida, shall be exempt from duty as long as vessels of the United States shall enjoy this exemption.

VI. The United States, in consideration of the cession of territory made by this treaty, shall pay to France_____ millions of *livres tournois*, in the manner following; namely, They shall pay _____ millions of *livres tournois* immediately on the exchange of the ratifications hereof; they shall assume, in such order of priority as the government of the United States may approve, the payment of claims which have been, or may be acknowledged by the French republic to be due to American citizens, or so much thereof as, with the payment to be made on the exchange of ratifications, will not exceed the sum of _____; and, in case a balance should remain due, after such payment and assumption, the same shall be paid at the end of one year from the final liquidation of the claims hereby assumed, which shall be payable in three equal annual payments—the first of which is to take place one year after exchange of ratifications, or they shall bear interest at the rate of sic per cent, per annum, from the date of such intended payments, until they shall be discharged. All the above-mentioned payments shall be made at the treasury of the United States, and at the rate of one dollar and ten cents for every six *livres tournois*.

VII. To incorporate the inhabitants of the hereby ceded territory with the citizens of the United States, on an equal footing, being a provision which cannot now be made, it is to be expected, from the character and policy of the United States, that such incorporation will take place without necessary delay. In the mean time they shall be secure in their persons and property, and in the free enjoyment of their religion.[72]

Finally, after recounting the various options and position of the United States on the issues of relations with both France and Spain, Madison concluded:

These instructions, though as full as they could be conveniently made, will necessarily leave much to your discretion. For the proper exercise of it, the president relies on your information, your judgment, and your fidelity to the interests of your country.[73]

Notice in the "Plan" that reference is made *only* to territory through purchase from France on left bank of the Mississippi River, New Orleans and/or including both East and West Florida; the territory on the right, or west bank of the river, is left in the possession of France. But, the territory on the west bank was useless without a port of access, although that was provided for France over a period of twelve years through New Orleans. But the bigger question is after the twelve years, then what? However, it was the last paragraph that would provide Monroe and Livingston with the authorization to conclude negotiations with France for the whole colony of Louisiana; it was made clear to them in Paris that for France, the bottom line was "all or nothing" regarding the sale of their colony. It was this position that Livingston and Monroe faced, and in their opinion, they had no choice but to use their "judgment" and proceed to negotiate for the whole. See their Report (May 13, 1803) to Secretary of State Madison, Primary Document 13 (page 179).

On January 12, 1803, the House of Representatives appropriated $2,000,000 for the purchase of New Orleans and adjacent lands to the east. In a later message to the Congress (October 17, 1803), and to quell the growing opposition to the purchase of Louisiana from Federalists, Jefferson argued that the House's action back in January had set a precedent and "was considered as conveying the sanction of Congress to the acquisition proposed." In another initiative a few days later (January 18, 1803), President Jefferson secretly requested $2,500 from Congress "for the purpose of extending the external commerce of the United States", and with which to send Meriwether Lewis and a small military party of 10–12 men to explore Louisiana, regardless of who possessed it.[74] Jefferson had a passionate appetite for information. His action to send Captain Meriwether Lewis (a fellow Virginian, a neighbor, and his private secretary) along with a small military party into Louisiana, which was still a Spanish possession even though by treaty and royal decree it was ceded to France, did not alter the fact that the President had authorized, and Congress had funded, a secret American military expedition to enter the territory of a foreign nation. It was the first American "black op!"

Thomas Jefferson

Thomas Jefferson was born on April 13, 1743, in Albermarle County, Virginia, the third of ten children by Peter Jefferson and Jane Randolph. An avid student, he went to the College of William and Mary from where he graduated in 1762 and later was admitted to the bar in 1767. In 1772, he married Martha Skelton, and in their eleven years of marriage, they had six children; following her death in 1782, Thomas Jefferson never remarried. He practiced law in Virginia, and served in the Virginia House of Burgesses from Albermarle. Then, in 1775, he represented Virginia as a delegate to the Second Continental Congress, and was appointed to join four other delegates in preparing the Declaration of Independence in 1776. He then returned to Virginia and in 1779, he was elected Governor of Virginia and served until 1781. Elected to the Continental Congress, he was the principal author of the Ordinance of 1784 that dealt with the issue of western lands. His ideas on developing the west to include future states also included a proposal for prohibiting slavery north of the Ohio River, which although not passed in 1784 was later included in the Northwest Ordinance of 1787. He was passionate about learning, gathering information and science. In 1785, he was appointed as U.S. Minister to France, where he worked until 1789 when he returned home and was appointed by President Washington to be the first Secretary of State. In this position, he served from 1790 to 1793, but disagreements with Alexander Hamilton over fiscal policy and consolidation of power by the Federalists, as well as division within the administration over American interests with the war in Europe between Britain and France, led him to resign in late 1793. He retired to his home Monticello in Albermarle where he became the leader of the opposition forces against Alexander Hamilton and took the name of "Democratic Republicans" to distinguish them from the Federalist power structure.

In the Presidential election of 1796, Jefferson lost to John Adams of Massachusetts, but there was a provision in the Constitution which provided that the person receiving the second most votes would be the Vice President, a position which Jefferson held from 1796 to 1801. Opposition to Jay's Treaty, implementation of new taxes, and, most importantly, the Federalist legislation known as the Alien and Sedition Acts in 1798, combined to lead Jefferson to become the undisputed leader of the opposition. Responding to what he regarded as Federalist "tyranny" and their connections to Britain, Jefferson authored the Kentucky Resolutions, which advocated the doctrine of "nullification" against Federal laws deemed unconstitutional within the states. He was accused of undermining the government of the United States and the presidency of John Adams. Deep divisions between the Federalists and Democratic Republicans took center stage in the elections of 1800. In the election, Jefferson wound up in an electoral tie vote with Aaron Burr of New York, which was only resolved on February 17, 1801, when Alexander Hamilton used his influence among Federalists to cast the deciding votes in favor of Jefferson. On March 4, 1801, Jefferson took the oath of Office, and became the Third President of the United States.

Jefferson would serve two terms as President, from 1801–1809. His first administration, 1801–1805, began by focusing on reversing Federalist policies and political appointments. A staunch believer in reducing the influence of the federal government in favor of the states, Jefferson, and a Democratic Republican Congress majority, went after those institutions which the Federalists had supported: an increased military, the national bank, an enlarged judiciary, increased taxes, repeal of the Alien and Sedition Acts and the national debt. The war in Europe, which by now was limited to France, with her ally Spain, and Great Britain still presented problems for the young republic and its new Democratic Republican President, and Jefferson attempted reverse Federalist policies at home and abroad. Then, a troubling rumor appeared on the scene from British sources in 1801: Spain had concluded a secret treaty with France for the retrocession of the Colony of Louisiana, and with it, the City of New Orleans, which controlled commerce from the western states and territories to the Gulf of Mexico. The "Mississippi Question" became the dominant national political issue of Jefferson's first administration. Along with Secretary of State James Madison, and his ministers in Paris, London and Madrid, Jefferson sought to find a diplomatic solution. Some in Congress and state or territorial legislatures in 1802 demanded a military solution, especially after Spain closed the port of New Orleans to American commerce. Yet, Jefferson did not waiver in his belief that a diplomatic solution on America's behalf might be found. As a result of his tireless efforts, and events in Europe and the West Indies, France decided to sell its colony of Louisiana to the United States in April, 1803. It was the greatest triumph of Jefferson's presidency. He followed up by sending Meriweather Lewis and William Clark to explore the new vast territory in 1804, and their safe return in 1806 with volumes of information they had gathered provided the country with the first glimpse of the magnitude of the Louisiana Purchase.

His second term, 1805–1809, was one problem after another. The renewal of war in Europe after May, 1803, led to increasing friction with Great Britain over American neutrality. Again, Jefferson opted to try a non-military solution, an embargo act restricting American commerce on the assumption that Britain needed American products, particularly agricultural ones, in order to survive. The embargo, however, only paralyzed American commerce and gave new life to a troubled Federalist party. In domestic and foreign affairs, Jefferson faced new challenges that his earlier ideas were incapable of resolving after 1806. Upon completion of his second term in 1809, he retired to his home at Monticello and began work for which he wished to be remembered, the founding of the University of Virginia. He died on July 4, 1826, the same day as his former friend and later rival, John Adams.

Jefferson also wrote to James Garrard, Governor of Kentucky, to inform him of his appointment of Monroe to negotiate "arrangements that may effectively secure our rights & interests on the Mississippi and in the country eastward of that."[75] He further informed the governor of recent diplomatic communications, which included information that he had received from Madrid informing him the king had not authorized the Intendant's action of revoking the right of deposit. All of these steps had the desired effect of neutralizing talk in Kentucky of secession or independent military action by some western inhabitants.

Monroe arrived in Paris on April 12, two days after an extraordinary meeting between First Consul Napoleon, Foreign Minister Talleyrand, and Director-General of the Public Treasury, François Barbé-Marbois (1745–1837). Barbé-Marbois had served in the administration of King Louis XVI, and then in public office during the French Revolution. In addition, he had been the Intendant for the Island of Saint-Domingue, 1784–1789, and knew full well the problems of the slave economy there.

Then, as France's consular representative in the United States,
1789–1795, he was knowledgeable
about the United States, and his
wife was an American from Philadelphia. Talleyrand, the French
Foreign Minister, opposed the sale

> Napoleon to Barbé-Marbois, April 10,
> 1803: "I renounce it [Louisiana] with the
> greatest regret; to attempt obstinately to
> retain it would be folly."

of Louisiana, along with Napoleon's brothers Joseph (1768–1844) and
Lucian (1778–1846), and Admiral Decrès, Minister of the Navy and
Colonies. Talleyrand's former negative dealings with Americans, including
the infamous XYZ Affair, therefore made Barbé-Marbois, Director-
General of the Public Treasury, an excellent choice to lead the French
negotiations. It was at this meeting that Napoleon said that he was thinking
of selling all of Louisiana to the Americans:

> They ask for only one town of Louisiana; but I already consider
> the Colony as completely lost, and it seems to me that in the
> hands of that growing power it will be more useful to the policy,
> and even the commerce of France than if I should try to keep it.[76]

Barbé-Marbois concurred in this decision; see his detailed account of
this meeting in Primary Document 9 (page 147).

Napoleon was well aware of the increasing American animosity,
including the potential for military action against New Orleans prior to
any French occupation of it. Livingston had made a point of informing
the French of the increasing hostility among not only the inhabitants in
the West, but also their representatives in Congress. In a letter to Talleyrand
(December 11, 1802), Livingston informed him of American outrage at
Spain's action by revoking the right of deposit, but then added a warning:

> It is, sir, particularly unfortunate that this difficulty should arise at
> the precise moment when France is about entering on the
> possession of the country. I very much fear that this circumstance,
> connected with that silence that the French government observes
> respecting its intentions, may induce suspicious persons to
> suppose that the court of Spain has acted in this manner
> altogether in concert with France. Although I too justly appreciate
> the uprightness of her government, to believe that it would
> approve the infraction of a treaty, and thus mark, by an act of
> hostility, the period of our becoming neighbors, the subject is,
> nevertheless, of a nature to require, on the part of France, the
> most prompt attention to these subjects, the disregard of which
> has excited the warmest sensations in the United States.[77]

It was a clear warning to France that if it was involved in this Spanish action, there would be repercussions, including driving the United States into Britain's lap. Livingston rattled the sabre, but failed to get any definitive response back. Foreign Minister Talleyrand later responded (March, 1803) to Livingston and stated that they were still looking into the matter; and, that the First Consul and France looked favorably on the continuation of their relationship with the United States, and awaited the arrival of Mr. Monroe.

French apprehension about the American frontiersmen's capacity for unilateral military action against New Orleans is indicated in a letter of December 2, 1802, from Admiral Decrès to Captain-General Victor:

> The inhabitants of Kentucky, especially must engage the attention of the Captain-General. The rapid current of the Ohio and the rivers whose shores they inhabit and which empty in the Mississippi, permit them so much more easily to attempt an expedition against New Orleans. A powder-horn, a pouch of bullets, their provisions of cold meal form their equipment. Great readiness is lent them by their custom of living in the forests and enduring fatigues. Beyond a doubt such neighbors merit being watched.[78]

The warning from Admiral Decrès to General Victor about the Kentuckians might well have come true if France had taken possession of Louisiana. Control of the Mississippi and New Orleans were not the only points of potential trouble. The most dangerous mistake France might have made in Louisiana, and its future impact on Franco-American relations, was its intended Indian policy. Prior to leaving France, Laussat prepared a report in September, 1802, in which he outlined plans that ought to guide French policy with the Indians which mirrored that of Spain previously. He recommended a plan for giving presents to the Indians. "It is essential," he wrote, "to start off with them in a manner which will maintain their favorable disposition and get them attached to us for the future, because they could become very useful."[79] Presents for the Indians in the form of medals, clothing, and tools were commonplace, but the French gifts included guns. Among the weapons were 4,000 regular muskets, 1,000 special muskets for the chiefs, 20,000 pounds of gunpowder, 25,000 flints, and a variety of other weapons. This policy, if implemented, would have been like waving the bloody red flag at the American frontiersman bull! In his instructions to General Victor, Napoleon ordered him to protect the colony with Indian alliances, but cautioned against any commitment that would bind France to protect them under all circumstances. He was told:

"everything that would occasion the establishment of quarrels with the United States must be avoided."[80] Like Spain's policy in 1795, for the French, the United States was not to become an ally of any other power, especially Britain! In New Orleans, Prefect Laussat was developing his own plans for the future management of Louisiana. As the chief fiscal officer in the colony, he proposed an action that would be implemented, i.e. revoking the "right of deposit." On April 18, 1803, he sent a lengthy report to Admiral Decrès in which he referred to his Spanish counterpart, Intendant Morales, as "a man of capacity and experience."[81] He indicated that he agreed with Morales that the "right of deposit" given to foreign merchants was a bad policy, and therefore went on to warn against any future French concessions to American shippers. He wrote of the American merchants: "They are poisoning these countries with English goods, with which French goods cannot compete." Any right of deposit, he argued was an open door through which "a smuggling trade without bounds" entered Louisiana.[82] Solution? Laussat proposed that France deal with the right of deposit issue, so sensitive to the Americans, by allowing it to continue but with conditions; his plan would require foreign merchants to pay a "storage fee" and place their merchandise in a government warehouse. With such government warehouses, and the storage fee "the loss of customs duties would be more or less made up" from losses due to "smuggling." Of course, he never got the opportunity to put his plan into operation because of events in Paris. Napoleon was right, this was neither the time nor the place to arouse the hostility of the United States, and the plans of Prefect Laussat would have done precisely that.

Bonaparte's immediate view in the spring of 1803 was that renewal of war with Britain was inevitable, perhaps even within a few weeks, and although France was a naval power, she could not protect both her interests in Europe and Louisiana. Any French military expedition that depended upon the French navy was unpredictable, the Egyptian and Syrian campaigns (1797–1801) and the British naval victory at Aboukir Bay (August 1, 1798) off the coast of Egypt demonstrated that. Ultimately, however, there was the continuing failure by French forces to pacify the slave rebellion in Saint-Domingue. The staggering losses of French troops to yellow fever and rebel forces proved decisive in his decision. Both diplomatic channels and private individuals, such as Pierre Samuel du Pont de Nemours (1739–1817), a friend of both the United States and France, had informed Napoleon of the potential for hostilities in the American west from any French military action.

Jefferson knew and trusted du Pont, and used him as diplomatic courier. In a letter to du Pont prior to his departure to France on April 25, 1802, Jefferson asked him:

> to impress on the government of France the inevitable
> consequences of their taking possession of Louisiana; and
> though, as I here mention, the cession of New Orleans and the
> Floridas to us would be a palliation, yet I believe it would be no
> more, and that this measure will cost France, and perhaps not
> very long hence, a war which will annihilate her on the ocean, and
> place that element under the despotism of two nations, which I
> am more reconciled to because my own would be one of them.[83]

See the text of this letter, Primary Document 10 (page 151). Jefferson used both official diplomatic channels and personal friends in France and the United States to convey his concerns to the French government. Jefferson concluded his letter by reminding du Pont that he was a man of peace, but there was the possibility that France's military occupation of Louisiana would thereby drive the United States into a military alliance with Britain.

Monroe's known support for the Westerners and their open threats to take matters into their own hands, with Congressional support in Washington, by invading New Orleans, put the American problem for France into perspective. Napoleon was a gambler, and the odds of holding Louisiana against a potential Anglo-American military alliance were slim to nonexistent. According to Barbé-Marbois, Napoleon, who hated Britain with a passion, informed him in a private conference that: "to emancipate nations from the commercial tyranny of England, it is necessary to balance her influence by a maritime power that may one day become her rival; that power is the United States."[84] Events in America seemed to substantiate Napoleon's views. The United States Senate debated a bill introduced by James Ross (Federalist from Pennsylvania) on February 16, 1803, which included several inflammatory remarks. His resolutions proposed that the President be authorized to raise 50,000 militia with which to secure navigation rights on the Mississippi by force, and $5,000,000 with which to undertake it. After some debate, Senator John Breckenridge (Democratic Republican from Kentucky) offered his own amendments that authorized the President to raise 80,000 militia, and included provision for funding, but cautioned that since negotiations were currently underway, he hoped the diplomatic process would work. This proposal had the advantage of the sword and the olive branch.

> "This little event, of France's possessing herself of Louisiana, is the embryo of a tornado which will burst on the countries on both sides of the Atlantic and involve in its effects the highest destinies."
>
> Jefferson's letter to Pierre Samuel du Pont, April 25, 1802.

Senator Breckenridge's proposals passed the Senate on February 25, by a vote of 15 yeas to 11 nays along party lines. A final bill was passed on February 26 that authorized the President to call up 80,000 militia, and appropriated funds with which to cover the costs if the diplomatic efforts failed.[85] Jefferson signed the bill on February 28. Monroe shrewdly carried a copy of the Senate bill with him to Paris.

From the beginning of the negotiations with France in 1802, the American interest had always been to: (1) confirm France's acquisition of Louisiana from Spain, a position which Talleyrand and his Spanish counterpart Godoy denied; and, (2) if it were true that France had acquired Louisiana, then to attempt to purchase New Orleans, or another port and lands on the east bank of the Mississippi that might serve American commercial interests. The large size of the Mississippi Territory, and the river systems that originated in the old southwest but which flowed south to the Gulf of Mexico offered alternatives. The Pearl River, the Alabama and the Tombigbee entered the Gulf in West Florida at Mobile, and these river systems drained the vast reaches of Mississippi and Alabama where there were thousands of American settlers. The right of deposit in New Orleans was of no value to them, but control of the river systems and access to the Gulf of Mexico via a port such as Mobile was. Jefferson, Secretary of State Madison, and the American negotiators assumed that France had also received West Florida as part of the treaty with Spain. They therefore were negotiating for New Orleans and lands to the east, West Florida. During the early years of the American Republic, commerce was conducted mainly by water transportation. There were only four routes, not roads but trails, which passed from the eastern seaboard across into the trans-Appalachian settlements, such as the Natchez Trace from Nashville westward. Road building was not only in its infancy, but was left to the individual states or to private parties. Therefore, the extensive rivers of the West and the South, of which the Mississippi was the largest and longest, did not negate the importance of other river systems as commercial routes that also terminated in the Gulf of Mexico, and depending upon your location, were important avenues of commerce. When French Foreign Minister Talleyrand asked the United States' negotiators on April 11 what they might be willing to pay for the whole of Louisiana, it came as not only a complete surprise, but purchasing the vast unknown lands on the west bank of Mississippi had not been authorized by President Jefferson. In the extensive instructions carried to France by Monroe from Madison, and those given to Livingston on April 18, 1802, by President Jefferson, both the Secretary of State and the President had referred only to "New Orleans and the Floridas."

On February 3, 1803, President Jefferson wrote to Livingston informing him of his decision to send James Monroe to assist in the discussions, and then reaffirmed the purpose of their mission:

> We must know at once whether we can acquire New Orleans or not. We are satisfied nothing else will secure us against a war at no distant period; and we cannot press this reason without beginning those arrangement which will be necessary if war is hereafter to result.[86]

He also informed Livingston of the political mischief and rhetoric by the Federalists. Jefferson's anguish is clear:

> A late suspension by the Intendant of New Orleans of our right of deposit there, without which the right of navigation is impracticable, has thrown this country into such a flame of hostile disposition as can scarcely be described. The Western country was peculiarly sensible to it as you may suppose. Our business was to take the most effectual pacific measures in our power to remove the suspension, and at the same time to persuade our countrymen that pacific measures would be most effectual and the most speedily so. The opposition [Federalists] caught it as a plank in a shipwreck, hoping it would enable them to tack the Western people to them. They raised the cry of war, were intriguing in all quarters to exasperate the Western inhabitants to arm and go down on their own authority and possess themselves of New Orleans, and in the meantime were daily reiterating, in new shapes, inflammatory resolutions for the adoption of the House.[87]

Then, Jefferson continued, Livingston's charge was to secure New Orleans and the land east of the Mississippi, and Monroe was instructed by Jefferson to offer up to $10 million for New Orleans and the Floridas. James Monroe arrived in Paris on April 12, and immediately conferred with Livingston. The next day, Monroe and Livingston met with Barbé-Marbois.

Monroe and Livingston were to secure at a minimum American access to the Mississippi and New Orleans, or at least some location in West Florida from which

> "Only force can give us New Orleans. We must employ force. Let us first get possession of the country, and negotiate afterwards."
>
> Robert Livingston to James Monroe on the latter's arrival in France, April 12, 1803

American commerce might have access to the Gulf. Finally, if negotiations with France failed, they were instructed to leave Paris and seek a treaty with Britain. Secretary of State Madison reiterated this alternative in a letter of April 18, 1803:

> If the French government, instead of friendly arrangements or views, should be found to meditate hostilities, or to have formed projects which will constrain the United States to resort to hostilities, such communications are then to be held with the British government as will sound its dispositions and invite its concurrence in the war.[88]

Monroe and Livingston were authorized with a blank check for purchasing New Orleans and adjacent lands to the east from France, but failing that, they were to negotiate an agreement with Britain. Among the items in the packet of instructions sent by Secretary of State Madison to James Monroe on April 18, 1803, were two blank commissions of appointment as representative plenipotentiary along with letters of "credence" to Great Britain:

> "A separate letter to you [Monroe] is also enclosed, authorizing you to enter into such communications and conferences with British ministers as may be possibly required by the conduct of France. The letter is made a separate one, that it may be used with the effect, but without the formality of a commission. It is hoped that sound calculations of interest, as well as the sense of right, in the French government, will prevent the necessity of using the authority expressed in this letter. In a contrary state of things the president relies on your own information to be gained on the spot, and on your best discretion, to open with advantage the communications with the British government, and to proportion the degree of an understanding with it, to the indications of an approaching war with France. It will only be observed to you, that if France should avow or evince a determination to deny to the United States the free navigation of the Mississippi, your consultations with Great Britain may be held, on the ground that war is inevitable."[89]

Fortunately, the letter and its commissions arrived after the treaty and conventions with France had been signed; however, it is indicative of the strong position being taken by the United States that if France balked, or in the meantime if war had erupted in Europe, Mr. Monroe should use his discretion accordingly. It was assumed in Washington, that if war had broken out, France "will no doubt be the more apt to concur in friendly accommodations with us." Resolution in favor of American interests in New Orleans, or in the Floridas for an outlet to the sea was still the priority. The commissions would have allowed Livingston and Monroe to negotiate in full immediately with Britain if the French negotiations failed. Livingston and Monroe were, as Jefferson stated, "fully possessed of every idea we have on the subject, and give them a shape admissible by us without being obliged to await new instructions hence."[90] There was never any discussion or intention in the instructions for the American plenipotentiaries to acquire land on the west bank of the Mississippi. Jefferson's letter, and the instructions from Secretary of State Madison therefore, provided Livingston and Monroe with all necessary authorization to negotiate in full. But no one in the United States or in Paris had any inkling that Napoleon would soon offer to sell the whole colony of Louisiana.

The American negotiators regarded their authorization from Jefferson as not exceeding their instructions to negotiate for the purchase of the whole Louisiana territory when it was surprisingly offered to them by France. It was a spur of the moment decision that they later defended to Secretary of State Madison on May 13, 1803. The question of the American negotiators having exceeded their authority is discussed in detail in their

Robert R. Livingston

Robert R. Livingston was born on November 27, 1746, in New York City and was the oldest child of nine. His early career included Recorder of New York City, and then he participated in the drafting of the Declaration of Independence. He returned to New York in order to become Chancellor of New York in 1777, a judicial position that he held until 1801. He served as U.S. Secretary of Foreign Affairs from 1781–1783, and became active in the political world as an adherent to the ideas of Thomas Jefferson, as opposed to those of fellow New Yorkers Alexander Hamilton and John Jay. He therefore was an important political leader among the Democratic Republicans and when Jefferson was elected President in 1800, he appointed Livingston as United States Minister to France in 1801, a position he held until 1804. It was in this capacity that he first learned of the retrocession of Louisiana from Spain to France, and he tirelessly worked to determine the circumstances of their secret treaty. He was constantly frustrated in this effort by the French Minister of Foreign Affairs, Talleyrand, and the two men disliked one another almost from the beginning. After 1804, Livingston returned to New York where he died on February 26, 1813.

James Monroe

James Monroe was born on April 28, 1758, in Virginia, where his family was one of several important planters. He joined the revolution, and was wounded. After the war he studied law, was elected as a delegate to the Continental Congress, and then participated in the ratification process for the new Constitution by joining the Anti-Federalists, along with people like Patrick Henry, because he regarded the document as giving too much power to the new government. Virginia finally ratified the Constitution in 1788 after Monroe and others agreed to withhold their opposition in return for inclusion of a Bill of Rights as amendments to the Constitution. He was elected from the state legislature in 1790 and served as a Senator in the United States Congress until 1794. Here too he opposed the Federalists, and became a member of the new Jeffersonian Republicans and was their floor leader of the soon to be called Democratic Republicans.

He served as United States Minister to France from 1794 to 1796, and when Franco-American relations deteriorated over the issue of American neutrality, he returned to Virginia. In 1799, he was elected Governor of Virginia a position he held until December, 1802, when he was asked by President Jefferson to join Livingston in France. It was during his governorship that the famous slave rebellion of Gabriel in 1800 occurred, which he suppressed. He was instrumental in the final negotiations with France after his arrival there in early April, 1803, and along with Livingston, he signed the Treaty and Two Conventions of April 30, 1803. Upon completion of the Louisiana Purchase, he succeeded Rufus King as United States Minister to Great Britain, where he served from 1803 to 1808. He was appointed by President James Madison as Secretary of State from 1811 to 1817, and briefly served concurrently as Secretary of War from 1814 to 1815 during the War of 1812. As an accomplished politician, and staunch Democratic Republican, he was elected as the Fifth President of the United States in 1816, served from 1817 to 1825, and was the author of the famous Monroe Doctrine in 1823. He died on July 4, 1831.

"Report of May 13, 1803." See Primary Document 13 (page 179) for the text. Livingston and Monroe argued that: France was unwilling to negotiate on anything other than the whole colony of Louisiana; during the negotiations, the original price had been set at 100,000,000 francs (the rate of exchange was 5.3333 francs to one American dollar), which they negotiated down to the final price of 60,000,000 francs; France had originally wanted the United States to assume the full debt owed to American shippers per the Convention of 1800, but which they managed to negotiate downward in the second convention; the right to enter all ports in the ceded territories for vessels of France and Spain without restrictions, but this provision was reduced for only for a twelve year

The full purchase price of Louisiana, principal and interest, was not paid off until 1823, by which time the final U.S. cost of Louisiana was $23,313,567.73.

period; and, that funds for the purchase should begin the payment schedule within the first year, but which they delayed for fifteen years instead. On the French view, see Part Two, Primary Document 11 (page 156) of the negotiations as recorded by Barbé-Marbois.

During the negotiations, Monroe was contacted by a representative of the Dutch and British banking firms of Hope and Baring, who informed him that they were willing to loan the United States the funds necessary, up to $10 million at 6 percent per year, with which to complete the transaction. This could be done by means of issuance of U.S. bonds, which would be acquired and sold by the Amsterdam firm of Hope and Company and the British banking House of Baring.[91] On its part, the British government agreed not to oppose this action, even with the knowledge that Napoleon would use his cash for military purposes, because the bigger political threat was with the prospect of the French once again in the middle of North America. James Monroe arrived in Paris on April 12, and met with Livingston. The next day, Livingston and Monroe met with their French counterpart. Barbé-Marbois later recalled the mood of the negotiations as one of friendship among the three plenipotentiaries, which "did not prevent their considering it a duty to treat, on both sides, for the conditions most advantageous to their respective countries."[92] Then, he described their first meeting and negotiations in part: "Deliberation succeeded to astonishment. The two joint plenipotentiaries [Livingston and Monroe], without asking an opportunity to concerting measures of the presence of the French negotiator, immediately entered on explanations, and the conferences rapidly succeeded one another."[93]

The negotiation had three objects. First, the cession of Louisiana, then the price and, finally, the indemnity due to Americans from France for the prizes and their cargoes. After having communicated their respective views on these different points, it was agreed to discuss them separately, and even to make three distinct treaties. The subject of the cession was considered first. Barbé-Marbois provided a discussion draft of a treaty, and the decision was made to use it as the template. The American negotiators provided their own draft of treaty provisions per the "Plan" given to them by Madison, but opted to incorporate their points through comments and changes to the French draft. The full powers given to the American plenipotentiaries only extended to an arrangement respecting the east bank of the Mississippi, including New Orleans. It was impossible for them to have recourse to their government for more specific instructions. Hostilities between France and Great Britain were on the eve of resuming; war was only a matter of time, and not much of that remained. For this reason, the issue of whether or not to include Spain in the discussions was dropped because of the time and distances involved in contacting Madrid.[94] In any case, Spain no longer possessed Louisiana since King Carlos IV had ordered it transferred to France. It was this situation that later precipitated the question from the Federalists in the United States Congress on Spain's position, and which, in 1804, prompted correspondence from the Spanish government to the United States regarding their displeasure at not being consulted by France and the United States. As the French negotiator put it, the conditions in Europe were such that: "The American plenipotentiaries had not to reflect long to discover that the circumstances, in which France was placed, were the most fortunate for their country."[95] As the negotiations proceeded, the issue of the purchase price became central. Napoleon, who had originally wanted 100 million francs, finally settled on 50 million francs as the price; Barbé-Marbois used Napoleon's original idea as a sum for the opening discussion, knowing that he could still reduce the amount if needed. The Americans thought that figure too high, and the amount was lowered to 60 million francs for Louisiana, plus an additional 20 million francs owed by France to citizens of the United States as a result of the Convention of 1800. On April 29, the negotiators agreed on a sale price of 60 million francs for the colony of Louisiana, and an additional 20 million francs for the United States to assume the claims of its citizens against the French government for losses "at sea" during the period of the quasi-war between the two nations.[96] All that remained was to include these terms into the two conventions as part of the treaty package, which was done on April 30, 1803. See Primary Document 11, Part Two (page 156).

The treaty of cession and two conventions were agreed to for France by François Barbé-Marbois, and for the United States by Robert Livingston and James Monroe. They were officially signed on May 2, 1803. But the treaty and conventions of April 30, 1803, deliberately left the boundary issues of Louisiana with Canada in the north, Texas and Mexico to the south and West Florida to the east up in the air. France sold to the United States property that had been retroceded to her in 1800 from Spain, the same property that she had ceded originally in 1762 to Spain. At no point during these years had either France or Spain undertaken to define or survey the boundaries of the colony.

The Treaty of Cession of April 30, 1803, in Article I provided a brief history of the provisions in the Treaty of San Ildefonso (October 1, 1800) and the promise of Spain to return "the Colony or Province of Louisiana with the Same extent that it now has in the hands of Spain & that it had when France possessed it." The boundary issue remained unsettled. When Livingston attempted to press the issue of the boundaries, Talleyrand refused to bite and referred him to future negotiation with Spain. According to Livingston, in a letter to Secretary of State Madison (May 20, 1803), Talleyrand gave him no direction: "You have made a noble bargain for yourselves, and I suppose you will make the most of it."[97] In other words, it was up to the United States to determine the details of any boundary issues with Spain regarding the Floridas in the future. The Treaty then reaffirmed that the French Republic "has an incontestable title to the domain and to the possession of the said Territory." Article I concluded:

> The First Consul of the French Republic desiring to give to the United States a strong proof of his friendship doth hereby cede to the United States in the name of the French Republic forever and in full Sovereignty the said territory with all its rights and appurtenances as fully and in the Same manner as they have been acquired by the French Republic in virtue of the above mentioned Treaty concluded with His Catholic Majesty.

The colony of Louisiana that France sold to the United States was therefore the same as it had existed in 1762, when she had ceded it to Spain. West and East Florida belonged to Britain at that time; it was only later during the war of the American Revolution that the Floridas had been captured by Spain, and retained per the peace Treaty of Paris in 1783. It was this fact that caused the American negotiators their grief over the status of the Floridas. Ambiguity regarding the status of West Florida boundaries became part of the document. The United States purchased "Louisiana with the same extent that it now has in the hands of Spain, and that it had when France possessed it; and Such as it Should be after Treaties subsequently entered into between Spain and other States." Not only was there obscurity, but there still was no clear delineation as to any actual boundaries of Louisiana. Louisiana had not been explored or mapped by either France or Spain, and therefore it had never been surveyed. Maps of that day were mere cartographical speculations. In other words, neither Livingston nor Monroe as American negotiators, nor Barbé-Marbois of France for that matter, knew the boundaries for the property that they had just purchased or sold when they all agreed to the terms of the treaty and conventions on April 30, 1803, and then signed the finished documents on May 2, 1803.

The Treaty of 30 April 1803 specified in Article II the transfer all public properties in Louisiana, buildings, fortifications, and even archival documents to the United States, which was consistent with any property transfer. The inhabitants were to be incorporated into the Union of the United States with all rights and properties enjoyed by the citizens of the United States, per Article III. Additional provisions specified the manner of the actual transfer of Louisiana from France to the United States, and certain commercial privileges for ships of France ("most favored nation" status) and Spain into the port of New Orleans. In Article IX, it was agreed that a Convention signed at the same time provided for payment by the United States of debts owed to American citizens by the French Republic ($3,750,000) prior to the Franco-American Convention of September 30, 1800. The specifics of the transfer were spelled out in the two Conventions. In the first Convention, Article 1 stated:

> The Government of the United States engages to pay to the French government in the manner specified in the following article the sum of Sixty millions of francs [$11,250,000] independent of the Sum which Shall be fixed by another Convention for the payment of debts due by France to citizens of the United States.

In Article 2, the arrangement specified that the United States stock for the purchase price was to be paid commencing fifteen years after the exchange of ratifications with the first payment of not less than three million dollars, and only after Louisiana "shall be taken possession of [in] the name of the Government of the United States." This provision, for payment only after the United States had taken possession, was crucial to quieting the debate in Congress, where the Federalist argument was that the nation might end up paying millions of dollars without clear title. The second Convention provided for the payment of debts to American citizens owed by France to be paid now by the United States Government. These debts were from the period of quasi-war between France and United States, 1797–1800, for "prizes made at sea." The specific methods for determining the validity of such future claims were enumerated, and the second Convention agreed to on April 30, 1803, as well. The deal was completed.

The purchase of Louisiana in 1803 however provided President Jefferson and the United States with a desperately needed opportunity to resolve the issues of navigation of the Mississippi and the status of New Orleans for frontiersmen without hostilities, and transformed the West for future American development and the spread of the American ideas of liberty under

"From this day the United States take their place among the powers of the first rank."
Robert Livingston upon signing the Louisiana Purchase Treaty, May 2, 1803

the Constitution. But such an opportunity was not universally applauded at home, and especially in the halls of Congress among President Jefferson's political opponents. The acquisition of Louisiana triggered a constitutional debate over the powers of the federal government. The ideological crisis for President Thomas Jefferson, a firm believer in the "strict constructionist" interpretation of the Constitution, was how to achieve a political solution consistent with his legal powers, and within what appeared to be an ever-changing window of opportunity. Jefferson, a strict constructionist, initially believed that a Constitutional amendment, authorizing the purchase of New Orleans and adjacent land, was necessary. The Constitution contained no provision for acquiring new land for the nation. Additionally, the amendment process would require placing the issue before Federalists in Congress and, ultimately, approval within their states. In one of those rare political ironies in American history, the Federalists, who during the administrations of Presidents Washington and Adams, espoused the "implied powers" doctrine for the Constitution found themselves on the other side of the fence when it came to support for the purchase of Louisiana. This precedent was available therefore for President Jefferson to use the "implied powers" clause (Article 1, Section 8) in the Constitution. The "implied powers" doctrine specified that the federal government had the power: "To make all laws which shall be necessary and proper for carrying into execution the forgoing powers," and therefore it placed the Louisiana issue, clearly within the legislative prerogatives of Congress. Any attempt along the path of a Constitutional amendment would be lengthy and perhaps even futile. While Jefferson had the votes in the Senate to pass the treaty, and enough seats in the House of Representatives for an appropriation, he was still concerned about using powers that he had earlier opposed. The option to use the "implied powers" clause, an interpretation that Hamilton had used with success in 1791 regarding the establishment of a national bank, and one with which President Washington had concurred. When Federalists in Congress during President Adams' administration passed the Alien and Sedition laws in 1798, citing a similar interpretation, Jefferson saw despotism and tyranny rising again from special interests and an attempt to silence political opposition. Of those persons tried and convicted of "sedition" after 1798, all of them were Democratic Republicans. To counter Federalists stretching of presumed federal powers in his mind, Jefferson wrote in The Kentucky Resolutions (November 16, 1798) as follows: "that the powers not delegated to the United States by the Constitution, nor prohibited by it to the States, are reserved to the States respectively, or to the people."[98]

An unanticipated result of the Kentucky Resolutions on the frontier, was that the Spanish governor in Natchez regarded it as evidence in the continuing political fight between Federalists and Democratic Republicans, between a power structure in the east against the political needs of the west, and therefore it appeared as a prelude to Kentucky declaring its independence.[99] He believed the old Wilkinson proposal for detaching Kentucky from the Union might be coming true! Much to the chagrin of Commissioner Ellicott, Spanish officials in Louisiana, with new secret instructions from Prime Minister Godoy to delay the transfer of some forts to the Americans, interpreted the political feud between political parties in Washington as reason to avoid compliance with the Pinckney Treaty. Spain still considered the possibility of an Anglo-American alliance as a threat to their possessions in West Florida. Fortunately, however, new instructions to proceed with the treaty compliance arrived soon from Spain.

As a strict constructionist, Jefferson's dilemma therefore was that nowhere in the Constitution was there a provision for the President of the United States to purchase land, along with its inhabitants, from a foreign power. On August 12, 1803, Jefferson wrote to Senator Breckenridge on the matter. "But, I suppose they [Congress] must then appeal to the nation for an additional article to the Constitution."[100] He therefore attempted twice to draft a constitutional amendment for the Louisiana Purchase. The initial plan included seeking a Constitutional amendment, authorizing the purchase of New Orleans and adjacent land, but this would require (per Article V of the Constitution) placing the issue before Federalists in Congress and, ultimately, requiring ratification from three-fourths of the legislatures within their states. Quite simply, this amendment process was lengthy, and, in the final analysis, the numbers needed for passage were not there because of Federalist domination in the legislatures of five states. He was persuaded by the Cabinet and other advisors, including Secretary of State Madison, to abandon this option in favor of using his Presidential treaty-making power as specified in the Constitution. Jefferson, running out of time because of events in Europe and potential challenges to his policy in Congress, reluctantly agreed. "It is the case of a guardian," he concluded, "investing the money of his ward in purchasing an important adjacent territory; and saying to him when of age, I did this for your good."[101] And, Congress was presently in the hands of Mr. Jefferson's Democratic Republican Party with substantial majorities in both the House and the Senate!

Federalists saw the acquisition of Louisiana as a continuing shift of the political center of gravity from the eastern states to those already in the west and those yet to be admitted. Some Federalists joined in celebration of America's diplomatic feat. Others pointed out that the United States already had too much land as it was. Louisiana was not only a great unknown land mass devoid of valuable commodities, it was a desert inhabited only by wild beasts and savages. "We are to give money of which we have too little of for land of which we already have too much," bemoaned the Federalist *Boston Columbian Centinel* (July 13, 1803). If this huge tract of land were to become part of the United States, it would drive down prices of the land still available in the east. And as new territories were created within this huge tract of land, and then states, the Democratic Republicans would be given credit. Already this pattern was evident in Kentucky, Tennessee, the Mississippi Territory and Ohio; in all of the newly emerging states and territories, the Democratic Republicans were dominant. Now the west had a powerful voice to represent them in national affairs, and hence the political intrigues that had been so common during the 1780s and 1790s disappeared. Soon the Federalist Party, without an expanding geographical base, would be a thing of the past! There was even some talk of creating a new confederation in the northeast based upon regional interests and states' rights. Roger Griswold, Connecticut Federalist, who would lead the fight against the Treaty in the House, predicted:

> The vast and unmanageable extent which the accession of Louisiana will give the United States; the consequent dispersion of our population, and the destruction of that balance which it is so important to maintain between Eastern and Western States, threatens, at no very distant day, the subversion of our Union.[102]

Per the second United States census of 1800, political power in Congress had already shifted, a process clearly in evidence with the Congressional elections in both 1800, and 1802. The 1802 elections for the Eighth United States Congress, U.S. House of Representatives, occurred between April, 1802, and December, 1803. The Eighth Congress met from March 4, 1803 to March 3, 1805.

The population growth of the trans–Appalachian West created a number of new districts in the House of Representatives, which increased the number of House members from 104 seats to 142; nearly all of the new seats went to Democratic Republicans. Between the U.S. census of 1790 and that of 1800, the population in the region of the trans–Appalachian West had tripled. The population in the region was estimated at about 800,000 people. In the Congressional elections of 1800 and that of 1802, the Democratic Republican Party of Jefferson gained 35 seats in the House and stood with a total of 103 seats; they controlled 72.5 percent of the House. This figure did not include one seat held by a non–voting representative from the Mississippi Territory. The Federalists, by comparison, increased their number of seats by only one, and stood with a total of 39 seats or only 27.5 percent of the House seats. In the Senate, the Democratic Republicans held 25 seats compared to 9 for the Federalists.[103] It was for this reason, that some Federalists decided to support frontiersmen with nationalistic speeches opposing the 1802 action of the Spanish Intendant (revoking the American "right of deposit") in the hope of gaining future political support from the West and South. By joining in the western chorus for free navigation of the Mississippi and access to the port of New Orleans, some Federalists hoped to appear as the real national party of action. This effort seemed to bear some fruit. In a letter to Congress from Natchez (April 13, 1803), the writer indicated that:

> The inhabitants residing near the western waters will necessarily be ruled by those [French] who dispose of their productions. Those who can do so are preparing to put themselves under the prudent and stable governments [Federalist states] of New England.[104]

In a burst of national enthusiasm at one point in the discussions over Spain's unilateral violation of Article XXII of the Pinckney Treaty (closing the port of New Orleans to foreigners), the Senate, with bipartisan support, had authorized President Jefferson to seize New Orleans by force. If Jefferson failed now in his diplomatic efforts, the Democratic Republicans would be blamed, and power again claimed by the Federalists, and their new supporters in the West and South, with their argument of "we told you so." Since the Seventh Congress had adjourned for the summer in March, 1803, President Jefferson issued a proclamation on July 16 calling for a Special Session of Congress to convene on October 17. The stage was now set for the anticipated debates on the purchase of Louisiana. Both Democratic Republicans and Federalists prepared for showdown.

Despite their bursts of aggressive, even nationalistic, actions against Spain and France, whom they had always distrusted anyway, conservative Federalists now became the party of "strict constructionist" idealism pertaining to the Constitution. Jefferson's diplomacy had won the day by acquiring New Orleans in the Treaty of April 30. Democratic Republicans, especially Secretary of State James Madison, now faced the problem of bringing their diplomatic triumph to a satisfactory conclusion at home. They therefore, as a political necessity, became the advocates of "implied" powers in the Constitution, and pointed to the President's specific treaty-making power, and his military role as commander-in-chief. New Orleans and navigation of the Mississippi were presented as being a national security interests. With a substantial majority in both houses of Congress, the Democratic Republicans, with time as their most serious enemy (the

MAP

SHOWING IN FIVE DEGREES OF DENSITY, THE DISTRIBUTION
WITHIN THE TERRITORY EAST OF THE 100TH MERIDIAN
OF THE

POPULATION OF THE UNITED STATES

excluding Indians not taxed.

Compiled from the Returns of Population at the First Census, 1790

Figure 4.1 The Population Map above illustrates the population density in 1790, the first year of the census under the Constitution required every ten years. The Congress passed the legislation authorizing the census, assigned by districts, and administered under the jurisdiction of the U.S. Marshals Service. The data required: name of the head of household and the members in each, free white males 16 years of age and older, free white females, all other persons by sex and color, and slaves. The 1790 census began on August 2, 1790. In the census, the population was 3,929,326.

Note in particular the population density between the Atlantic Ocean and the Appalachian Mountains, with a small representation of population beginning in the area south and east of the Ohio River, but west of the Appalachians.

Source: U.S. Census Bureau: www.census.gov/history/www/reference/maps/1790_population-map.html. Accessed July 20, 2013.

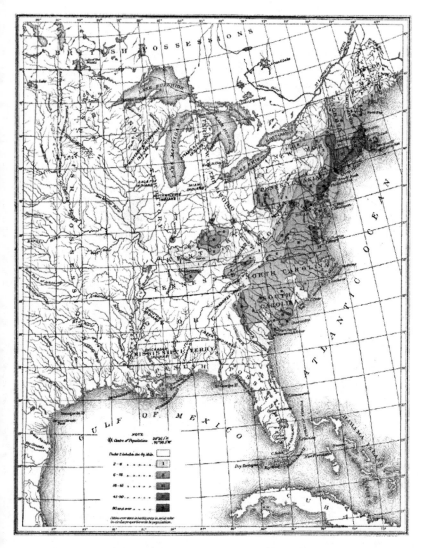

Figure 4.2 Article 1, Section 2 of the Constitution required a census be taken every ten years; in the second U.S. census of August 4, 1800, the population stood at 5,308,483 people, many of whom were located in the trans-Appalachian West. Note by way of contrast (map above) that there are now new shaded areas of population density in the South and West in comparison with the census population map of 1790. By the time of the second census, not only had the population increased in the ten years since 1790, but that increase had resulted in the addition to two new states into the Union. Kentucky entered in 1792, and Tennessee in 1796. In addition, as a result of the boundary changes following the Pinckney Treaty with Spain in 1795, enough American settlers had entered into the new area to have it designated as the Mississippi Territory in 1798. In 1803, Ohio entered the Union as a state as well. The population density map of 1800 clearly shows the movement of Americans into the South and West, and thereby illustrates the importance and urgency of the United States acquiring an outlet to the Gulf of Mexico for commercial and communication purposes. Because the population was growing east of the Mississippi River only, Jefferson was under immense pressure to meet their needs in this area of the Floridas. This explains his instructions to Livingston and Monroe in 1803 to acquire by purchase New Orleans and/or "adjacent lands to the east."

Source: U.S. Census Office, prepared in 1903. David Rumsey Historical Map Collection: www.davidrumsey. com/luna/servlet/detail/RUMSEY~8~1~32056:Distibution-of-the-population-1800. Accessed Juy 20, 2013.

Treaty of 30 April 1803 with France had a six-month period until expiration) for U.S. ratification, they had no intention of throwing the issue of the Louisiana Purchase to the states via the amendment process. In addition, Europe was again at war.

In the ensuing national debate, Jefferson argued that possession of the Mississippi River and New Orleans were crucial to the national security of the United States. In his message to the Special Session of Congress (October 17, 1803), he recapped the events of the past two years:

> Previous, however, to this period, we had not been unaware of the danger to which our peace would be perpetually exposed whilst so important a key to the commerce of the western country remained under a foreign power. Difficulties too were presenting themselves as to the navigation of other streams, which arising within our territories, pass through those adjacent. Propositions had therefore been authorized for obtaining, on fair conditions, the sovereignty of New Orleans, and of other possessions in that quarter, interesting in our quiet, to such extent as was deem practicable; and the provisional appropriation of two millions of dollars to be applied and accounted for by the President of the United States, intended as part of the price, was considered as conveying the sanction of Congress for the acquisition proposed. The enlightened Government of France saw, with discernment, the importance to both nations of such liberal arrangements as might best and permanently promote the peace, interests, and friendship of both; and the property and sovereignty of all Louisiana, which had been restored to them, has, on certain conditions, been transferred to the United States, bearing date this 30th April last. . . Whilst the property and sovereignty of the Mississippi and its waters secure an independent outlet for the produce of the Western States, and an uncontrolled navigation through their whole course, free from collision with other Powers, and the dangers to our peace from that the source, the fertility of the country, its climate and extent, promise, in due season, important aids to our Treasury, an ample provision for our posterity, and a wide spread for the blessings of freedom and equal laws.

In this same message, he concluded with the issue of costs:

> Should the acquisition of Louisiana be Constitutionally confirmed and carried into effect, a sum of nearly thirteen millions of dollars

will be added to our public debt, most of which is payable after fifteen years, before which term, the present existing debts will all be discharged by the established operation of the Sinking fund.[105]

The cost of acquiring Louisiana, Federalists pointed out, was greater than that of the United States Treasury. Jefferson countered Federalist opponents with an argument that the proposed sale of United States bonds, which the Dutch and British banking houses were willing to purchase, and treasury payments would not begin for fifteen years, therefore provided adequate safeguards. Finally, he stated that monies raised over the next fifteen years from increasing population and wealth, augmentation of duties and other revenues from Louisiana, should all be such as to avoid the necessity of raising any new taxes. His words—"no new taxes"—won the day in the United States Senate. The issue of Louisiana's boundaries with British Canada, and the Floridas with Spain would take time to resolve, but free navigation of the Mississippi and control of the port of New Orleans had been achieved through Senate ratification of the Treaty and two Conventions. See Primary Documents 3, 4, and 5. The Senate, as expected, formally ratified the Treaty and two Conventions on October 20, 1803, by a vote of 24 in favor to 7 opposed. However, in order to carry out the provisions therein, the next step in the process was to have the documents communicated to the Representatives for the exercise of their functions, as to those conditions "which within the powers [appropriations] vested by the Constitution in Congress." From October 21 to November 7, 1803, the debate along party lines centered on issues of both money and the future government for a new territory in the House of Representatives. How quickly everyone had forgotten the prophetic words of President Washington in his "Farewell Address" (September 19, 1796). "I have already intimated to you the danger of parties in the state, with particular reference to the founding of them on geographical discriminations."[106]

On Monday, October 24, the political gloves came off in response to President Jefferson's Message when Roger Griswold (1762–1812), Federalist Representative from Connecticut, introduced a resolution that the House be given all of the appropriate documents. This included a request for a copy of the "deed of cession from Spain" and such other documents that would demonstrate Spain's approval or disapproval to the purchase of Louisiana by the United States. Who had legal title to Louisiana? Griswold asked. All that the documents showed thus far was "a promise made by Spain to France." In addition to any legal deeds of transfer, Representative Griswold demanded all of the documents since 1800, such as:

> copies of such correspondence between the Government of the
> United States and the Government or Minister of Spain (if any
> such correspondence has taken place) as will show the assent or
> dissent of Spain to the purchase of Louisiana by the United
> States; together with copies of such other documents as may be
> in the Department of State, or any other Department of this
> Government, tending to ascertain whether the United States
> have, in fact, acquired any title to the province of Louisiana by
> treaties with France, of the thirtieth of April, one thousand eight
> hundred and three.

Finally, Mr. Griswold pointed out: "If the terms stipulated by France had not been complied with, and Spain has not delivered the province to France, then it results that France had no title, and of consequence that the United States has acquired no title from France. If this is correct," he continued, "the consequence will be that we have acquired no new territory or new subjects, and that it is perfectly idle to spend time in passing laws for the possessing the territory, and governing the people."[107] He concluded his remarks by noting that currently Spain was in fact still in possession of Louisiana! Whether Congressman Griswold was aware of it or not, the Spanish governor of Louisiana, Don Manuel de Salcedo, had already issued a general proclamation to the citizens of Louisiana on May 18, 1803, informing them of the colony's retrocession to France. See Primary Document 6 (page 139). This proclamation was based upon King Carlos IV's directive (October 15, 1802) to all Spanish officials to proceed with the transfer of Louisiana pursuant to the treaty with France of 1800. And, it was known in Washington that French Prefect Laussat in New Orleans had established his credentials for the assumption of his duties there, and awaited only the arrival of the French military Expedition. This was necessary because Captain-General Victor, not Laussat, had been authorized by Napoleon to receive Louisiana from Spain. However, on August, 18, 1803, Laussat received documents from France informing him of the sale of Louisiana to the United States, and which included his official commission, signed by Napoleon on June 6, to act as the commissioner for the French Republic to receive Louisiana from Spain, and to cede it to the United States thereafter.

In response to Griswold's resolution, Virginia's Representative John Randolph, Jr. (1773–1833), a Democratic Republican, Jefferson's party leader in the House, and Chairman of the House Ways and Means Committee, rose to speak. Congressman Randolph summarized the reasons for rejecting the Griswold Resolution.

Figure 4.3 Appointment of Prefect Laussat by Napoleon Bonaparte, First Consul, to act as Commissioner of the French Government for the transfer of Louisiana to the United States (June 6, 1803), signed by Admiral Denis Decres. Photocopy of original document from the Laussat Papers, courtesy of The Historic New Orleans Collection.

The Executive has laid before this House an instrument, which he tells us has been duly ratified, conveying to the United States the country known under the appellation of Louisiana. The first article affirms the right of France, to the sovereignty of this territory, to be derived under the Treaty of St Ildefonso, which it quotes. The third article makes provision for the future government, by the United States, of its inhabitants; and the fourth provides the manner in which territory and these inhabitants are to be transferred by question, which is supported by the strongest possible evidence, and pledging herself to put us in possession of that right, so soon as shall be performed those stipulations, on our part, in consideration of which France has conveyed to us her sovereignty over this country and people. From the nature of our Government, these stipulations can only be fulfilled by laws to the

> passing of which the Legislature alone is competent. And when
> these laws are about to be passed, endeavors are made to
> impede, or frustrate, the measure, by setting on foot inquiries
> which mean nothing, or are unconnected with the subject, and
> this is done by those who have always contended that there was
> no discretion vested in this House by the Constitution, as to
> carrying treaties into effect.

After recounting his understanding of the role of the House, which was not to delay a treaty made by the Executive, and ratified by the Senate, he hoped that the House would not adopt Griswold's resolution. Congressman Randolph then stated that:

> he held in the highest veneration the principle established in the
> case of the British treaty, and the men [Federalists] by whom it
> was established, that, in all matters requiring legislative aid, it was
> the right and duty of this House to deliberate, and upon such
> deliberation, to afford, or refuse, that aid, as in their judgments
> the public good might require.

He cited Federalist precedent for his views as being consistent with the Constitution. "To illustrate this remark, let us advert to the case of the Treaty of London, generally known as Mr. Jay's Treaty. That instrument had excited the public abhorrence. The objections to carrying into effect believed insuperable. This sentiment pervaded the House of Representatives." He then concluded: "If, then, we are satisfied as to the terms of this treaty, and with the conduct of our Ministers abroad, let us pass the laws necessary for carrying it into effect."[108] Pennsylvania Representative John Smilie (Democratic Republican) then took the floor and reminded the Representatives that this subject of the President's powers regarding treaty documents had been raised years earlier when the House had been given the British Treaty (Jay's Treaty of 1795) in March, 1796:

> At that day, it had been argued by certain gentlemen [Federalists]
> that the right of passing or not passing the necessary laws for
> carrying a treaty into effect did not belong to that House, but that
> they were under an absolute obligation to pass them.[109]

Smilie concluded by citing none other than "Mr. Federalist" himself, former President George Washington, whose message to the House on March 30, 1796, which Smilie quoted, was very clear:

that the power of making treaties is exclusively vested in the
President, by and with the advice and consent of the Senate,
provided that two-thirds off the Senators present concur; and that
every treaty so made and promulgated thenceforth becomes the
law of the land.[110]

Representative Smilie argued that Constitutional precedent on this matter for the role of the House was clear, and that this interpretation had been acquiesced in by the House ever since. Therefore, he would vote against Congressman Griswold's resolution requiring that the Spanish papers be delivered by the President. Responding to Mr. Randolph's comments, Representative Griswold again took the floor and emphasized the need for an absolutely clear title. "We require to know if Spain refuses to deliver Louisiana to France, can France transmit it to us? We desire to know whether there is any prospect of a refusal on the part of Spain."[111]

Joining the debate also was Representative Joseph H. Nicholson (Democratic Republican, Maryland) who reiterated the conclusions offered by Mr. Randleph. He then added:

If gentlemen are consistent with themselves, if they have not
forgot the lessons which they inculcated upon the ratification of
the British Treaty, this House has no right to call for papers, no
right to make inquiry, no right to deliberate, but must carry this
treaty into effect, be it good or bad; must vote for all the
necessary measures [appropriations], whether they are calculated
to promote the interests of the United States or not.

Finally, he stated in part:

What, said Mr. N [icholson], has Spain to do in this business?
Gentlemen ask if she has acquiesced in our purchase, and call
for her correspondence with our Government. What is the
acquiescence of Spain to us? If the House is satisfied from the
information laid on the table, that Spain had ceded Louisiana to
France, and that France had since ceded it to the United States,
what more do they require? Are we not an independent nation?
Have we not a right to make treaties for ourselves without asking
leave of Spain? What is it to us whether she acquiesces or not?
She is no party to the treaty of cession, she has no claim to the
ceded territory. Are we to pause till Spain thinks proper to
consent, or are we to inquire, whether, like a cross child, she has
thrown away her rattle, and cries for it afterward?[112]

Congressman Nicholson's nationalistic fervor carried the day. He concluded with a reminder from the Treaty itself, that "if France shall fail to put us into actual possession, the United States are not bound to pay a single dollar." After a lengthy discussion on Spain's actions, and American interests, the resolution in the House to have the President deliver a copy of the Treaty of San Ildefonso and any instruments showing that the Spanish government had ordered Louisiana to be delivered to France was defeated by a vote of 57 to 35.

By this time, it was rumored that the Spanish court was opposed to the French cession by sale of Louisiana to the United States. Such rumors were widely spread in Washington, and caused concern among the Spanish and French diplomats. But, Spain's principle policy objective remained: to keep the United States out of any alliance with Britain, her mortal enemy on a global basis. It was for this reason that the Spanish Minister of State wrote to Charles Pinckney, the American Minister to Spain, denying any efforts on her part to renounce the deal with France. He then went on to state that King Carlos IV wished to give "a new proof of his benevolence and friendship towards the United States." The rumors persisted however until the actual transfer of Louisiana from Spain to France on November 30, 1803.

Representative Griswold's resolution was seen as a Federalist political maneuver to delay a vote on providing the necessary funds with which to complete the treaty and convention. Opposing the Treaty and the two Conventions by the Federalists is politically difficult to understand in view of the fact that the provisions for settlement of the maritime losses from French naval seizures provided in Convention 2 would benefit the shipping and banking interests in the Northeast, precisely the Federalist strongholds. It was this provision that caused the Federalist ranks to split. On his part, Representative Griswold and a few other Federalists looked to the future of only their section of the country and their party with despair as the political winds blowing from the West grew stronger.

On Friday, October 28, 1803, a Senate bill entitled: "An act to enable the President of the United states to take possession of the territories ceded by France to the United States, by the treaty concluded at Paris on the thirtieth of April last, and for the temporary government thereof," was read for the third time. On the question of "do pass," the vote was 89 yeas and 23 nays. The House authorized the creation of stock, U.S. government bonds, in the amount of $11,250,000. The following day, October 29, 1803, an engrossed bill for carrying into effect the "Convention" between the United States and France (to pay claims against the French government by United States' citizens) passed with a House vote of 85 yeas to 7 nays.[113] Then the actual purchase price for Louisiana was approved by action in the House:

An Act authorizing the creation of a stock, to the amount of eleven million two hundred and fifty thousand dollars, for the purpose of carrying into effect the convention of the thirtieth of April, one thousand eight hundred and three, between the United States of America and the French Republic, and making provision for the payment of the same.

This first Act met the requirements of the Treaty for payment to France for possession of Louisiana in the amount of $11,250,000 as agreed to in the Convention for that purpose. The second Act met the requirements of the Convention for payment by United States government to its citizens for former claims against the French government in the amount of $3,750,000. The appropriations necessary with which to implement both Conventions were agreed to as part of the Treaty of April 30, 1803, approved by House and Senate, and signed by President Jefferson on November 10, 1803.

On October 31, President Jefferson signed into law:

an act to enable the President of the United States to take possession of the territories ceded by France to the United states, by the treaty concluded at Paris on the thirtieth of April last, and for the temporary government thereof.

Also on October 31, 1803, Jefferson appointed William C.C. Claiborne, Governor of the Mississippi Territory, and General James Wilkinson, U.S. Army, to act as commissioners on behalf of the United States to receive Louisiana, and thereby to establish formal possession by the government of the United States.

Additional legislation establishing the laws of the United States within the territories was debated in the House. Between November 1 and 10, both houses of Congress offered a series of amendments regarding the laws to be established within the newly acquired territories, but concurred on the amount of stock to be issued. On November 2, 1803, the Senate passed an act for making payment to citizens of the United States "by virtue of the convention of the 30th April, 1803, between the United States and the French Republic." It was about this time (November 14, 1803) that Jefferson prepared a special message for Congress outlining in detail, as he knew it, accounts of Louisiana's boundaries, geography and history. President Jefferson signed all of the legislation into law on November 10, 1803. In Washington, therefore, the United States completed all of the executive and legislative steps necessary in order to take possession of Louisiana, and fulfill the terms of both the Treaty and the Conventions

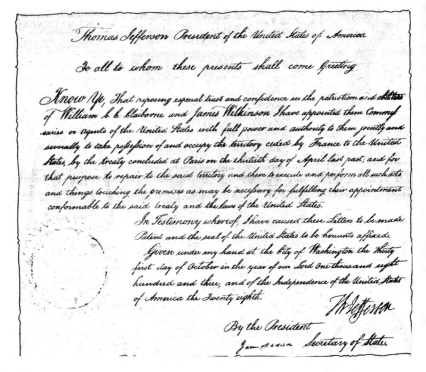

Figure 4.4 Appointment of William C.C. Claiborne and General James Wilkinson as Commissioners for the United States of America to receive Louisiana from the French Government (October 31, 1803), signed by Thomas Jefferson, President of the United States, and James Madison, Secretary of State. Courtesy of The Historic New Orleans Collection.

of 30 April, 1803 with France. Events now turned to what was happening in New Orleans.

French Colonial Prefect Laussat had arrived in New Orleans on March 26, 1803. He immediately presented his credentials to the Spanish governor, and began to carry out the duties and prepared for what he believed to be the imminent arrival of the French military Expedition under Captain-General Victor. One of the controversies swirling in New Orleans during the fall of 1802 and into spring, 1803, was that of the American "right of deposit." According to Laussat, it was Governor Salcedo, not the Intendant Morales, who had ordered this provision (Article XXII of the Pinckney Treaty) revoked on October 16, 1802. In May, 1803, dispatches from Madrid ordered Spanish officials to restore the right of deposit, and the affair was concluded. But there were now other more disturbing issues. By the end of May, rumors of the renewal of hostilities between Britain and France arrived in New Orleans aboard incoming ships. In addition to the war, rumors of France's cession of Louisiana to the United States circulated widely in the press on July 4, and it was the subject of conversation from increasing numbers of Americans arriving in New Orleans. On August 18, 1803, Laussat received confirmation of the cession of Louisiana from Louis Andre Pichon, French *charge d'affairs*, in Washington, D.C. With the resumption of hostilities between Britain and France, and the inability to protect her colony of Louisiana, Prefect Laussat mused: "with the cession of this colony, we fortified the United States, already a feared rival of the British Empire and added the most beautiful of its gem to the crown of the American Confederation."[114]

Throughout the rest of the summer and into the fall of 1803, New Orleans awaited events that would settle its future. Final dispatches from Paris for the Louisiana retrocession from Spain to France, and then from France to the United States, were received by Prefect Laussat on November 4. These instructions informed Laussat that he should take possession of Louisiana from Spain as soon as possible. On November 30, 1803, the retrocession of the Colony of Louisiana from Spain to France was held in the Cabildo (city hall) in New Orleans. Laussat accepted the colony on behalf of France from the Spanish commissioners, Governor Salcedo and the Marquis de Casa-Calvo. Laussat described the events:

> At 11:45, on the morning of November 30, 1803, I set out on foot for the city hall [Cabildo], escorted by approximately sixty Frenchmen. The brig Argo fired a salute as we passed. We arrived at the Place [d'Armes, now known as Jackson Square]. The crowed was considerable. The Spanish troops were standing at attention on one side, the militia on the other. The commissioners of H.C.M. came midway across the room to meet me. M. de Salcedo sat down in the armchair in the middle, I sat in another on his right, and the Marquis de Casa-Calvo in a third to his left. I presented my credentials and the order from the king of Spain. The secretary, Don Andres Lopez de Armesto, was given the order to read the powers of his nation's commissioners, and upon my order [Joseph] Daugerot, clerk of the navy, read my appropriate powers. The Marquis de Casa-Calvo formally announced that subjects who did not choose to remain under the Spanish dominion were, from that moment on, rightfully released from their oath of allegiance. At the same time, the governor handed me, on a silver tray, the keys to Fort Saint Charles and Fort Saint Louis. Thereupon he relinquished his place to me, and I accepted it.

> Don Andres read in Spanish the official proceedings of the
> cession as agreed upon and transcribed in advance, and
> immediately thereafter Daugerot read the French version. We
> signed and affixed the seals. Then we rose and went out on the
> side of the balconies of the city hall. Upon our appearance, the
> Spanish Flag, which had been flying atop the flagstaff, was
> lowered, and the French flag was raised.[115]

French possession of Louisiana lasted for only twenty days, from November 30 to December 20. Yet, during that brief period, Prefect Laussat took the time to appoint a municipal government for the City of New Orleans, and recalling the terrible fires in the city of 1788 and 1794, he created the first fire department and several other administrative procedures. Another one of Laussat's decrees during his twenty-day administration was to have future ramifications as well. On December 15, the municipal council and mayor of New Orleans ordered that twenty-eight articles for the enforcement of slavery in Louisiana from the *Code Noir* ("Black Code" of 1724) for the administration of justice, police, discipline and commerce of Negro slaves be promulgated by Prefect Laussat. This request to Laussat was based on the continuing fear of white owners of slave rebellions like that in Haiti. On December 16, he promulgated a decree declaring that the *Code Noir* to be in effect, except for any provisions that might be in future conflict with the Constitution of the United States. Laussat explained:

> The members of the local government tormented me to sanction
> yet one more decree relative to the regulation of the Negroes.
> They pointed out that they daily felt an extreme need for it. They
> came back to the charge several times. I kept refusing on the
> grounds that this was on the eve of my laying down my
> ephemeral power. Finally, I gave in. I explained the motives for
> my conduct in the preamble of the decree that I drew up for the
> purpose. A good deal of trouble was taken to hasten printing and
> publication of this decree. It will be my testament, in the name of
> the French Republic, on behalf of this dear Louisiana.[116]

On December 19, the American commissioners, William C.C. Claiborne and General James Wilkinson, along with a contingent of American dragoons arrived. It was agreed that the transfer ceremony of Louisiana from France to the United States would be held the following day, and follow the same general pattern as that which had been observed earlier with the Spanish/French ceremony. See the text of the "Process-

Verbal," which was submitted to President Jefferson from Claiborne in January, 1804:

> Process-Verbal of the cession of Louisiana from France to the United States of America, represented by Commissioners William C.C. Claiborne and General James Wilkinson. Signed by William C.C. Claiborne, Ja [mes] Wilkinson, and D [ecius] Wadsworth for the United States of America; Prefect Laussat and Joseph Daugerot on behalf of France (December 20, 1803).

This official narrative of the transfer events on December 20, 1803, is provided in the report to President Jefferson, later submitted to Congress, and signed by William C.C. Claiborne and James Wilkinson for the United States.

William C.C. Claiborne was born in Virginia (1773–1817), and studied law. He was elected to the House of Representatives from Tennessee in 1797–1801, and was a Democratic Republican. He was appointed by Jefferson as governor for the Mississippi Territory in 1801, and it was from that position that he provided intelligence to the President on affairs in Louisiana. Once again, Jefferson exhibited his uncanny ability to secure able men to accomplish

William C.C. Claiborne

William Charles Cole Claiborne's date of birth remains in dispute, but is generally assumed to have been between November 23, 1772 and November 23, 1774, in Virginia. Like many young men of his day, he worked in a variety of jobs, studied law at the College of William and Mary, traveled from New York City to Philadelphia, and then went west to Tennessee. In 1797, he was elected to the House of Representatives from Tennessee, and served until 1801. A Democratic Republican, Jefferson appointed him as governor and superintendent of Indian affairs in the Mississippi Territory where he served 1801–1803. He was well respected in this position for his progressive administration, and it was this aspect of his career that brought him to the attention of President Jefferson again in 1803 when someone was needed to administer the newly acquired Territory of Orleans, the lands south of the 33rd parallel, from 1804 to 1812. Although he got off to a troubled start in New Orleans, he gradually won over the diverse population of the city, successfully annexed portions of West Florida into the Territory in 1810, and put down a slave rebellion in 18ll. After Louisiana became a state in 1812, he was elected as its first governor, and served from 1812 to 1816. He was elected to the United States Senate from Louisiana, and served only to his death on November 23, 1817.

James Wilkinson

James Wilkinson was born on March 24, 1757, in Maryland. He studied medicine but joined the Continental Army during the American Revolution, where he participated in a number of engagements between 1776–1777. Despite his military actions, he seemed to have an insatiable desire to pursue his own ends, and by 1778 he had fallen from grace in the command of General Horatio Gates and he was forced to resign. A year later, he was appointed as a supply officer with the rank of general, but faced charges of corruption in that capacity and was again forced to resign in 1781. He returned to Pennsylvania, briefly held the rank of general in the militia and served in the state assembly, but moved to the Kentucky district in 1784. It was his infamous business trip to New Orleans in 1787, a colony of Spain, and there he met with Governor Esteban Miro. Wilkinson's dealings with Miro, which included promises to promote Americans to settle in Spanish Louisiana, and trade concessions for himself, were only discovered later. The most dangerous part of Wilkinson's "plan" was for Spain to support the separation of Kentucky from the United States, and in order to convince Governor Miro of his trust, he signed an oath of allegiance to the King of Spain. Returning to Kentucky, he actively engaged in local politics in the state convention of 1788 where he opposed the U.S. Constitution, and secretly sought land grants from Spain near Natchez for himself and several of his followers. Wilkinson's plans with Spanish officials fell through, but did receive funds from them and continued to provide some intelligence about American interests for years.

With his military experience, he did engage in several operations against Indians in the 1790s. During the "quasi-war" with France, Wilkinson was promoted to the rank of general in the Ohio River Valley, on the probable grounds that if a war with France and her ally Spain were to break out, he would then lead the American expedition to capture New Orleans. Because of his location in Illinois between 1801 to 1802, he was assigned by President Jefferson to join William C.C. Claiborne to take possession of Louisiana as the senior American military officer. He continued to serve in Louisiana for several years, was implicated in the famous Burr Conspiracy in 1805–1806, participated in the War of 1812, and then headed for Mexico which gained its independence from Spain in 1821. There, he again became involved in land schemes reminiscent of his earlier days in Kentucky, and died on December 28, 1825, in Mexico City. Although his political and financial dealings with Spain were rumored during his Kentucky and Louisiana days, it was not until later after his death that the documents surfaced regarding his Spanish connections.

his goals, and to place his complete confidence in them. From his position as governor of the Mississippi Territory, Claiborne was sent as a commissioner for the United States by Jefferson to take possession of Louisiana. He served as governor of the Territory of Orleans from 1804–1812.

A more personal account of the transfer ceremonies from France to the United States on December 20 is provided by Prefect Laussat in his *Memoires*. He described the events in detail:

> The day was beautiful and temperature as balmy as a day in May. Lovely ladies and city dandies graced all the balconies on the Place [d'Armes]. The Spanish officers could be distinguished in the crowd by their plumage. At none of the preceding ceremonies had there been such a throng of curious spectators. The eleven rooms of the city hall were filled with all the beautiful women of the city.
>
> The Anglo-American [American only] troops at last appeared . . . To the roll of drums they emerged in ranks down along the river front at the Place [d'Armes] and, facing the militia, which was standing with its back to the city hall, arranged themselves there in battle formation.
>
> The commissioners Claiborne and Wilkinson were received at the foot of the stairs of the city hall by the major of engineers, Vinache; the commander of the militia, Livaudais; and the secretary of the French commission, Daugerot. I came forward to greet them, halfway across the meeting room. Claiborne seated himself in an armchair on my right and Wilkinson seated himself in another on my left. I announced the purpose of the ceremony. The commissioners presented their powers to me; their secretary read them aloud. Immediately after, I ordered to be read (1) the treaty off transfer, (2) my powers, and (3) the act of exchange of ratifications. Then I declared that I was transferring the country to the United States, repeating solemnly the terms in which my powers were conceived.
>
> I handed over the keys to the city, tied together with tricolor ribbons, to Mr. Wilkinson and, immediately, I absolved from their oath of allegiance to France the inhabitants who chose to remain under the domination of the United States. The minutes were read, first in French by Daugerot, and then in English by Wadsworth. Both sides, together with the respective secretaries, affixed their signatures. We moved to the main balcony of the city hall. As we appeared, the French colors were lowered and the American flag was raised. When they reached the same level, both banners paused for a moment. A cannon shot was the signal for salvoes from the forts and the batteries.[117]

Louisiana was now officially part of the United States of America, and its inclusion would change forever the country and its people. Governor Claiborne spoke briefly to the crowd and informed them that they would be incorporated into the United States as soon as possible, that in the meantime they would enjoy all "the rights, advantages and immunities of citizens of the United States," and that they would be protected for "their liberty, property, and the religion which they profess." Claiborne's address, in his capacity as Governor of the Mississippi Territory, "exercising the powers of Governor General and Intendant of the province of Louisiana," set the tone for Louisiana now under the jurisdiction of the United States:

> Whereas, by stipulations between the Governments of France and Spain, the latter ceded to the former the colony and province of Louisiana, with the same extent which it had at the date of abovementioned treaty in the hands of Spain, and that it had when France possessed it, and such as it ought to be after the treaties subsequently entered into between Spain and other States; and whereas the Government of France has ceded the same to the United States by a treaty duly ratified, and bearing date of 30th April, in the present year, and the possession of said colony and province is now in the United States, according to the tenor of the last mentioned treaty; and whereas the Congress of the United States, on the 31st day of October, in the present year, did enact that until the expiration of the Congress then sitting, (unless provisions for the temporary Government of the said territories be sooner made by Congress,) all the military, civil, and judicial powers, exercised by the then existing Government of the same, shall be vested in such person or persons, and shall be exercised in such manner, as the President of the United States shall direct, for the maintaining and protecting the inhabitants of Louisiana in the free enjoyment of their liberty, property, and religion; and the President of the United States has by his commission, bearing date of the same 31st day of October, invested me with all the powers, and charged me with the several duties heretofore held and exercised by the Governor General and Intendant of the province:
>
> I have, therefore, thought fit to issue this proclamation, making known the premises, and to declare, that the Government heretofore exercised over the said province of Louisiana, as well under the authority of Spain as of the French Republic, has ceased, and that of the United States of America is established over the same; that the inhabitants thereof will be incorporated in

the union of the United States, and admitted as soon as possible, according to the principles of the federal constitution, to the enjoyment of all the rights, advantages, and immunities of citizens of the United States; that in the meantime, they shall be maintained and protected in the free enjoyment of their liberty, property and the religion which they profess; that all laws and municipal regulations, which were in existence at the cession of the late Government, remain in full force; and all civil officer charged with their execution, except those whose powers have been especially vested in me, and except also such officers as have been of the Governor for the time being, or until provision shall otherwise be made. Entrusted with the collection of the revenue, are continued in their functions, during the pleasure of the Governor for the time being, or until provision shall otherwise be made.[118]

Perhaps no one has described what had just transpired better than Robert Livingston. "We have lived long," he wrote from Paris (May 2, 1803) upon execution of the Treaty and the Conventions,

but this is the noblest work of our whole lives. The treaty which we have just signed has not been obtained by art or dictated by force; equally advantageous to the two contracting parties, it will change vast solitudes into flourishing districts. From this day the United States takes her place among the powers of the first rank.[119]

On January 16, 1804, President Jefferson informed Congress of the smooth taking of possession of Louisiana on behalf of the United States by Governor William C.C. Claiborne and General Wilkinson on December 20, 1803. On the same day Jefferson informed Congress, the *National Intelligencer and Washington Advertiser* reported the completion of the Louisiana Purchase to its readers: "Never have mankind contemplated so vast and important an accession of empire by means so pacific and just." In his message to Congress, Jefferson described the preparations for the transfer, and its outcome as follows:

In execution of the act of the present session of Congress for taking possession Louisiana, as ceded to us by France, and for the temporary government thereof, Governor Claiborne, of the Mississippi territory, and General Wilkinson, were appointed commissioners to receive possession. They proceeded, with such regular troops as had been assembled at Fort Adams, from the

nearest posts, and with some militia of the Mississippi territory, to
New Orleans. To be prepared for anything unexpected, which
might arise out of the transaction, a respectable body of militia
was ordered to be in readiness in the states of Ohio, Kentucky,
and Tennessee, and a part of those of Tennessee was moved on
to the Natchez. No occasion, however, arose for their services.
Our commissioners, on their arrival at New Orleans, found the
province already delivered by the commissioners of Spain to that
of France, who delivered it over to them on the 20th day of
December, as appears by their declaratory act accompanying
this. Governor Claiborne being duly invested with the powers
heretofore exercised by the governor and intendant of Louisiana
assumed the government on the same day, and, for the
maintenance of law and order, immediately issued the
proclamation and address now communicated.

"On this important acquisition," Jefferson concluded, "so favorable
to the immediate interests of our western citizens, so auspicious to the
peace and security of the nation in general, which adds to our country
territories so extensive and fertile, and our citizens new brethren to partake
of the blessings of freedom and self-government, I offer to Congress and
our country my sincere congratulations.[120]

On March 26, 1804, the Territory of Orleans, land south of 33rd
parallel, was created as part of the United States by Act of Congress and
signed by President Jefferson. Areas to the north of the 33rd parallel were
designated in the same Act as the District of Louisiana, which later became
the Louisiana Territory; in 1812, the year in which the Orleans Territory
became the State of Louisiana, the name was changed to the Missouri
Territory in order to more clearly designate the land area.

In Louisiana, now under the direction of the United States, things
did not go so well. Louisianians were deeply suspicious of their new
American government. William C.C. Claiborne remained as the territorial
governor, and by 1805 had instituted a legislative council, which he
appointed to advise him. The fundamental problem was that the people
of Louisiana had no experience in self-government during their years under
either the French or the Spanish. When Louisiana became a territory, per
the provisions of the Northwest Ordinance of 1787, the citizens assumed
that they would be admitted into the Union as a new state in short order.
But, in fact, statehood was not granted by Congress until April 30, 1812.

The transfer ceremony of Louisiana from France to the United States
on December 20, 1803, was followed by number of social events in New
Orleans. Prefect Laussat described the first event in his *Memoires:*

> The celebration closed with a dinner and *soiree* in which all
> society took part without distinction of Spaniards, Americans, or
> Frenchmen. We raised a solemn toast to the three nations and
> saluted them to the deafening noise of the cannons.[121]

But future incidents did not go so well. At another social event on January 24, 1804, according to Laussat, "It was an infernal brawl" between Frenchmen and the Americans. Then, he concluded:

> The principal responsibility for the fracas belonged to the
> American leaders. They played a role in it, encouraged it
> participated in it. Claiborne kept repeating, "To bring these folks
> to their senses, we'll have to aim cannons at them and knock
> down the walls of the city from top to bottom."[Daniel] Clark, their
> interpreter, let it be rumored around that "until two or three
> Frenchmen have been hanged, we will not rule over this
> country."[122]

Fortunately, saner heads prevailed, order was restored, and such problems were reduced to minor incidents thanks to the efforts of Governor Claiborne.

Another problem that confronted the former colony was that of its whole system of laws. Louisiana's tradition was based upon French and Spanish codes and laws, particularly the latter since Spain had possessed the colony and administered it since 1769. It was Governor O'Reilly who abolished the existing French codes, and substituted them with the Laws of Castile, and Laws of the Indies. From 1769 to 1803, several generations of Louisiana citizens had known no other, and in the practice of implementation during these years, Spanish officials, who often held court in their houses, looked to written sources and practices in Spain, Mexico City, or Cuba. The codes, traditions, and practices of the American system were therefore totally foreign to the local population, and produced no shortage of problems. This is one of the reasons it took so long for Louisiana to be admitted into the Union. Claiborne made the effort to govern his diverse inhabitants with skill, compassion and patience. In that effort, he gradually came to see the necessity for maintaining some aspects of the former Spanish civil codes, while moving slowly into the Anglo-American common law. The transition from a European colony to statehood was an arduous process, but it worked.

CHAPTER 5

The Louisiana Purchase

A Global Context, Summary

In summary, the acquisition of Louisiana by the United States in 1803, with its boundaries and resources unknown, was an unprecedented accomplishment. The size of the United States doubled, and some 50,000 new inhabitants were added to its population. The ramifications of the Louisiana Purchase were both domestic and international. New commercial opportunities from raw materials and markets for United States goods seemed endless. At home, the divisiveness and hostility in the West produced by the foreign possession of New Orleans and control of the Mississippi River, either from Spain or potentially France, and therewith foreign control of American commerce from the Ohio and Mississippi Valleys, had been eliminated. Threats of direct action from radical frontiersmen, or those seeking to carve out their fortunes in the West by alliances with either a foreign power, or possibly fomenting rebellion and even secession from the Union, that had been regarded as realities in the 1780s and early 90s, were now a thing of the past. Spanish officials played on such feelings of frustration and resentment, and resorted to alliances with Indian tribes, bribery of Americans as spies, and sometimes domination by force. The potential for local frontiersmen therefore to take drastic action of some kind may have been overblown, but with the distances and length of time for communications, no one knew for sure. James Pitot was in Natchez in 1798, and reported on conditions there; he described American intentions for the possible invasion of Louisiana. Spanish Governor Gayoso similarly reported on such conditions.

President Jefferson was keenly aware of the problems, especially after the Spanish Intendant revoked the American right of deposit in October, 1802. Rumors abounded under such circumstances. Prefect Laussat in his *Journal* (May, 1803), written prior to his being informed of the Purchase, recounted his conversation with Samuel Young, an American resident in Louisiana:

> an opulent proprietor whose family was well established, told me
> boldly that he had no doubt the western states would one day
> form a nation independent from those in the east. It was then a
> common opinion that one did not conceal.[123]

Later that month, Laussat recorded his conversation with American
General Jonathan Dayton, a Federalist U.S. Senator from New Jersey, who
was in New Orleans at the end of May, in order to learn more about the
region. One of the questions Dayton put to Laussat was the possibility of
France encouraging westerners to abandon the United States. Laussat
recorded Dayton's concerns:

> Last, they were especially suspicious that we [France] might want
> to foment divisive wars between their western and eastern states;
> arouse separatist ideas among the states; stir up the Indians; and
> kindle underhandedly enmities and troubles against their
> government.

After stating that this American fear had been raised with him
many times, Laussat responded that: "It is not, therefore, in our interest
to provoke it. What is more, our mission is to nurture unceasingly the
best possible understanding between ourselves and the United States
government."[124] But France had not yet taken possession of Louisiana, it
remained at this time still under Spanish administration, and another of
the persistent rumors was that Spain might yet refuse to retrocede Louisiana
to France. As illustrated by the case with General James Wilkinson in the
1780s, and others, the possibility of Spanish intrigue was not taken lightly—
Commissioner Ellicott, for example, reported in 1798 from Natchez that
as many as four American officers might be involved in such plots.

The reports of Ellicott to the government in Washington on Spanish
delaying tactics, Wilkinson's role, and prospects of Indian attacks, all led
to additional American army units
being sent to the area. The passage
of the Alien and Sedition Acts in
1798 by the Federalist Congress
had been motivated in part by the
recurring rumors of meddling in
American affairs by foreign agents.
The real concern was the possible
presence of a European power
at the mouth of the Mississippi,
which by its very position and use

> "Is it possible to find a Military Gentleman
> in our army possessed of sobriety, talents,
> and prudence? I have only to add that for
> the honor of the United States it will be
> necessary to send officers to this country
> who are not mad."
>
> American Boundary Commissioner
> Andrew Ellicott to Secretary of
> State, Natchez, July 4, 1797

of its military forces could halt American commerce. That European power in 1803 was France. It was a prospect that was not taken lightly, and in fact it was a condition that could not be allowed to continue. Fortunately, diplomacy triumphed over military action.

The history of political intrigues in the Mississippi Valley between 1793 and 1803, both actual and rumored, were however too numerous to ignore And, some of them involved Frenchmen. There were too many examples of potential trouble for the United States, and the possibility of actions to separate a portion of the West from the Union—George Rogers Clark and recruitment for his French Revolutionary Legion, with the support of the French emissary to the United States, Citizen Edmond Genet in 1793–1794; the "conspiracy" of Colonel Blunt in Tennessee; Wilkinson's "plans" in the 1780s; the rumor of up to 2,000 French Brigands landing on the Florida coast to stir up the Indians in the mid-1790s; and the incident with William Augustus Bowles and his Indian allies against Spain in 1802 on behalf of England. Secretary of State Madison was determined to bring an end to the prospect of future European meddling. In his instructions to Robert Livingston and James Monroe (March 2, 1803), which Monroe took with him to France, Madison addressed the future of Franco-American relations on this very subject, and which was to be conveyed to the French. The substance and tone of Madison's letter reflects the seriousness with which such incidents in the past were regarded in Washington:

> The French government is not less mistaken if it supposes that the western part of the United States can be withdrawn from their present union with the Atlantic part, into a separate government, closely allied with France.
>
> Our western fellow-citizens are bound to the Union, not only the ties of kindred and affection, which for a longtime will derive strength from the stream of emigration peopling that region; but by two considerations which flow from clear and essential interests.
>
> One of this considerations is, the passage through the Atlantic ports of the foreign merchandise consumed by the western inhabitants, and the payments thence made to a treasury in which would lose their participation by erecting a separate government. The bulky production of the western country may continue to pass down the Mississippi; but the difficulties of the ascending navigation of that river, however free it may be made, will cause the imports for consumption to pass through the Atlantic States.

This is the course through which they are now received, nor will the impost to which they will be subject, change the course even if the passage up the Mississippi should be duty free. It will not equal the difference in the freight through the latter channel. It is true that mechanical and other improvements in the navigation of the Mississippi may lessen the labor and expense of ascending the stream: but it is not the least probable, that savings of this sort will keep pace with improvements in canals and roads, by which the present course of imports will be favored. Let it be added, that the loss of the contribution thus made to a foreign treasury, would be accompanied with the necessity of providing by less convenient revenues for the expense of a separate government, and of the defensive precautions required by the change of situation.

The other of these considerations results from the insecurity to which the trade from the Mississippi would be exposed by such a revolution in the western part of the United States. A connection of the western people as a separate state with France, implies a connection between the Atlantic states and Great Britain. It is found, from long experience, that France and Great Britain are nearly half the time at war. The case would be the same with their allies. During nearly one time, therefore, the trade of the western country from the Mississippi, would have no protection but that of France, and would suffer all the interruptions which nations, having the command of the sea, could inflict on it.

It will be the more impossible for France to draw the western country under influence, by conciliatory regulations of the trade through the Mississippi; because the regulations which would be regarded by her as liberal, and claiming returns of gratitude, would be viewed on the other side as falling short of justice. If this should not be at first the case, it soon would be so. The western people believe, as do their Atlantic brethren, that they had a natural and indefeasible right to trade freely through the Mississippi. They are conscious of their power to enforce their rights against any nation whatever. With these ideas in their minds, it is evident that France will not be able to excite either a sense of favor, or of fear, that would establish an ascendancy over them. On the contrary, it more than probable that the different views of their respective rights would quickly lead to disappointments and disgusts on both side, and thence to collisions and controversies fatal to the harmony of the two nations. To guard against these consequences is a primary

> motive with the United States in wishing the arrangement
> proposed. As France has equal reasons to guard against them,
> she ought to feel an equal motive to concur in the
> arrangement.[125]

Even after the United States took possession, an incident to separate western lands for their own purposes involved former Vice President Aaron Burr and James Wilkinson, for a time, until he realized in late 1806 what this foolish policy might do to his career. When events along the border became too well-known, Wilkinson bailed out and informed Washington in 1806 of Burr's conspiracy to set up an independent nation in the West. Burr was ultimately arrested, tried and acquitted on the charges because of lack of proof, but clearly the intent was there. With the Americans in control of New Orleans and the Mississippi, the stimuli for such actions in the past by inhabitants from the west were no longer present. Incidents, such as that by Burr, served as a reminder of earlier problems and troubles, but at least now there was no foreign power involved. Once President Jefferson and Congress confirmed the acquisition of New Orleans by the United States, and took possession on December 20, 1803, the potential for any separatist movements in the West that might have had any chance of foreign or local support and success were all but eliminated. The centerpiece for the plots and conspiracies had always been possession or control of New Orleans. Even if personal self-interest in acquiring western lands had been the primary motive, such lands were useless for development without some avenue of access to the Gulf of Mexico. The acquisition of land east of the Mississippi River by itself was of little value, but this changed if it was possible to negotiate with whomever controlled New Orleans. The possession of New Orleans by the United States for all of its people as far north as Ohio, and the freedom of their commerce uninterrupted to the Gulf, closed the chapter on western conspiracy and intrigue! Finally, the American settlers in the west had a new and legal tool with which they could have their voices heard: the Democratic Republican Party controlled Washington. Federalist fears of a new power structure had come true!

But, the Louisiana Purchase did not end the talk of secessionist ideas and states' rights. Following the successful acquisition of Louisiana, and with it the potential for several new territories and then states to enter the Union, the Federalists in the northeast states knew a new day had arrived for their political rivals. A small group of Congressional Federalists from Connecticut, New Jersey, New York, and Massachusetts discussed in 1804 creating a new North East Confederation, including Canada, which would coincide with their sectional political interests, and with their traditional strong economic and political ties to Britain. This idea of secession from the Union withered away in 1806 as a result of intense nationalism, as reflected in the National Jubilee in 1804, and outrage produced by the infamous and abortive Burr Conspiracy in 1806; but, it would re-emerge in 1814 among some Federalists at the Hartford Convention in the aftermath of the War of 1812. The result was the death of the Federalist Party, and reflected in their last effort to offer their candidate for the Presidency in 1816, who was soundly defeated. It began in 1817 the new "era of good feeling" in domestic politics.

The Louisiana Purchase added a new dimension to United States foreign policy initiatives for the future. The treaty-making power of the President, with ratification by the Senate per the Constitution, had been firmly established during President Washington's administration. The precedents set in Jay's Treaty, or Pinckney's Treaty, were clear. What was new with the Louisiana case was the provision for financially obligating the government of the United States with monetary payments to a foreign power in the Treaty and Conventions of April 30, 1803. This issue was debated in the House, and resolved by the fact that it was not the prerogative of the House to challenge the President's action since the Senate had ratified the treaty. Rather, by a vote in the House, its only role was to approve or not the necessary appropriations with which to carry the treaty into effect. Acquiring new territory for the United States by a treaty involving its purchase, along with those who inhabited the area, was a new precedent as well. President Washington had defended his treaty-making prerogative before the Congress in Jay's Treaty. President Jefferson simply added a corollary to Presidential treaty-making powers by providing a new mechanism, purchasing power by means of Congressional appropriations. It was a new dimension to American policy, and one that Andrew Jackson later considered when the prospect of acquiring Texas occurred; he wanted to buy Texas from Mexico, not fight a war over it. The Louisiana Purchase similarly had a huge impact on the domestic politics of the United States. The enthusiasm over the acquisition of Louisiana stirred patriotic feelings in many parts of the country. Here was the new opportunity for the American yeoman, the individual farmer/settler who had created the west, and the citizen envisioned by Thomas Jefferson as constituting the future of the country and the protection of its liberties. National celebrations in honor of the Louisiana Purchase were held around the country in 1804 as part of national "Jubilee." Lewis and Clark began their epic journey to the west in 1804. It was another stepping stone on the road to the development of American expansionism and nationalism for the nineteenth century.

The impact of the Louisiana Purchase upon the Native Americans residing in the newly acquired territory was to place them in the path of

American western expansion, with the same results as their brethren in the east. Yet, American expansionism was not the exclusive action plan of any one political party. Prior to 1803, Federalist Presidents George Washington and John Adams had expanded the United States. Even the Congress under the Articles of Confederation had done so with the land Ordinances of 1784, 1785, and the Northwest Ordinance of 1787. President Washington did it with Jay's Treaty, in the northwest by removal of the last British troops from the region in 1795; removal of the Indians in Ohio by military action and in the Treaty of Grenville in 1795; and, in the Pinckney Treaty of 1795, he expanded the U.S. into present-day Mississippi and Alabama at the expense of Spain. John Adams authorized the boundary survey necessary, and created the Mississippi Territory in 1798. Westward expansion had been a part of the Federalist agenda from the beginning of the United States under the Constitution. Kentucky entered the Union in 1792, Tennessee in 1796, and the Mississippi Territory in 1798. The population of the United States was moving to the west and the south; what divorced the Federalists from the general population was their international ties to Britain, and domestic policies—their taxes, land speculation, monetary policies, and their assault, both actual and perceived, on individual liberties as reflected in the Alien and Sedition Acts of 1798. These policy decisions had both domestic and foreign repercussions. Spain and France sought to keep the U.S. away from ties to Britain, and in this effort they were supported by Jefferson's Democratic Republican Party. Federalists, especially under the party leadership of Alexander Hamilton, pushed the party into too many tight corners. Voters in the west and south, however, turned to the Democratic Republicans as their party, one of the individual farmer, and with increased numbers as they settled the frontier; then, they were in a position to gain control of the federal government, which they did in the elections of 1800 and 1802.

Spain's gamble to have the French protect her possessions in Mexico, Central America and South America from future Anglo-American intrusions was a miscalculated policy step doomed to fail. Spain's own European troubles and dependency upon France led to the loss of her fleet to the British at Trafalgar in 1805, and military occupation by France with Joseph Bonaparte placed on the Spanish throne by a French army in 1808. The global impacts of these decisions and actions for Spain were disastrous. Internationally, the loss of Louisiana, both as a colonial possession and as buffer zone to Mexico, was the beginning of the end of Spain's role in the Western Hemisphere. Only the Floridas remained, and then in 1819 they too would be lost to the Americans.

Finally, looking at another global impact, France's retreat from Louisiana in 1803, and Saint-Domingue—which became the independent nation of Haiti in 1804—witnessed the issue of slavery and Negro rebellions in slave territories as an open question in need of resolution in the future. Barbé Marbois, who had been the intendant for Saint-Domingue prior to the French Revolution, warned Napoleon of the eternal problems with a slave economy in the meeting on April 10, 1803.

> "Before long, the United States will give Spain trouble; the acquisition of Louisiana has increased their ambition."
> French Prefect Laussat, *Memoires*,
> March 27, 1804

Jefferson, himself a slave owner but someone who detested the institution, attempted to deal with the problem as well. The prohibiting of slavery in the region

> "The occupation of Louisiana—a colony with slaves—will occasion us more expense than it will afford us profit."
> Barbé-Marbois to Napoleon,
> meeting of April 10, 1803

per the Northwest Ordinance in 1787 was due to his effort. And, shortly after the American acquisition of Louisiana, Congress prohibited the importation of slaves into the Territory, a policy that led to a lucrative slave trade through smuggling. But, the fear of slave rebellions first in the West Indies, and then in Virginia, and its spread to other states which had a slave dominated economy, including recently acquired Louisiana, led Jefferson to propose an alternative strategy. Gabriel's slave rebellion (1800) in Virginia, in which twenty-seven slaves were executed, had a profound impact on him. Jefferson's concerns and responses the slave rebellion in Saint-Domingue, which in January, 1804, declared its independence as the nation of Haiti from France, haunted him. The intellectual precepts of the French Revolution and the ideas of liberty that it originally represented were dear to him. But, the application of its tactics, rebellion that turned to racial violence, was unacceptable. It was Jefferson who wrote then Governor James Monroe of Virginia in 1801 indicating that he thought the slave executions following Gabriel's revolt had gone far enough. It was a dilemma. Following Pinckney's Treaty and the setting of the boundary between Spanish Florida and the United States at 31 degrees north latitude instead of 32 degrees 30 minutes north as the Spanish claimed, the result was that Federalist President John Adams' administration created the Mississippi Territory. And, with it, the extension of slavery into this area south of Ohio River. The American expansion into the south and west after 1798, which would soon include Louisiana, was done with slavery included in the process. Jefferson wrote at one point that maintaining slavery "was like holding a wolf by the ears; you didn't like it, but you dare not let it go." The expansion of the United States, with the Mississippi Territory and eventually in Louisiana with slavery, prompted Jefferson, who detested the institution, to look for solutions. In a letter to Rufus King, in London (July 13, 1802), Jefferson, at the height of the controversy over Louisiana, ever the man of peace and diplomacy, outlined a global proposal for dealing with slavery, and thereby avoiding the future potential for slave rebellions, such as that precipitated by the French Revolution in Haiti, for the United States and resolution in a humanitarian manner:

To Rufus King

Washington, July 13, 1802.

DEAR SIR,

The course of things in the neighboring islands of the West Indies, appear to have given a considerable impulse to the minds of the slaves in different parts of the United States. A great disposition to insurgency has manifested itself among them, which, in one instance, in the State of Virginia, broke out into actual insurrection. This was easily suppressed, but many of those concerned (between twenty and thirty, I believe) fell victims to the law. So extensive an execution could not but excite sensibility in the public mind, and begat a regret that the laws had not provided for such cases, some alternative, combing more mildness with equal efficacy. The Legislature of the State at a subsequent meeting took the subject in consideration, and have communicated to me through the Governor of the State, their wish that some place could be provided, out of the limits of the United States, to which slaves guilty of insurgency might be transported; and they particularly looked to Africa as offering the most desirable receptacle. We might, for this purpose, enter into negotiations with the natives, on some part of the coast, to obtain a settlement; and, by establishing an African company, combine with it commercial operations, which might not only reimburse expenses, but procure profit also. But there being already such an establishment on that coast by the English Sierra Leone company, made for the express purpose of colonizing civilized blacks to that country, it would seem better, by incorporating our emigrants with theirs, to make one strong, rather than two weak colonies. This would be the more desirable because the blacks settled at Sierra Leone having chiefly gone from the States, would often receive among those we should send, their acquaintances and relatives. The object of this letter therefore is to ask the favor of you too enter into conference with such persons private and public as would be necessary to give us permission to send thither the persons under contemplation. It is material to observe that they are not felons, or common malefactors, but persons guilty of what the safety of society, under actual circumstances, obliges us to treat as a crime, but which their feelings may represent in a far different shape. They are such as will be a valuable acquisition to the settlement already existing there, and well calculated to co-operate in the plan of civilization.

As the expense of so distant transportation would be very heavy, and might weigh unfavorably in deciding between modes of punishment, it is very desirable that it should be lessened as much as practicable. If the regulations of the place would permit these emigrants to dispose of themselves, as the Germans and others do who come to this country poor, by giving their labor for a certain to someone who will pay their passage; and if the master of the vessel could be permitted to carry articles of commerce from this country and take back others from that, which might yield him a mercantile profit sufficient to cover the expenses of the voyage, a serious difficulty would be removed. I will ask you attention therefore to arrangements necessary for this purpose.

The consequences of permitting emancipations to become extensive, unless the condition of emigration be annexed to them, furnish also matter of solicitation to the Legislature of Virginia, as you will perceive by their resolution enclosed to you. Although provision for the settlement of emancipated negroes might perhaps be obtainable nearer home than Africa, yet is desirable that we should be free to expatriate this description of people also to the colony of Sierra Leone, if considerations respecting either themselves or us should render it more expedient. I will pray you therefore to get the same permission extended to the reception of these as well as the first mentioned. Nor will be a selection of bad subjects; the emancipations, for the most part, being either of the whole slaves of the master, of such individuals as have particularly deserved well: the latter is most frequent.

The request of the Legislature of Virginia having produced to me the occasion of addressing you, I avail myself of it to assure you of perfect satisfaction with the manner in which you have conducted the several matters confided to you by us; and to express my hope that through your agency we may be able to remove everything inauspicious to a cordial friendship between this country and the one in which you are stationed; a friendship dictated by too many considerations not to be felt by the wise and the dispassionate of both nations. It is therefore with the sincerest pleasure I have observed on the part of the British government various manifestations of just and friendly disposition towards us. We wish to cultivate peace and friendship with all nations, believing that course most conducive to the welfare of our own. It is natural that these friendships should bear some proportion to the common interests of the parties. The interesting relations between Great Britain and the United States, are certainly of the first order; and as such are estimated, and will be faithfully cultivated by us. . . .[126]

While an excellent example of Jefferson's fertile mind, this proposal failed to recognize that in Louisiana, many of those whites who fled the violence in the West Indies took their slaves with them. The Spanish colonies had their own "Black Code" which protected the institution of slavery. French Prefect Laussat, during his twenty days of administration in Louisiana, submitted to the pressure from local white slave owners, and issued a *Code Noir* just three days prior to the transfer of the colony. After Louisiana became part of the United States, the Constitution (Article 1, section 2) then protected slaves as "property." The legacy of the slave revolution in Haiti, not only derailed France's plans for her West Indies enterprise, but had a lasting impact in Louisiana, the United States and on President Jefferson as well.

Not the least of this influence of the slave rebellion in Saint-Domingue was the decision by Bonaparte to sell Louisiana to the United States. Napoleon's dreams of a new French Empire turned inward, both in France and in Europe. Such a dream of global empire and glory stopped at the water's edge, however, because of the British navy. The old analogy of the "tiger" and the "shark" was a reality in 1803.

Nothing reflected America's new global image better than the City of New Orleans itself. Its population of creoles, Americans, freemen-of-color, Spanish descendants, Negro slaves, and Indians testified to this. The global trade and commerce operating from New Orleans, and which ultimately led her to become the fifth largest port in the United States demonstrated a new economic vitality and global influence.

The successful acquisition of Louisiana insured President Jefferson a second term in office, the continued growth of the Democratic Republican Party, and a further decline of the Federalists. The mission of Lewis and Clark, the Corps of Discovery (1804–1806) and their reports and maps opened the gates to West for the continued westward expansion of the

United States. The United States, exactly as Jefferson or even Napoleon, had predicted, was the new power on the scene. France turned her global attention again to European matters, and with the exception of maintaining a limited interest in the West Indies after the loss of Saint-Domingue in 1804, she was no longer a political contender. Only Britain remained, and events during the War of 1812 and thereafter would lead to a future understanding between the United States and Britain. The "critical moment" of the Louisiana Purchase was over, and the future for the United States, in her domestic and foreign affairs, was now firmly committed to the American fulfillment of western expansion and of her "manifest destiny" at home and global identity abroad. Robert Livingston was correct when he wrote from Paris (May 2, 1803) that the acquisition of Louisiana meant that the United States had taken "their place among the powers of the first rank."

Documents

Treaty of San Lorenzo el Real

The Treaty of San Lorenzo el Real, also known as Pinckney's Treaty (Thomas Pinckney), was signed on October 27, 1795; it was later ratified by the United States Senate on March 7, 1796; and became effective on August 3, 1796. Spain was facing her old nemesis Britain after becoming an ally of France in 1795, and wanted to neutralize her frontier disputes with the United States and thereby avoid hostilities. In addition, Spain's weak military power after years of war in Europe had drained her resources. She began her retreat from colonies in the West Indies by relinquishing the western portion of the Island of Hispaniola to France at the end of the seventeenth century. In the Treaty of Basel (July 22, 1795), Spain transferred the remaining two-thirds of the island to France, which was now completely French as "Saint-Domingue" or Haiti. Prior to the secret treaty of San Il Defonzo in 1800, Spain had also made overtures regarding cession of Louisiana to France as well. Spain was divesting herself of colonies she could no longer afford to administer and defend; but, in 1795, she retained her possessions of Louisiana, West and East Florida, Cuba, Central America, Mexico and South America. This treaty opened the floodgates to American expansionism, and by defining the northern border of Spanish Florida at 31 degrees north, it opened a new area, including Natchez, in what was to become the Mississippi Territory in 1798. The text of the treaty stresses over and over again the importance of peace and goodwill between the two nations. For Spain, such peace with the United States was necessary, and a priority.

Treaty of Friendship, Limits, and Navigation, signed at San Lorenzo el Real October 27, 1795. Original in English and Spanish Submitted to the Senate February 26, 1796. Resolution of advice and consent March 5, 1796. Ratified by the United States March 7, 1796. Ratified by Spain April 25, 1796. Ratifications exchanged at Aranjuez April 25, 1796. Proclaimed August 2, 1796.

"His Catholic Majesty and the United States of America desiring to consolidate on a permanent basis the Friendship and good correspondence which happily prevails between the two Parties, have determined to establish by a convention several points, the settlement whereof will be productive of general advantage and reciprocal utility to both Nations. With this intention his Catholic Majesty has appointed the most Excellent Lord Don Manuel de Godoy and Alvarez de Faria, Rios, Sanchez Zarzosa, Prince de la Paz Duke de la Alcudia Lord of the Soto de Roma and of the State of Albala: Grandee of Spain of the first class: perpetual Regidor of the City of Santiago: Knight of the illustrious Order of the Golden Fleece, and Great Cross of the Royal and distinguished Spanish order of Charles the III. Commander of Valencia del Ventoso, Rivera, and Aceuchal in that of Santiago: Knight and Great Cross of the religious order of St John: Counsellor of State: First Secretary of State and Despacho: Secretary to the Queen: Superintendent General of the Posts and High Ways: Protector of the Royal Academy of the Noble Arts, and of the Royal Societies of natural history, Botany, Chemistry, and Astronomy: Gentleman of the King's Chamber in employment: Captain General of his Armies: Inspector and Major of the Royal Corps of Body Guards &a &a &a and the President of the United States with the advice and consent of their Senate, has appointed Thomas Pinckney a Citizen of the United States, and their Envoy Extraordinary to his Catholic Majesty. And the said Plenipotentiaries have agreed upon and concluded the following Articles."

ART. I.

There shall be a firm and inviolable Peace and sincere Friendship between His Catholic Majesty his successors and subjects, and the United States and their Citizens without exception of persons or places.

ART. II.

To prevent all disputes on the subject of the boundaries which separate the territories of the two High contracting Parties, it is hereby declared and agreed as follows: to wit: The Southern boundary of the United States which divides their territory from the Spanish Colonies of East and West Florida, shall be designated by a line beginning on the River Mississippi at the Northernmost part of the thirty first degree of latitude North of the Equator, which from thence shall be drawn due East to the middle of the River Apalachicola or Catahouche, thence along the middle thereof to its junction with the Flint, thence straight to the head of St Mary's River, and thence down the middle thereof to the Atlantic Ocean. And it is agreed that if there should be any troops, Garrisons or settlements of either Party in the territory of the other according to the above mentioned boundaries, they shall be withdrawn from the said territory within the term of six months after the ratification of this treaty or sooner if it be possible and that they shall be permitted to take with them all the goods and effects which they possess.

ART. III.

In order to carry the preceding Article into effect one Commissioner and one Surveyor shall be appointed by each of the contracting Parties who shall meet at the Natchez on the left side of The River Mississippi before the expiration of six months from the ratification of this convention, and they shall proceed to run and mark this boundary according to the stipulations of the said Article. They shall make Plats and keep journals of their proceedings which shall be considered as part of this convention, and shall have the same force as if they were inserted therein. And if on any account it should be found necessary that the said Commissioners and Surveyors should be accompanied by Guards, they shall be furnished in equal proportions by the Commanding Officer of his Majesty's troops in the two Floridas, and the Commanding Officer of the troops of the United States in their Southwestern territory, who shall act by common consent and amicably, as well with respect to this point as to the furnishing of provisions and instruments and making every other arrangement which may be necessary or useful for the execution of this article.

ART. IV.

It is likewise agreed that the Western boundary of the United States which separates them from the Spanish Colony of Louisiana, is in the middle of the channel or bed of the River Mississippi from the Northern boundary of the said States to the completion of the thirty first degree of latitude North of the Equator; and his Catholic Majesty has likewise agreed that the navigation of the said River in its whole breadth from its source to the Ocean shall be free only to his Subjects, and the Citizens of the United States, unless he should extend this privilege to the Subjects of other Powers by special convention.

ART. V.

The two High contracting Parties shall by all the means in their power maintain peace and harmony among the several Indian Nations who inhabit the country adjacent to the lines and Rivers which by the proceeding Articles form the boundaries of the two Floridas; and to obtain this effect both Parties oblige themselves expressly to restrain by force all hostilities on the part of the Indian Nations living within their boundaries: so that Spain will not order her Indians to attack the Citizens of the United States, nor the Indians inhabiting their territory; nor will the United States permit these last mentioned Indians to commence hostilities against the Subjects of his Catholic Majesty, or his Indians in any manner whatever.

And whereas several treaties of Friendship exist between the two contracting Parties and the said Nations of Indians, it is hereby agreed that in future no treaty of alliance or other whatever (except treaties of Peace) shall be made by either Party with the Indians living within the boundary of the other; but both Parties will endeavor to make the advantages of the Indian trade common and mutually beneficial to their respective Subjects and Citizens observing in all things the most complete reciprocity: so that both Parties may obtain the advantages arising from a good understanding with the said Nations, without being subject to the expense which they have hitherto occasioned.

ART. VI.

Each Party shall endeavor by all means in their power to protect and defend all Vessels and other effects belonging to the Citizens or Subjects of the other, which shall be within the extent of their jurisdiction by sea or by land, and shall use all their efforts to recover and cause to be restored to the right owners their Vessels and effects which may have been taken from them within the extent of their said jurisdiction whether they are at war or not with the Power whose Subjects have taken possession of the said effects.

ART. VII.

And it is agreed that the Subjects or Citizens of each of the contracting Parties, their Vessels, or effects shall not be liable to any embargo or detention on the part of the other for any military expedition or other public or private purpose whatever; and in all cases of seizure, detention, or arrest for debts contracted or offences committed by any Citizen or Subject of the one Party within the jurisdiction of the other, the same shall be made and prosecuted by order and authority of law only, and according to the regular course of proceedings usual in such cases. The Citizens and Subjects of both Parties shall be allowed to employ such Advocates, Solicitors, Notaries, Agents, and Factors, as they may judge proper in all their affairs and in all their trials at law in which they may be concerned before the tribunals of the other Party, and such Agents shall have free access to be present at the proceedings in such causes, and at the taking of all examinations and evidence which may be exhibited in the said trials.

ART. VIII.

In case the Subjects and inhabitants of either Party with their shipping whether public and of war or private and of merchants be forced through stress of weather, pursuit of Pirates, or Enemies, or any other urgent necessity for seeking of shelter and harbor to retreat and enter into any of the Rivers, Bays, Roads, or Ports belonging to the other Party, they shall be received and treated with all humanity, and enjoy all favor, protection and help, and they shall be permitted to refresh and provide themselves at reasonable rates with victuals and all things needful for the sustenance of their persons or reparation of their Ships, and prosecution of their voyage; and they shall no ways be hindered from returning out of the said Ports, or Roads, but may remove and depart when and whither they please without any let or hindrance.

ART. IX.

All Ships and merchandise of what nature so ever which shall be rescued out of the hands of any Pirates or Robbers on the high seas shall be brought into some Port of either State and shall be delivered to the custody of the Officers of that Port in order to be taken care of and restored entire to the true proprietor as soon as due and sufficient proof shall be made concerning the property there.

ART. X.

When any Vessel of either Party shall be wrecked, foundered, or otherwise damaged on the coasts or within the dominion of the other, their respective Subjects or Citizens shall receive as well for themselves as for their Vessels and effects the same assistance which would be due to the inhabitants of the Country where the damage happens, and shall pay the same charges and dues only as the said inhabitants.

ART. XI.

The Citizens and Subjects of each Party shall have power to dispose of their personal goods within the jurisdiction of the other by testament, donation, or otherwise; and their representatives being Subjects or Citizens of the other Party shall succeed to their said personal goods, whether by testament or *by intestate* and they may take possession thereof either by themselves or others acting for them, and dispose of the same at their will paying such dues only as the inhabitants of the Country wherein the said goods are shall be subject to pay in like cases, and in case of the absence of the representatives, such care shall be taken of the said goods as would be taken of the goods of a native in like case, until the lawful owner may take measures for receiving them. And if question shall arise among several claimants to which of them the said goods belong the same shall be decided finally by the laws and Judges of the Land wherein the said goods are. And where on the death of any person holding real estate within the territories of the one Party, such real estate would by the laws of the Land descend on a Citizen or Subject of the other were he not disqualified by being an alien, such subject shall be allowed a reasonable time to sell the same and to withdraw the proceeds without molestation, and exempt from all rights of detraction on the part of the Government of the respective states.

ART. XII.

The merchant Ships of either of the Parties which shall be making into a Port belonging to the enemy of the other Party and concerning whose voyage and the species of goods on board her there shall be just grounds of suspicion shall be obliged to exhibit as well upon the high seas as in the Ports and havens not only her passports but likewise certificates expressly strewing that her goods are not of the number of those which have been prohibited as contraband.

ART. XIII.

For the better promoting of commerce on both sides, it is agreed that if a war shall break out between the said two Nations one year after the proclamation of war shall be allowed to the merchants in the Cities and Towns where they shall live for collecting and transporting their goods and merchandises, and if anything be taken from them, or any injury be done them within that term by either Party, or the People or Subjects of either, full satisfaction shall be made for the same by the Government.

ART. XIV.

No subject of his Catholic Majesty shall apply for or take any commission or letters of marque for arming any Ship or Ships to act as Privateers against the said United States or against the Citizens, People, or inhabitants of the said United States, or against the property of any of the inhabitants of any of them, from any Prince or State with which the said United States shall be at war.

Nor shall any Citizen, Subject, or Inhabitant of the said United States apply for or take any commission or letters of marque for arming any Ship or Ships to act as Privateers against the subjects of his Catholic Majesty or the property of any of them from any Prince or State with which the said King shall be at war. And if any person of either Nation shall take such commissions or letters of marque he shall be punished as a Pirate.

ART. XV.

It shall be lawful for all and singular the Subjects of his Catholic Majesty, and the Citizens People, and inhabitants of the said United States to sail with their Ships with all manner of liberty and security, no distinction being made who are the proprietors of the merchandises laden thereon from any Port to the Places of those who now are or hereafter shall be at enmity with his Catholic Majesty or the United States. It shall be likewise lawful for the Subjects and inhabitants aforesaid to sail with the Ships and merchandises aforementioned, and to trade with the same liberty and security from the Places, Ports, and Havens of those who are Enemies of both or either Party without any opposition or disturbance whatsoever, not only directly from the Places of the Enemy aforementioned to neutral Places but also from one Place belonging to an Enemy to another Place belonging to an Enemy, whether they be under the jurisdiction of the same Prince or under several, and it is hereby stipulated that Free Ships shall also give freedom to goods, and that every thing shall be deemed free and exempt which shall be found on board the Ships belonging to the Subjects of either of the contracting Parties although the whole lading or any part thereof should appertain to the Enemies of either; contraband goods being always excepted. It is also agreed that the same liberty be extended to persons who are on board a free Ship, so that, although they be Enemies to either Party they shall not be made Prisoners or taken out of that free Ship unless they are Soldiers and in actual service of the Enemies.

ART. XVI.

This liberty of navigation and commerce shall extend to all kinds of merchandises excepting those only which are distinguished by the name of contraband; and under this name of contraband or prohibited goods shall be comprehended arms, great guns, bombs, with the fuses, and other things belonging to them, cannon ball, gun powder, match, pikes, swords, lances, spears, halberds, mortars, petards, grenades, saltpeter, muskets, musket ball bucklers, helmets, breast plates, coats of mail, and the like kind of arms proper for arming soldiers, musket rests, belts, horses with their furniture and all other warlike instruments whatever. These merchandises which follows shall not be reckoned among contraband or prohibited goods; that is to say, all sorts of cloths and all other manufactures woven of any wool, flax, silk, cotton, or any other materials whatever, all kinds of wearing apparel together with all species whereof they are used to be made, gold and silver as well coined as un-coined, tin, iron, copper, brass, coals, as also wheat, barley, oats, and any other kind of corn and pulse: tobacco and likewise all manner of spices, salted and smoked fish, salted fish, cheese and butter, beer, oils, wines, sugars, and all sorts of salts, and in general all provisions which serve for the sustenance of life. Furthermore all kinds of cotton, hemp, flax, tar, pitch, ropes, cables, sails, sail cloths, anchors, and any parts of anchors, also ships masts, planks, wood of all kind, and all other things proper either for building or repairing ships, and all other goods whatever which have not been worked into the form of any instrument prepared for war by land or by sea, shad not be reputed contraband, much less such as have been already wrought and made up for any other use: all which shall be wholly reckoned among free goods, as likewise all other merchandises and things which are not comprehended and particularly mentioned in the foregoing enumeration of contraband goods: so that they may be transported and carried in the freest manner by the subjects of both parties, even to Places belonging to an Enemy, such towns or Places being only excepted as are at that time besieged, blocked up, or invested. And except the cases in which any Ship of war or Squadron shall in consequence of storms or other accidents at sea be under the necessity of taking the cargo of any trading Vessel or Vessels, in which case they may stop the said Vessel or Vessels and furnish themselves with necessaries, giving a receipt in order that the Power to whom the said ship of war belongs may pay for the articles so taken according to the price thereof at the Port to which they may appear to have been destined by the Ship's papers: and the two contracting Parties engage that the Vessels shall not be detained longer than may be absolutely necessary for their said Ships to supply themselves with necessaries: that they will immediately pay the value of the receipts: and indemnify the proprietor for all losses which he may have sustained in consequence of such transaction.

ART. XVII.

To the end that all manner of dissensions and quarrels may be avoided and prevented on one side and the other, it is agreed that in case either of the Parties hereto should be engaged in a war, the ships and Vessels belonging to the Subjects or People of the other Party must be furnished with sea letters or passports expressing the name, property, and bulk of the Ship, as also the name and place of habitation of the master or commander of the said Ship, that it may appear thereby that the Ship really and truly belongs to the Subjects of one of the Parties; which passport shall be made out and granted according to the form annexed to this Treaty. They shall likewise be recalled every year, that is, if the ship happens to return home within the space of a year. It is likewise agreed that such ships being laden, are to be provided not only with passports as above mentioned but also with certificates containing the several particulars of the cargo, the place whence the ship sailed, that so it may be known whether any forbidden or contraband goods be on board the same; which certificates shall be made out by the Officers of the place whence the ship sailed in the accustomed form; and if any one shall think it fit or advisable to express in the said certificates the person to whom the goods on board belong he may freely do so: without which requisites they may be sent to one of the Ports of the other contracting Party and adjudged by the competent tribunal according to what is above set forth, that all the circumstances of this omission having been well examined, they shall be adjudged to be legal prizes, unless they shall give legal satisfaction of their property by testimony entirely equivalent.

ART. XVIII.

If the Ships of the said subjects, People or inhabitants of either of the Parties shall be met with either sailing along the coasts on the high Seas by any Ship of war of the other or by any Privateer, the said Ship of war or Privateer for the avoiding of any disorder shall remain out of cannon shot, and may send their boats aboard the merchant Ship which they shall so meet with, and may enter her to number of two or three men only to whom the master or Commander of such ship or vessel shall exhibit his passports concerning the property of the ship made out according to the form inserted in this present Treaty: and the ship when she shall have showed such passports shall be free and at liberty to pursue her voyage, so as it shall not be lawful to molest or give her chance in any manner or force her to quit her intended course.

ART. XIX.

Consuls shall be reciprocally established with the privileges and powers which those of the most favored Nations enjoy in the Ports where their consuls reside, or are permitted to be.

ART. XX.

It is also agreed that the inhabitants of the territories of each Party shall respectively have free access to the Courts of Justice of the other, and they shall be permitted to prosecute suits for the recovery of their properties, the payment of their debts, and for obtaining satisfaction for the damages which they may have sustained, whether the persons whom they may sue be subjects or Citizens of the Country in which they may be found, or any other persons whatsoever who may have taken refuge therein; and the proceedings and sentences of the said Court shall be the same as if the contending parties had been subjects or Citizens of the said Country.

ART. XXI.

In order to terminate all differences on account of the losses sustained by the Citizens of the United States in consequence of their vessels and cargoes having been taken by the Subjects of his Catholic Majesty during the late war between Spain and France, it is agreed that all such cases shall be referred to the final decision of Commissioners to be appointed in the following manner. His Catholic Majesty shall name one Commissioner, and the President of the United States by and with the advice and consent of their Senate shall appoint another, and the said two Commissioners shall agree on the choice of a third, or if they cannot agree so they shall each propose one person, and of the two names so proposed one shall be drawn by lot in the presence of the two original Commissioners, and the person whose name shall be so drawn shall be the third Commissioner, and the three Commissioners so appointed shall be sworn impartially to examine and decide the claims in question according to the merits of the several cases, and to justice, equity, and the laws of Nations. The said Commissioners shall meet and sit at Philadelphia and in the case of the death, sickness, or necessary absence of any such commissioner his place shall be supplied in the same manner as he was first appointed, and the new Commissioner shall take the same oaths, and do the same duties. They shall receive all complaints and applications, authorized by this article during eighteen months from the day on which they shall assemble. They shall have power to examine all such persons as come before them on oath or affirmation touching the complaints in question, and also to receive in evidence all written testimony authenticated in such manner as they shall think proper to require or admit. The award of the said Commissioners or any two of them shall be final and conclusive both as to the justice of the claim and the amount of the sum to be paid to the claimants; and his Catholic Majesty undertakes to cause the same to be paid in specie without deduction, at such times and Places and under such conditions as shall be awarded by the said Commissioners.

ART. XXII.

The two high contracting Parties hoping that the good correspondence and friendship which happily reigns between them will be further increased by this Treaty, and that it will contribute to augment their prosperity and opulence, will in future give to their mutual commerce all the extension and favor which the advantage of both Countries may require; and in consequence of the stipulations contained in the IV. article his Catholic Majesty will permit the Citizens of the United States for the space of three years from this time to deposit their merchandise and effects in the Port of New Orleans, and to export them from thence without paying any other duty than a fair price for the hire of the stores, and his Majesty promises either to continue this permission if he finds during that time that it is not prejudicial to the interests of Spain, or if he should not agree to continue it there, he will assign to them on another part of the banks of the Mississippi an equivalent establishment.

ART. XXIII.

The present Treaty shall not be in force until ratified by the Contracting Parties, and the ratifications shall be exchanged in six months from this time, or sooner if possible.

In Witness whereof We the underwritten Plenipotentiaries of His Catholic Majesty and of the United States of America have signed this present Treaty of Friendship, Limits and Navigation and have "hereunto affixed our seals respectively.

Done at San Lorenzo el Real this seven and twenty day of October one thousand seven hundred and ninety five."

THOMAS PINCKNEY
[Seal]

EL PRINCIPE DE LA PAZ
[Seal]

Source: www.earlyamerica.com/earlyamerica/milestones/sanlorenzo/text.html. Accessed July 20, 2013.

Secret Treaty of San Ildefonso, Spain and France, signed October 1, 1800, returning Louisiana back to France in exchange for Spanish properties in Italy

*F*or Spain, this treaty represented her primary interest in European affairs, and interests of the royal family. With the most powerful army in Europe, the treaty utilized France as her ally against their common enemy, Britain; by occupying Louisiana, it positioned a French army between the Anglo- Americans and Mexico, the crown jewel in her colonial empire. It continued a pattern of Spain ridding herself of unprofitable colonies, in that she was on the point of bankruptcy with a huge national debt brought on by years of war. For France, and Napoleon Bonaparte, the treaty recognized the new order not only in Europe, but a resumption of French imperial designs and power in the Western Hemisphere. Napoleon, at this point, still believed in France's mission to rival Britain on a global basis. It was not until mid-October, 1802, that King Carlos IV instructed Spanish officers in Louisiana to prepare for the actual retrocession of the colony to France after the Italian properties had been ceded to Spain. On May 18, 1803, the Spanish Governor of Louisiana, Don Manuel de Salcedo, issued a proclamation to the citizens informing them of their impending transfer back to France.

Preliminary and Secret Treaty between the French Republic and His Catholic Majesty the King of Spain, Concerning the Aggrandizement of His Royal Highness the Infant Duke of Parma in Italy and the Retrocession of Louisiana.

"His Catholic Majesty having always manifested an earnest desire to procure for His Royal Highness the Duke of Parma an aggrandizement which would place his domains on a footing more consonant with his dignity; and the French Republic on its part having long since made known to His Majesty the King of Spain its desire to be again placed in possession of the colony of Louisiana; and the two Governments having exchanged their views on these two subjects of common interest, and circumstances permitting them to assume obligations in this regard which, so far as depends on them, win assure mutual satisfaction, they have authorized for this purpose the following: the French Republic, the Citizen Alexandre Berthier General in Chief, and His Catholic Majesty, Don Mariano Luis de Urquijo, knight of the Order of Charles III, and of that of St. John of Jerusalem, a Counselor of State, his Ambassador Extraordinary and Plenipotentiary appointed near the Batavian Republic, and his First Secretary of State ad interim, who, having exchanged their powers, have agreed upon the following articles, subject to ratification.

ARTICLE 1

The French Republic undertakes to procure for His Royal Highness the Infant Duke of Parma an aggrandizement of territory which shall increase the population of his domains to one minion inhabitants, with the title of King and with all the rights which attach to the royal dignity; and the French Republic undertakes to obtain in this regard the assent of His Majesty the Emperor and King and that of the other interested states that His Highness the Infant Duke of Parma may be put into possession of the said territories without opposition upon the conclusion of the peace to be made between the French Republic and His Imperial Majesty.

ARTICLE 2

The aggrandizement to be given to His Royal Highness the Duke of Parma may consist of Tuscany, in case the present negotiations of the French Government with His Imperial Majesty shall permit that Government to dispose thereof; or it may consist of the three Roman legations or of any other continental provinces of Italy which form a rounded state.

ARTICLE 3

His Catholic Majesty promises and undertakes on his part to retrocede to the French Republic, six months after the full and entire execution of the above conditions and provisions regarding His Royal Highness the Duke of Parma, the colony or province of Louisiana, with the same extent that it now has in the hands of Spain and that it had when France possessed it, and such as it ought to be according to the treaties subsequently concluded between Spain and other states.

ARTICLE 4

His Catholic Majesty will give the necessary orders for the occupation of Louisiana by France as soon as the territories which are to form the arrondissement [district] of the Duke of Parma shall be placed in the hands of His Royal Highness. The French Republic may, according to its convenience, postpone the taking of possession; when that is to be executed, the states directly or indirectly interested will agree upon such further conditions as their common interests and the interest of the respective inhabitants require.

ARTICLE 5

His Catholic Majesty undertakes to deliver to the French Republic in Spanish ports in Europe, one month after the execution of the provision with regard to the Duke of Parma, six ships of war in good condition built for seventy-four guns, armed and equipped and ready to receive French crews and supplies.

ARTICLE 6

As the provisions of the present treaty have no prejudicial object and leave intact the rights of an, it is not to be supposed that they win give offense to any power. However, if the contrary shall happen and if the two states, because of the execution thereof, shall be attacked or threatened, the two powers agree to make common cause not only to repel the aggression but also to take conciliatory measures prosper for the maintenance of peace with all their neighbors.

ARTICLE 7

The obligations contained in the present treaty derogate in no respect from those which are expressed in the Treaty of Alliance signed at San Ildefonso on the 2nd Fructidor, Year 4 (August 19, 1796); on the contrary they unite anew the interests of the two powers and assure the guaranties stipulated in the Treaty of Alliance for all cases in which they should be applied.

ARTICLE 8

The ratifications of these preliminary articles shall be effected and exchanged within the period of one month, or sooner if possible, counting from the day of the signature of the present treaty. In faith whereof we, the undersigned Ministers Plenipotentiary of the French Republic and of His Catholic Majesty, in virtue of our respective powers, have signed these preliminary articles and have affixed thereto our seals. Done at San Ildefonso the 9th Vendemiaire, 9th year of the French Republic (October 1, 1800)."

ALEXANDRE BIRTHIER [Seal of France]

MARIANO LUIS DE URQUIJO [Seal of Spain]

Source: Avalon Project, Documents in Law, History and Diplomacy. Yale Law School. http://avalon.law.yale.edu/19th_century/ildefens.asp. Accessed July 20, 2013.

DOCUMENT 3

Treaty between the United States of America and the French Republic, agreed to April 30, 1803, for the sale of Louisiana

Napoleon's decision (April 10, 1803) to sell the whole of Louisiana and New Orleans presented to the American envoys by Talleyrand, the Foreign Minister (April 11, 1803) and its resulting negotiations between French and American diplomats, involved extensive discussions as to the final price and terms. After three weeks of negotiations, the result was the Treaty and two Conventions of April 30th, 1803. After haggling down from 100 million francs, the price was finally settled at 60 million francs ($11,250,000) for Louisiana, and the United States agreed to pay another 20 million francs ($3,750,000) in damages owed by France to American shippers from the years of the "quasi-war," (1797–1800), a total commitment by the United States of $15 million in U.S. dollars.

Note: This document, and Documents 4 and 5, transcribed here, are the treaty of cession and two conventions, one for the payment of 60 million francs ($11,250,000), the other for claims American citizens had made against France for 20 million francs ($3,750,000).

Louisiana Purchase Treaty and Conventions of April 30, 1803; signed for the United States by Robert Livingston and James Monroe; signed for France by Charles Maurice Talleyrand and François Barbé-Marbois on May 2, 1803.

TREATY BETWEEN THE UNITED STATES OF AMERICA AND THE FRENCH REPUBLIC

"The President of the United States of America and the First Consul of the French Republic in the name of the French People desiring to remove all Source of misunderstanding relative to objects of discussion mentioned in the Second and fifth articles of the Convention of the 8th Vendémiaire an 9 (30 September 1800) relative to the rights claimed by the United States in virtue of the Treaty concluded at Madrid the 27 of October 1795, between His Catholic Majesty & the Said United States, & willing to Strengthen the union and friendship which at the time of the Said Convention was happily re-established between the two nations have respectively named their Plenipotentiaries to wit The President of the United States, by and with the advice and consent of the Senate of the Said States; Robert R. Livingston Minister Plenipotentiary of the United States and James Monroe Minister Plenipotentiary and Envoy extraordinary of the Said States near the Government of the French Republic; And the First Consul in the name of the French people, Citizen François Barbé Marbois Minister of the public treasury who after having respectively exchanged their full powers have agreed to the following Articles.

ARTICLE I

Whereas by the Article the third of the Treaty concluded at St Ildefonso the 9th Vendémiaire an[year] 9 (1st October) 1800 between the First Consul of the French Republic and his Catholic Majesty it was agreed as follows:

"His Catholic Majesty promises and engages on his part to cede to the French Republic six months after the full and entire execution of the conditions and Stipulations herein relative to his Royal Highness the Duke of Parma, the Colony or Province of Louisiana with the Same extent that it now has in the hand of Spain, & that it had when France possessed it; and Such as it Should be after the Treaties subsequently entered into between Spain and other States."

And whereas in pursuance of the Treaty and particularly of the third article the French Republic has an incontestable title to the domain and to the possession of the said Territory—The First Consul of the French Republic desiring to give to the United States a strong proof of his friendship doth hereby cede to the United States in the name of the French Republic forever and in full Sovereignty the said territory with all its rights and appurtenances as fully and in the Same manner as they have been acquired by the French Republic in virtue of the above mentioned Treaty concluded with his Catholic Majesty.

ART: II

In the cession made by the preceding article are included the adjacent Islands belonging to Louisiana all public lots and Squares, vacant lands and all public buildings, fortifications, barracks and other edifices which are not private property—The Archives, papers & documents relative to the domain and Sovereignty of Louisiana and its dependences will be left in the possession of the Commissaries of the United States, and copies will be afterwards given in due form to the Magistrates and Municipal officers of such of the said papers and documents as may be necessary to them.

ART: III

The inhabitants of the ceded territory shall be incorporated in the Union of the United States and admitted as soon as possible according to the principles of the federal Constitution to the enjoyment of all these rights, advantages and immunities of citizens of the United States, and in the mean time they shall be maintained and protected in the free enjoyment of their liberty, property and the Religion which they profess.

ART: IV

There Shall be Sent by the Government of France a Commissary to Louisiana to the end that he do every act necessary as well to receive from the Officers of his Catholic Majesty the Said country and its dependences in the name of the French Republic if it has not been already done as to transmit it in the name of the French Republic to the Commissary or agent of the United States.

ART: V

Immediately after the ratification of the present Treaty by the President of the United States and in case that of the first Consul's shall have been previously obtained, the commissary of the French Republic shall remit all military posts of New Orleans and other parts of the ceded territory to the Commissary or Commissaries named by the President to take possession—the troops whether of France or Spain who may be there shall cease to occupy any military post from the time of taking possession and shall be embarked as soon as possible in the course of three months after the ratification of this treaty.

ART: VI

The United States promise to execute Such treaties and articles as may have been agreed between Spain and the tribes and nations of Indians until by mutual consent of the United States and the said tribes or nations other Suitable articles Shall have been agreed upon.

ART: VII

As it is reciprocally advantageous to the commerce of France and the United States to encourage the communication of both nations for a limited time in the country ceded by the present treaty until general arrangements relative to commerce of both nations may be agreed on; it has been agreed between the contracting parties that the French Ships coming directly from France or any of her colonies loaded only with the produce and manufactures of France or her Said Colonies; and the Ships of Spain coming directly from Spain or any of her colonies loaded only with the produce or manufactures of Spain or her Colonies shall be admitted during the Space of twelve years in the Port of New-Orleans and in all other legal ports-of-entry within the ceded territory in the Same manner as the Ships of the United States coming directly from France or Spain or any of their Colonies without being Subject to any other or greater duty on merchandize or other or greater tonnage than that paid by the citizens of the United States.

During that Space of time above mentioned no other nation Shall have a right to the Same privileges in the Ports of the ceded territory— the twelve years Shall commence three months after the exchange of ratifications if it Shall take place in France or three months after it Shall have been notified at Paris to the French Government if it Shall take place in the United States; It is however well understood that the object of the above article is to favor the manufactures, Commerce, freight and navigation of France and of Spain So far as relates to the importations that the French and Spanish Shall make into the Said Ports of the United States without in any Sort affecting the regulations that the United States may make concerning the exportation of the produce and merchandize of the United States, or any right they may have to make Such regulations.

ART: VIII

In future and forever after the expiration of the twelve years, the Ships of France shall be treated upon the footing of the most favored nations in the ports above mentioned.

ART: IX

The particular Convention Signed this day by the respective Ministers, having for its object to provide for the payment of debts due to the Citizens of the United States by the French Republic prior to the 30th Sept. 1800 (8th Vendémiaire an 9) is approved and to have its execution in the Same manner as if it had been inserted in this present treaty, and it Shall be ratified in the same form and in the Same time So that the one Shall not be ratified distinct from the other.

Another particular Convention Signed at the Same date as the present treaty relative to a definitive rule between the contracting parties is in the like manner approved and will be ratified in the Same form, and in the Same time and jointly.

ART: X

The present treaty Shall be ratified in good and due form and the ratifications Shall be exchanged in the Space of Six months after the date of the Signature by the Ministers Plenipotentiary or Sooner if possible.

In faith whereof the respective Plenipotentiaries have Signed these articles in the French and English languages; declaring nevertheless that the present Treaty was originally agreed to in the French language; and have thereunto affixed their Seals.

Done at Paris the tenth day of Floreal in the eleventh year of the French Republic; and the 30th of April 1803."

Robt R Livingston [seal of the United States of America]

Jas. Monroe [sea of the United States of Americal]

Barbé Marbois [seal of the French Republic]

Source: National Archives and Records Administration, www.archives.gov/exhibits/american_originals/louistxt.html. Accessed July 20, 2013.

Convention between the United States of America and the French Republic for the payment of $11,250,000 to the latter for the purchase of Louisiana, April 30, 1803

A CONVENTION BETWEEN THE UNITED STATES OF AMERICA AND THE FRENCH REPUBLIC

" "The President of the United States of America and the First Consul of the French Republic in the name of the French people, in consequence of the treaty of cession of Louisiana which has been Signed this day; wishing to regulate definitively everything which has relation to the Said cession have authorized to this effect the Plenipotentiaries, that is to say the President of the United States has, by and with the advice and consent of the Senate of the Said States, nominated for their Plenipotentiaries, Robert R. Livingston, Minister Plenipotentiary of the United States, and James Monroe, Minister Plenipotentiary and Envoy-Extraordinary of the Said United States, near the Government of the French Republic; and the First Consul of the French Republic, in the name of the French people, has named as Plenipotentiary of the Said Republic the citizen François Barbé Marbois: who, in virtue of their full powers, which have been exchanged this day, have agreed to the followings articles:

ART: 1

The Government of the United States engages to pay to the French government in the manner Specified in the following article the sum of Sixty millions of francs independent of the Sum which Shall be fixed by another Convention for the payment of the debts due by France to citizens of the United States.

ART: 2

For the payment of the Sum of Sixty millions of francs mentioned in the preceding article the United States shall create a Stock of eleven millions, two hundred and fifty thousand Dollars bearing an interest of Six percent per annum payable half yearly in London Amsterdam or Paris amounting by the half year to three hundred and thirty Seven thousand five hundred Dollars, according to the proportions which Shall be determined by the French Government to be paid at either place: The principal of the Said Stock to be reimbursed at the treasury of the United States in annual payments of not less than three millions of Dollars each; of which the first payment Shall commence fifteen years after the date of the exchange of ratifications:—this Stock Shall be transferred to the government of France or to Such person or persons as Shall be authorized to receive it in three months at most after the exchange of ratifications of this treaty and after Louisiana Shall be taken possession of the name of the Government of the United States.

It is further agreed that if the French Government Should be desirous of disposing of the Said Stock to receive the capital in Europe at Shorter terms that its measures for that purpose Shall be taken So as to favor in the greatest degree possible the credit of the United States, and to raise to the highest price the Said Stock.

ART: 3

It is agreed that the Dollar of the United States Specified in the present Convention shall be fixed at five francs 3333/100000 or five livres eight Soustournois.

The present Convention Shall be ratified in good and due form, and the ratifications Shall be exchanged the Space of Six months to date from this day or Sooner it possible.

In faith of which the respective Plenipotentiaries have Signed the above articles both in the French and English languages, declaring nevertheless that the present treaty has been originally agreed on and written in the French language; to which they have hereunto affixed their Seals.

Done at Paris the tenth of Floreal eleventh year of the french Republic

30th April 1803."

Robt R Livingston [seal of the United States of America]

Jas. Monroe [seal of the United States of America]

Barbé Marbois [seal of the French Republic]

Source: National Archives and Records Administration, www.archives.gov/exhibits/american_originals/louistxt.html. Accessed July 20, 2013.

Convention between the United States of America and the French Republic whereby the former agrees to pay claims against the latter nation from citizens of the United States for damages incurred during the "quasi war" (1797–1800) in the amount of $3,750,000, April 30, 1803

CONVENTION BETWEEN THE UNITED STATES OF AMERICA AND THE FRENCH REPUBLIC

"The President of the United States of America and the First Consul of the French Republic in the name of the French People having by a Treaty of this date terminated all difficulties relative to Louisiana, and established on a Solid foundation the friendship which unites the two nations and being desirous in compliance with the Second and fifth Articles of the Convention of the 8th Vendémiaire ninth year of the French Republic (30th September 1800) to Secure the payment of the Sums due by France to the citizens of the United States have respectively nominated as Plenipotentiaries that is to Say The President of the United States of America by and with the advice and consent of their Senate Robert R. Livingston Minister Plenipotentiary and James Monroe Minister

Plenipotentiary and Envoy Extraordinary of the Said States near the Government of the French Republic: and the First Consul in the name of the French People the Citizen François Barbé Marbois Minister of the public treasury; who after having exchanged their full powers have agreed to the following articles.

ART: 1

The debts due by France to citizens of the United States contracted before the 8th Vendémiaire ninth year of the French Republic (30th September 1800) Shall be paid according to the following regulations with interest at Six per Cent; to commence from the period when the accounts and vouchers were presented to the French Government.

ART: 2

The debts provided for by the preceding Article are those whose result is comprised in the conjectural note annexed to the present Convention and which, with the interest cannot exceed the Sum of twenty millions of Francs. The claims comprised in the Said note which fall within the exceptions of the following articles, Shall not be admitted to the benefit of this provision.

ART: 3

The principal and interests of the Said debts Shall be discharged by the United States, by orders drawn by their Minister Plenipotentiary on their treasury, these orders Shall be payable Sixty days after the exchange of ratifications of the Treaty and the Conventions Signed this day, and after possession Shall be given of Louisiana by the Commissaries of France to those of the United States.

ART: 4

It is expressly agreed that the preceding articles Shall comprehend no debts but Such as are due to citizens of the United States who have been and are yet creditors of France for Supplies for embargoes and prizes made at Sea, in which the appeal has been properly lodged within the time mentioned in the Said Convention 8th Vendémiaire ninth year, (30th Sept 1800).

ART: 5

The preceding Articles Shall apply only, First: to captures of which the council of prizes Shall have ordered restitution, it being well understood that the claimant cannot have recourse to the United States otherwise than he might have had to the Government of the French republic, and only in case of insufficiency of the captors—2d the debts mentioned in the Said fifth Article of the Convention contracted before the 8th Vendémiaire an 9 (30th September 1800) the payment of which has been heretofore claimed of the actual Government of France and for which the creditors have a right to the protection of the United States;—the Said 5th Article does not comprehend prizes whose condemnation has been or Shall be confirmed: it is the express intention of the contracting parties not to extend the benefit of the present Convention to reclamations of American citizens who Shall have established houses of Commerce in France, England or other countries than the United States in partnership with foreigners, and who by that reason and the nature of their commerce ought to be regarded as domiciled in the places where Such house exist.—All agreements and bargains concerning merchandize, which Shall not be the property of American citizens, are equally excepted from the benefit of the said Conventions, Saving however to Such persons their claims in like manner as if this Treaty had not been made.

ART: 6

And that the different questions which may arise under the preceding article may be fairly investigated, the Ministers Plenipotentiary of the United States Shall name three persons, who Shall act from the present and provisionally, and who shall have full power to examine, without removing the documents, all the accounts of the different claims already liquidated by the Bureaus established for this purpose by the French Republic, and to ascertain whether they belong to the classes designated by the present Convention and the principles established in it or if they are not in one of its exceptions and on their Certificate, declaring that the debt is due to an American Citizen or his representative and that it existed before the 8th Vendémiaire 9th year (30 September 1800) the debtor shall be entitled to an order on the Treasury of the United States in the manner prescribed by the 3d Article.

ART: 7

The Same agents Shall likewise have power, without removing the documents, to examine the claims which are prepared for verification, and to certify those which ought to be admitted by uniting the necessary qualifications, and not being comprised in the exceptions contained in the present Convention.

ART: 8

The Same agents Shall likewise examine the claims which are not prepared for liquidation, and certify in writing those which in their judgments ought to be admitted to liquidation.

ART: 9

In proportion as the debts mentioned in these articles Shall be admitted they Shall be discharged with interest at Six per Cent: by the Treasury of the United States.

ART: 10

And that no debt shall not have the qualifications above mentioned and that no unjust or exorbitant demand may be admitted, the Commercial agent of the United States at Paris or such other agent as the Minister Plenipotentiary or the United States Shall think proper to nominate shall assist at the operations of the Bureaus and co-operate in the examinations of the claims; and if this agent Shall be of the opinion that any debt is not completely proved, or if he shall judge that it is not comprised in the principles of the fifth article above mentioned, and if notwithstanding his opinion the Bureaus established by the French Government should think that it ought to be liquidated, he shall transmit his observations to the board established by the United States, who, without removing documents, shall make a complete examination of the debt and vouchers which Support it, and report the result to the Minister of the United States.— The Minister of the United States Shall transmit his observations in all Such cases to the Minister of the treasury of the French Republic, on whose report the French Government Shall decide definitively in every case.

The rejection of any claim Shall have no other effect than to exempt the United States from the payment of it, the French Government reserving to itself, the right to decide definitively on Such claim So far as it concerns itself.

ART: 11

Every necessary decision Shall be made in the course of a year to commence from the exchange of ratifications, and no reclamation Shall be admitted afterwards.

ART: 12

In case of claims for debts contracted by the Government of France with citizens of the United States Since the 8th Vendémiaire 9th year/30 September 1800 not being comprised in this Convention may be pursued, and the payment demanded in the Same manner as if it had not been made.

ART: 13

The present convention Shall be ratified in good and due form and the ratifications Shall be exchanged in Six months from the date of the Signature of the Ministers Plenipotentiary, or Sooner if possible.

In faith of which, the respective Ministers Plenipotentiary have signed the above Articles both in the French and English languages, declaring nevertheless that the present treaty has been originally agreed on and written in the French language, to which they have hereunto affixed their Seals.

Done at Paris, the tenth of Floreal, eleventh year of the French Republic.

30th April 1803."

Robt. R Livingston [seal of the United States of America!]

Jas. Monroe [seal of the United States of America]

Barbé Marbois [seal of the French Republic]

Source: National Archives and Records Administration, www.archives.gov/exhibits/american_originals/louistxt.html. Accessed July 20, 2013.

Proclamation by Don Manuel de Salcedo, Spanish Governor of Louisiana, to the citizens informing them of the colony's transfer to France, and advising them of their opportunities, May 18, 1803

Don Manuel de Salcedo, Spanish Governor of Louisiana, issued the following proclamation to the citizens of Louisiana on May 18, 1803. Salcedo was following orders received from the Captain-General of Cuba to transition Louisiana from Spanish to French rule in accordance with the instructions from the King of Spain, Carlos IV, which he had issued on October 15, 1802. This document not only ended speculation that Spain might balk at turning the colony of Louisiana over to the French, but it coincided with the termination of Intendant Morales order cancelling the American right of deposit in New Orleans. Once King Carlos IV gave assurances that Intendant Morales was not following his directive, the "right of deposit" was restored, and Governor Salcedo therefore proceeded to proclaim the transfer of Louisiana to France on May 18, 1803. He was, of course, unaware that France had just signed the Treaty and Conventions of 30 April 1803 selling Louisiana to the United States. It was the worst Spanish nightmare come true! See the full text below.

May 18, 1803

"Don Manuel de Salcedo, Brigadier of the Royal Armies, Military and Civil Governor of the Province of Louisiana and West Florida, Inspector of the Veteran Troops and Militias of same, Royal Vice Patron, Judge

Sub-delegate of the General Superintendency of the Post Office, etc., and Don Sebastian Calvo de la Puerta y O'Farrill, Marquis de Casa-Calvo, Knight of the Order of Santiago, Brigadier of the Royal Armies and Colonel of the Regiment of Infantry stationed in Havana, Commissoned by His Majesty to deliver this Province to the French Republic.

We hereby make it known to all vassals of the King, Our Lord, of any class and condition that they may be, that His Majesty has resolved that the retrocession of the Province of Louisiana be done to the mutual satisfaction of both powers; and that the vassals shall continue to enjoy same proofs of protection and affection which have always been experienced by the inhabitants of this Province. His Majesty has also been kind enough to determine, among other things, certain points which we believe to be our duty to bring to public knowledge for the guidance and dispositions of those who may be interested.

First, His Majesty, bearing in mind the obligations imposed by the treaties and wishing to avoid the disputes that may arise, has deigned to resolve: That the delivery of the Colony and Island of New Orleans must be made to Division General Victor, or to another officer legitimately authorized by the Government of the French Republic; that the transfer of the Province be confirmed in the same terms under which France ceded it to His Majesty, by virtue of which the boundaries of both banks of the Rivers St. Louis or Mississippi shall remain as they were, irrevocably fixed on February 10, 1763, by Article 7 of the Treaty of Paris. Consequently, the settlements from the Rivers Manchac or Iberville to the line which separates the American Territory from that of the dominions of the king shall remain under the power of Spain and be annexed to West Florida.

Second, all the individuals who are presently employed in any branch of government and who wish to continue under the dominion of the King shall be transferred to the City of Havana or other points in the possessions of His Majesty, unless they prefer to remain the service of France, which they can freely do. However, if for the present those who wish to be transferred are unable to do because of other pressing matters, they shall report it to their superiors, so that a decision may be rendered on the case.

Third, due to the generous piety of the King, the pensions of the widows and retired persons shall not be discontinued, and in due time the recipients shall be informed of the manner in which this will be arranged.

Fourth, His Majesty expects from the sincere friendship and intimate alliance between us and the French Republic, and hopes that for the benefit and tranquility of the inhabitants, the French government will order its governor and other colonial officials to permit the ecclesiastics and other religious groups to continue to exercise their duties and enjoy the privileges, prerogatives, and exemptions granted them in the titles of their establishment; to permit the ordinary judges and established tribunals to continue to administer justice in accordance with the laws and customs of the Colony; to allow the inhabitants to retain possession of their property and to confirms all the concessions granted to them by my governors, although they may not have received my royal confirmation; finally, His Majesty hopes that the French Government will give its new subjects the same protection and affection which they enjoyed while they were under his rule.

Fifth, in order that all parties be able to make the final decisions on matters pertaining to their interest, we hereby make it equally known that they must come any one of us, so that we may render judgement in accordance in accordance with the Royal Orders and other instructions in our possessions.

And, in order that this proclamation be made known to everyone, we ordered it published and announced with the greatest solemnity and other requisites at the sound of the military drums, as well as having ordered that it be posted in the designated places."

Given in New Orleans on May 18, 1803

Manuel de Salcedo　　　　El Marques de Casa-Calvo

By order of their Lordships.

Carlos Ximenex, War Notary

Source: New Orleans Public Library, "'A Great and Growing City': New Orleans in the Era of the Louisiana Purchase," http://nutrias.org/exhibits/purchase/1sptr.html. Accessed July 20, 2013.

Congressional act enabling the President to take possession of the Louisiana territory

*O**n** Friday, October 28, 1803, a Senate bill entitled: "An act to enable the President of the United states to take possession of the territories ceded by France to the United States, by the treaty concluded at Paris on the thirtieth of April last, and for the temporary government thereof," was read the third time. On the question of "do pass," the vote was 89 yeas and 23 nays. The House then authorized the creation of stock, U.S. government bonds, in the amount of $11,250,000, as required by the First Convention passed as the actual purchase price for Louisiana. The following day, October 29th, 1803, an engrossed bill for carrying into effect the Second convention between the United States and France (to pay claims against the French government by United States' citizens) passed with a House vote of 85 yeas to 7 nays.[113] Then the actual purchase price for Louisiana was approved by action in the House.*

An act to enable the President of the United States to take possession of the territories ceded by France to the United States, by the treaty concluded at Paris on the thirtieth of April last, and for the temporary government thereof.

"Be it enacted by the Senate and House of Representatives of the United States of America in Congress assembled, That the President of the United States be, and he is herby, authorized to take possession of, and occupy the territories ceded by France to the United States, by the treaty concluded at Paris on the thirtieth day of April last, between the two nations, and that he may for that purpose, and in order to maintain in the said territories the authority of the United States, employ any part of the army or navy of the United States, and of the force authorized by an act passed the third of March last, entitled "An act directing a detachment from the militia of the United States, and for erecting certain arsenals," which he may deem necessary; and so much of the sum appropriated for the purpose of carrying this act into effect; to be applied under the direction of the President of the United States.

Sec. 2. And be it further enacted, That until the expiration of the present session of Congress, unless provision for the temporary government of the said territories be sooner made by Congress, all the military, civil, and judicial powers exercised by the officers of the existing government of the same, shall be invested in such person and persons, and shall be exercised in such manner, as the President of the United States shall direct, for maintaining and protecting the inhabitants of Louisiana in the free enjoyment of their liberty, property, and religion."

NATHL. MACON,
Speaker of the House of Representatives

JOHN BROWN,
President of the Senatate, pro tempore.

Approved, October 31, 1803

Source: *Annals of Congress, 8th Congress, 1st Session, pages 1247& 1248; Senate Journal, 302–3* (October 31, 1803).

Two Congressional acts authorizing the financial portions of the Louisiana Purchase

The first Act below met the requirements of the Treaty for payment to France for possession of Louisiana in the amount of $11,250,000 as agreed to in the Convention for that purpose. The second Act met the requirements of the Convention for payment by United States government to its citizens for former claims against the French government in the amount of $3,750,000. The appropriations necessary with which to implement both Conventions were agreed to as part of the Treaty of April 30, 1803, approved by House and Senate, and signed by President Jefferson on November 10, 1803.

1.

An act authorizing the creation of a stock to the amount of eleven millions two hundred and fifty thousand dollars, for the purpose of carrying into effect the convention of the thirtieth of April, one thousand eight hundred and three, between the United States of America and the French Republic, and making provision for the payment of the same.

Be it enacted, *etc,* That for the purpose of carrying into effect the convention of the thirtieth day of April, one thousand eight hundred and three, between the United States of America and the French Republic, the Secretary of the Treasury be, and he is hereby authorized to cause to be constituted certificates of stock, signed by the Register of the Treasury, in favor of the French Republic, or its assignees for the sum of eleven millions two hundred and fifty thousand dollars bearing an interest of six per centum per annum, from the time when possession of Louisiana shall have been obtained in conformity with the treaty of the thirtieth day of

April, one thousand eight hundred and three, between the United States of America and the French Republic, and in other respects conformable with the tenor of the convention aforesaid; and the President of the United States is authorized to cause the said certificates of stock to be delivered to the Government of France, or to such person or persons as shall be authorized to receive them, in three months, at most after the exchange of ratifications of the treaty aforesaid, and after Louisiana shall be taken possession of in the name of the Government of the United States; and credit or credits to the proprietors thereof shall thereupon be entered and given on the books of the Treasury of the United States, by the proprietor or proprietors of such stock, his, her, or their attorney; and the faith of the United States is hereby pledged for the payment of the interest, and for the reimbursement of the principal of said stock, in conformity with the provisions of the said convention; Provided, however, That the Secretary of the Treasury may, with the approbation of the President of the United States, consent to discharge said stock in four equal annual installments, and also shorten the periods fixed by the convention for its reimbursement; And provided also, That every proprietor of the said stock may, until otherwise directed by law, on surrendering his certificate of such stock, receive another to the same amount, and bearing an interest of six per centum per annum, payable quarterly at the Treasury of the United States."

NATHL. MACON,
Speaker of the House of Representatives.

JOHN BROWN,
President of the Senate, pro tempore.

Approved, October 31, 1803.

2.

An Act making provision for the payment of claims of citizens of the United States on the Government of France, the payment of which has been assumed by the United States, by virtue of the Convention of the thirtieth of April, one thousand eight hundred and three, between the United States and French Republic.

Be it enacted, etc., That a sum not exceeding three millions seven hundred and fifty thousand dollars (including a sum off two millions of dollars appropriated by the act of the twenty-sixth for the expenses attending the intercourse between the United States and foreign nations) to be paid out of any moneys in the Treasury not otherwise appropriated, be, and the same hereby is, appropriated, for the purpose of discharging the claims of citizens of the United States against the Government of France, the payment of which has been assumed by the Government of the United States, by virtue of a Convention made the thirtieth day of April, one thousand eight hundred and three, between the United States of America and the French Republic, respecting the said claims.

Source: *Annals of Congress, 8th Congress, 1st Session, pages 1247& 1248; Senate Journal, 302–3* (October 31, 1803).

Letter from President Jefferson to Robert Livingston in Paris, April 18, 1802

*T*his communication from Jefferson to Livingston outlines the current situation and provides instructions on how to proceed. Jefferson recognized and understood the unrest in the West, and knew he needed to head off a crisis there. In this letter to Livingston, Jefferson states that war is inevitable; "There is on the globe one single spot, the possessor of which is our natural and habitual enemy. It is New Orleans, . . . France, placing herself in that door, assumes to us the attitude of defiance." This letter constitutes the basic formula for American action regarding the situation and status of Louisiana, and Franco-American relations regarding the subject. It outlines in detail President Jefferson's concerns regarding the French possession of Louisiana. The failure of either France or Spain to acknowledge the terms of their secret treaty required Jefferson to instruct Minister Livingston as to his course of action, and possible alternatives. The letter also conveys a sense of urgency in the matter, and therefore provides Livingston with his instructions. Notice in particular that depending upon what he learns from French officials, Livingston is authorized to negotiate for New Orleans and lands to the east; or, failing that, the possibility of an outlet in West Florida on the Gulf. There is no mention of American interest regarding lands on the west bank of the Mississippi.

"To the United States Minister to France (Robert E. Livingston.)

Washington, April 18, 1802.

DEAR SIR

A favorable and confidential opportunity offering by M. Dupont de Nemours, who is revisiting his native country, gives me an opportunity of sending you a cypher to be used between us, which will give you some trouble to understand, but once understood, is the easiest to use, the most indecipherabel, and varied by a new key with the greatest facility, of any I have ever known. I am in hopes the explanaataion enclosed will be sufficient.

But writing by Mr. Dupont, I need use no cypher. I require from him to put this into your own and no other hand, let the delay occasioned by that be what it will.

The cession of Louisiana and the Floridas by Spain to France, works most sorely on the United States. On this subject the Secretary of State has written to you fully, yet I cannot forebear recurring to it personally, so deep is the impression makes on my mind. It completely reverses all the poliitical relations of the United States, and will form a new epoch in our poliitical course. Of all nations of any consideration, France is the one which, hitherto, has offered the fewest points on which we could have any conflict of right, and most points of communion of interests. From these causes, we have ever looked to her as our mutual friend, as one with which we never could have an occasion of difference. Her growth, therefore, we viewed as our own, her misfortunes ours. There is on the globe one single spot, the possessor of which is our natural and habitual enemy. It is New Orleans, through which the produce of three-eighths of our territory must pass to market, and from its fertility it will ere long yield more than half of our whole produce, and contain more than half of our inhabitants. France, placing herself in that door, assumes to us the attitude of defiance. Spain might retaine it quietly for years. Her pacific dispositions, her feeble state, would induce her to increase our facilities there, so that her possession of the place would be hardly felt by us, and would not, perhaps,be very long before some circumstance might arise, which might make the cession of it to us the price of something of more worth to her. Not so can it ever be in the hands of France: the impetuosity of her temper, the energy and restlessness of her character, placed in a point of eternal friction with us, and our character, which, though quiet and loving peace and the pursuit of wealth, is high-minded, despising wealth in competition with insult or injury, enterprising and energetic as any nation on earth; these circumstances render it impossible that France and the United States can continue long friends, when they meet in so irritable a position. They, as well as we, must be blind if they do not see this; and we must be very improvident if we do not begin to make arrangements on that hypothesis. The day that France takes possession of New Orleans, fixes the sentence which is to restrain her forever within her low-water mark. It seals the union of two nations, who, in conjunction, can maintain exclusive possession of the ocean. From that moment, we must marry ourselves to the British fleet and nation. We must turn all our attention to maritime force, for which our resources place us on very high ground; and having formed and connected together a power which may render reinforcement of her setrtlement here impossible to France, make the first cannon which shall be fired in Europe the signal for the tearing up any settlement she may have made, and for holding the two continents of America in question for the common purposes of the United British and American nations. This is not a state of things we seek or desire. It is one which measure, if adopted by France, forces on us necessarily, as any other cause, by the laws of nature, brings on its necessary effect. It is not from a fear of France that we depreciate this measure proposed by her. For however greater her force is than ours, compared in the abstract, it is nothing in comparison of ours, when to excerted on our soil. But it is from a sincere love of peace, and a firm persuasion, that bound to France by the interests and the strong sympathies still existing in the minds of our citizens, and holding relative position which insure their continuance, we are secure of a long course of peace. Whereas, the change of friends, which will be rendered necessary if France changes that position, embaarks us necessarily as a belligerent power in the first war in Europe. In that case, France will have help in the possession of New Orleans during the interval of a peace, long or short, at the end of which it will be wrested from her. Will this short-lived possession have been an equivalent to her for the transfer of such a weight into the scale of her enemy? Will not the amalgamation of a young, thriving nation, continue to that enemy the health and force which are at present so evcidently on the decline? And will a few years' possession of New Orleans add equally to the strength of France? She may say she needs Louisiana for the supply of her West Indies. She does not need it in time of peace, and in war she could not depend on them, because they would be easily intercepted. I should suppose that all these considerations might, in some proper form, be brought into view of the government of France. Though stated by us, it ought not to give offence; because we do not bring them forward as a menace, but as consequences not controllable by us, but inevitable from the course of things. We mention them, not as things which we desire by any means, but as things we depreciaate; and we beseech a friend to look forward and prevent them for our common interest.

If France considers Louisiana, however, as indispensable for her views, she might perhaps be willing to look about for arrangements which might reconcile it to our interests. If anything could do this, it would be the ceding to us the island of New Orlelans and the Floridas. This would certainly, in a great degree, remove he causes of jarring and irritation between us, and perhaps for such a length of time, as might produce other meaans of making the measure permanently conciliatory to our interests and friendships. It would at any rate, relieve us sfrom the necessity of taking immediate measures for countervailing such an operarion by arrangements in another quarter. But still we should consider New Orleans and the Floridas as no equivalaent for the risk of a quarrel with Fraance, produced by her vicinage.

I have no doubt you have urged these considerations, on every proper occasion with the government where you are. They are such as must have effect, if you can find means of producing thorough reflection on them by that government. The idea here is, that the troops sent to St. Domingo, were to proceed to Louisiana after finishing their work in tht island. If this were the arrangement, it will give you time to return again and again to the charge. For the conquest of St.Domingo will not be a short work. It will take considerable time, and wear down aa great number of soldiers. Every eye in the United Stataes is now fixed on the affairs of Louisian. Perhaps nothing since the revolutionary war, has produced more uneasy sensations through th body of the nation. Notwithstanding temporaary bickerings have taken place with France, she has still strong hold on the affections of our citizens generally. I have thought it not amiss, by way of supplement to the letters of the Secretary of State, to write you this private one,to impress you with the importance we affix to this transaction. I pray you to cherish Dupont. He has the best dispositon for the continuance of friendship between the two nations, and perhaps you may be able to make good use of him.

Accept assurance of my affectionate esteem and high consideration."

Th. Jefferson

Source: "The Letters of Thomas Jefferson: 1743–1826, The Affair of Louisiana." www.let.rug.nl/usa/P/tj3/writings,brf/jefl146.html. Accessed July 20, 2013.

Letter from President Jefferson to Pierre Samuel du Pont de Nemours, April 25, 1802

*P*ierre Samuel du Pont de Nemours (1739–1817) was a French intellectual whose career included writings in education, political economy, and government. As one of the French thinkers during the Enlightenment, he was well known in educational circles both in France and the United States. He participated in the French Revolution, but because of his family ties, he was arrested and nearly executed by the radicals in 1794. Released from jail after the fall of the radicals, he and his family eventually moved to the United States, where he became acquainted with Thomas Jefferson and corresponded with him frequently. Because of his French government ties, at one time he was President of the National Constituent Assembly, and his relocation to the United States, du Pont had extensive connections in both countries. In the United States, his son, Eleuthere Irenee du Pont, a chemist, founded the company that still bears his name. President Jefferson thought highly of du Pont, and because both men shared many of the same values, including a love for liberty, Jefferson used him as a courier to French policy makers, including Napoleon, during 1802–1803. Pierre Samuel du Pont has been given credit for working behind the scenes in both France and America to avoid the possibility of a war between the two countries over Louisiana. The letter of April 25, 1802, below was intended to be shared by du Pont with French officials as a private citizen, who therefore had no hidden agenda other than the maintenance of peace and goodwill between the two countries.

"To Monsieur Dupont de Nemours.

Washington, April 25, 1802.

DEAR SIR,

The week now closed, during which you had give me a hope of seeing you here, I think it safe to enclose you my letters for Paris, lest should fail of the benefit of so dedsirabe conveyance. They are addressed to Kosciusko, Madame de Corny, Mrs. Short, and Chancellor Livingston. You will perceive the unlimited confidence I repose in your good faith, and in your cordial dispositions to serve both countries, when you observe that I leave the letters for Chancellor Livingston open for your perusal. The first page respects a cyupher, as do the loose sheets folded within the letter. These are interesting to him and myself only, therefore are not for your perusal. It is the second, third, and ourth pages which I wish you to read to possess yourself of completely, and then seal the letter with wafers stuck under the flying seal, that it may beseen by nobody else if any accident should happen to you. I wish you to be possessed of subject, because you may be able to impress on the government of France the inevitable consequences of their taking possession of Louisiana; and though, as I here mention, the cession of New Orleans and the Floridas to us would be a palliation, yet I believe it would be no more, and that this measure will cost France, and perhaps not very long hence, a war which will annihilate her on the ocean, and place that element under the despostism of two nations, which I am not reconciled to the more because my own would be one of them. Add to this the exclusive appropriation of both continents of America as a consequence. I wish the present order of things to contiue, and with a view to this I value highly a state of friendship between France and us. You know too well how sincere I have ever been in these dispositions to doubt them. You know, too, how much I value peace, and how unwillingly I should see any event taake place which would render war a necessary resource; and that all our movements should change their character and object. I am thus open with you, because I trust that you will have it in your power to impress on the government considerations, in the scale against which the possession of Louisiana is nothing. In Europe, nothing but Europe is seen, or supposed to have any right in the affairs of nations; but this little event, France's possessing herself of Louisiana which is thrown in as nothing, as an mere make-weight in the general settlement of accounts,—this speck which now appears as an almost invisible point in the horizon, is the embryo of a tornado will will burst on the countries on both sides of theAtlantic, and involve in its effects their highest destinies. That it may yet be avoided is my sincere prayer; and if you can be the means of informing the wisdom of Bonapart of all its consequences, you have deserved wll of both countries. Peace and abstince fromEuropean inteferences are our objects, and so will continue while the present order of things in America remain uninterrupted. There is another service you can render. I am told that Talleyrand is personally hostile to us. This, I suppose, has been occasioned by the XYZ history. But he should consider that that was the artifice of a party[Federalists], willing to sacrifice him to the consolidation of their power. This nation has done him justice by dismissing them; that those in power are precisely those who disbelieved that story, and saw in it nothing but an attempt to deceive their country; that entertain towards him personally the most friendly dispositions; that as to the government of France, we know to little of the state of things there to understand what it is, and have no inclination to meddle in their settlement. Whatever government they establish, we wish to be well with it. One more request,—that you deliver the letter of Chancellor Livingston with your own hands, and, moreover, that you charge Madame Dupont, if any accident should happen to you, that she deliver the letter with her own hands. If it passes only through hers and yours, I shall have perfect confidence in its safety. Present her my most sincere respects, and accept yourself assurances of my constant affection, and my prayers, that a genial sky and propitious gales may place you, after a pleasant voyage, in the midst of your friends."

Th. Jefferson

Source: Thomas Jefferson Papers: www.yamaguchy.com/library/jefferson/1802. html. Accessed July 20, 2013.

Excerpts from the memoirs of François Barbé-Marbois

*F*rançois Barbé-Marbois (1745–1837) served Napoleon Bonaparte as Minister of the Public Treasury. In the account, Part One below, he describes in detail his participation in the meeting of April 10, 1803, with First Consult Bonaparte on the subject of Louisiana. It was at this meeting that Napoleon sought his advice, along with that of Admiral Denis Decrès, Minister of the Navy and Colonies, regarding his decision to sell Louisiana to the United States. In the account, Part Two below, he discusses the negotiations between himself and Robert Livingston and James Monroe. In later years, he corresponded with Monroe whom he regarded as a friend, and received from him copies of the papers and documents currently in the United States which he then included in his History. In 1829, Barbé-Marbois published his memoires as: The History of Louisiana, Particularly Of The Cession Of That Colony To The United States of America. The excerpts quoted below are from the 1830 Edition, published in Philadelphia, and reprinted by the Louisiana State University Press in 1977 as a volume in the Louisiana American Revolution Bicentennial Commission Series, Edited with an Introduction by E. Wilson Lyon, 263–266, 281–286 and 292–298. Part One: provides insight into Napoleon's momentous decision to sell Louisiana to the United States; Part Two: narrates the tone and process of the negotiation process on the primary issues of the Treaty content, and boundary problems. Throughout this portion of the discussion, Barbé-Marbois interjects comments and observations on the articles in light of later events, but these are so noted. Taken together, they provide insight into the negotiations, the resulting provisions, and potential for the future. For the specific provisions of the treaty and two conventions, see Primary Documents (3, 4 and 5).

PART ONE:

"On Easter Sunday, the 10th of April, 1803, after having attended to the solemnities and ceremonies of the day, he called those two counselors to him, and addressing them with that vehemence and passion which he particularly manifested in political affaire said; 'I know the full value of Louisiana, and I have been desirous of repairing the fault of the French negotiator who abandoned it in 1763. A few lines of a treaty have restored it to me, and I have scarcely recovered it when I must expect to lose it But if it escapes from me, it shall one day cost dearer to those who oblige me to strip myself of it than to those to whom I wish to deliver it. The English have successively taken from France, Canada, Cape Breton, Newfoundland, Nova Scotia, and the richest portions of Asia. They are engaged in exciting troubles in St. Domingo. They shall not have the Mississippi which they covet. Louisiana is nothing in comparison with their conquests in all parts of the globe, and yet the jealousy they feel at the restoration of this colony to the sovereignty of France, acquaints me with their wish to take possession of it, and it this that they will begin the war. They have twenty ships of war in the Gulf of Mexico, they sail over those seas as sovereigns, while our affairs in St. Domingo have been growing worse every day since the death of Leclerc. The conquest of Louisiana would be easy, if they only took the trouble to make a descent there. I have not a moment to lose in putting it out of their reach. I know not whether they are not already there. It is their usual course, and if I had been in their place, I would not have waited. I wish if there is still time, to take from them any idea that they may have of ever possessing that colony. I think of ceding it to the United States. I can scarcely say that I cede it to them, for it is not yet in our possession. If, however, I leave the least time to our enemies, I shall only transmit an empty title to those republicans whose friendship I seek. They only ask of me one town in Louisiana, but I already consider the colony as entirely lost, and it appears to me that in the hands of this growing power, it will be more useful to the policy and even to the commerce of France, than if I should attempt to keep it. . . . .'

"We should not hesitate, said the last minister [Barbé-Marbois], to make a sacrifice of that which is about slipping from us. War with England is inevitable; shall we be able with the very inferior naval forces to defend Louisiana against that power? The United States, justly discontented with our proceedings, do not hold out to us a solitary haven, not even an asylum, in case of reverses. They have just become reconciled with us [Convention of 1800], it is true; but they have a dispute with the Spanish government, and threaten New Orleans, of which we shall only have momentary possession. At the time of the discovery of Louisiana the neighboring provinces were as feeble as herself; they are now powerful, and Louisiana is still in her infancy. The country is scarcely at all inhabited; you have not fifty soldiers there. Where are your means of sending garrisons thither?

Can we restore fortifications that are in ruins, and construct a long chain of forts upon a frontier of four hundred leagues? If England lets you [Napoleon] undertake these things, it is because they will drain your resources, and she will feel a secret joy in seeing you exhaust yourself in efforts of which she alone will derive the profit. You will send out a squadron; but while it is crossing the ocean, the colony will fall, and the squadron will in turn be in danger. Louisiana is open to the English from the north by the great lakes, and if, to the south, they show themselves at the mouth of the Mississippi, New Orleans will immediately fall into their hands. What consequence is it to the inhabitants to whom they are subject, if their country is not to cease to be a colony? The conquest would be still easier to the Americans; they can reach the Mississippi by several navigable rivers, and to be masters of the country it will be sufficient for them to enter it. The population and resources of one of these two neighbors every day increase; and the other has maritime means sufficient to take possession of everything that can advance her commerce. The colony has existed for a century, and in spite of efforts and sacrifices of every kind the last accounts of its population and resources attest its weakness. If it becomes a French colony and acquires increased importance, there will be in its very prosperity a germ of independence, which will not be long in developing itself. The more it flourishes, the less chances we will have of preserving it. Nothing is more uncertain than the fate of the European colonies in America. The exclusive right which the parent states exercise over these remote settlements becomes every day more and more precarious. The people feel humbled at being dependent on a small country in Europe, and will liberate themselves, as soon as they have a consciousness of their strength."

PART TWO:

"In the space of twenty-five years, the United States had, by treaties with the European powers and the Indians, gradually advanced to the Mississippi. By the proposed cession, vast regions to the west were about to belong to them without dispute. It relieved them from the necessity of erecting forts and maintaining garrisons on a French frontier. While ambition and passion for conquests expose the nations of Europe to continual wars, commerce, agriculture, equitable as, and a wise liberty, must guaranty to the United States all the benefits of the social state, without any of its dangers. A serious but pacific struggle might then take place between the enlightened and improved industry of the old nations, and the territorial riches of a new people; and this rival ship, useful to the world, was going to be exercised in the most extensive career that has ever been opened to the efforts of man.

At the same time, a consideration of another description was presented to the view of the negotiators. They were about once more to dispose of Louisiana, not only without consulting its inhabitants, but without tits being possible that they should suspect, at the distance of two thousand leagues, that their dearest interests were then to be decided on. The three ministers expressed their sincere regrets at this state of things. But a preliminary of this nature was rendered impossible by circumstances, and to defer the cession would have been to make Louisiana a colony of England—to render that power predominant in America, and to weaken for centuries the state whose aggrandizement in the part of the globe the whole world must desire. This difficulty, which could not be solved, was at once set aside.

As soon as the negotiation was entered on, the American ministers declared that they were ready to treat on the footing of the cession of the entire colony, and they did not hesitate to take on themselves the responsibility of augmenting the sum that they had been authorized to offer. The draft of the principal treaty was communicated to them. They had prepared another one, but consented to adopt provisionally as the basis of their conferences that of the French negotiator, and they easily agreed on the declaration contained in the first article; 'The colony or province of Louisiana is ceded by France to the United States, with all its right appurtenances, as fully and in the same manner as they been acquired by the French republic, by virtue of the third article of the treaty concluded with His Catholic Majesty at St. Ildephonso, on the 1st of October, 1800.' Terms so general seemed, however, to render necessary some explanations, relative to the true extent of Louisiana. The Americans at first insisted on this point. They connected the questions of limits with a guarantee on the part of France, to put them in possession of the province, and give them the enjoyment of it.

In treaties of territorial cession, the guarantee of the grantor is a usual clause. Publicists even assert that where it is omitted in terms, it is not the less obligatory of right.

There were some historical and diplomatic researches on the first occupation and earliest acts of sovereignty. But they were only attended with the results usual in such cases. Travelers and historians had not left on this subject any but vague and general notions; they had only narrated some accidents of navigation, some acts of occupation, to which contradictory ones might be opposed. According to old documents, the bishopric of Louisiana extended to the Pacific Ocean, and the limits of the diocess defined were secure from all dispute. But this was at most a matter in expectancy, and the Indians in these regions never had any suspicion of the spiritual jurisdiction, which it was designed to exercise over them. Besides, it had no connection with the rights of sovereignty and property. One Important point was, however, beyond all discussion; according to the then existing treaties, the course of the Mississippi, in descending this river to the thirty-first degree of north latitude, formed the boundary line, leaving to the United States the country on the left bank; to the right, on the other hand, there were the vast regions without well defined boundaries, although France had formerly included a great part of them in what was called Upper Louisiana: this was particularly the case with the territories to the south of the Missouri.

The limits of Louisiana and Florida, to the south of the thirty-first degree, were not free from some disputes, which possessed importance on account of the neighborhood of the sea, and embouchure of the rivers. However, this country, disregarded by the European powers, that successively possessed it, was scarcely mentioned in the conferences. France had had only the smallest portion of it. The name of Florida could not have been inserted in the treaty without preparing great difficulties for the future.

The boundary to the north and north-west was still less easy to describe. Even the course of the Mississippi might give rise to some border disputes; for that great river receives beyond the forth-third degree several branches, then regarded as its sources. A geographical chart was before the plenipotentiaries. They negotiated with entire good faith; they frankly, agreed that these matters were full of uncertainty, but they by no means of quieting the doubts. The French negotiator said; 'Even this map informs us that many of these countries are not better known at this day than when Columbus landed at the Bahamas; no one is acquainted with them. The English themselves have never explored them. The circumstances are too pressing to permit us concert matters on this subject with the court of Madrid. It would be too long before this discussion would be terminated, and perhaps that government would wish to consult the viceroy of Mexico. Is it not better for the United States to abide by a general stipulation, and, since these territories are still this day for the most part in the possession of the Indians, await future arrangements, or leave the matter for the treaty stipulations that the United States may make with them and Spain? In granting Canada to the English, at the peace of 1763, we only extended the cession to the country that we possessed. It is, however, a consequence of that treaty, that England has occupied territory to the west as far as the great Northern Ocean.' Whether the American plenipotentiaries had themselves desired what was proposed to them, or that these words afforded them a ray of light, they declared that they kept to the terms of the 3rd article of the treaty of St. Ildephonso, which was inserted entire in the first article of the treaty of cession.

M. Marbois, who offered the draft, said several times; 'The first article may in time give to difficulties, they are at this day insurmountable; but if they do not stop you, I, at least, desire that your government should know that you have been warned of them.'

It is in fact important not to introduce ambiguous clauses into treaties: however, the American plenipotentiaries made no more objections; and, if, in appearing to be resigned to these general terms through necessity, they considered them really preferable to more precise stipulations, it must be admitted that the event has justified their foresight. The shores of the Western Ocean were certainly not included in the cession; but the United States are already established there.

The French negotiator, in rendering an account of the conference to the first consul, pointed out to him the obscurity of this article and the inconveniencies of so uncertain a stipulation. He [Napoleon] replied, 'that if an obscurity did not already exist, it would perhaps be good policy to put one there.'

[There follows a general description of Louisiana, its position in the relationship between France and Spain, and then with the United States. This discussion was added later by Barbé-Marbois in his *History* from notes and documents, including correspondence with James Monroe, who sent him some of his letters. The two men remained friends. The author.]

"By the 2nd article, 'all public lots and squares, vacant lands, and all public buildings, fortifications, barracks, and other edifices that were not private property, were included in the cession. The archives, papers, and documents relative to the domain and sovereignty of Louisiana and its dependencies were to be left in the possession of the commissioners of the United States and copies were afterwards to be given in due form the magistrates and municipal officers, of such of the said paper and documents as might be necessary to them.'

The plenipotentiaries, being all three plebeians, easily agreed on the stipulations of the 3rd article, founded on a perfect equality between the inhabitants of the ceded territories.

It provided, 'that they should be incorporated in the Union of the United States, and admitted as soon as possible, according to the principles of the federal constitution, to the enjoyment of all the rights, advantages, and immunities of citizens of the United States; and, they should in the meantime, be maintained and protected in the free enjoyment of their liberty, property, and the religion which they profess.'

These provisions prepared the way for a great change in the constitution of Louisiana, or rather guaranteed to it the advantage of having a length a constitution, laws, and self-government. There was not a single family in the colony but must profit sooner or later by this revolution.

The first consul, left to his natural disposition, was always inclined to an elevated and generous justice. He himself prepared the article which has been just recited. The words which he employed on the occasion are recorded in the journal of the negotiation, and deserve to be preserved. 'Let the Louisianians know that we separate ourselves from them with regret; that we stipulate in their favor everything that they can desire, and let them hereafter, happy in their independence, recollect that they have been Frenchmen, and that France, in ceding them, has secured for them advantages which they could not have obtained from an European power, however paternal it might have been. Let them retain for us sentiments of affection; and may their common origin, descent, language, and customs perpetuate the friendship.'

[After several passages on the role of the Indians, the discussion focused on the specific provisions to be included in the treaty. Barbé-Marbois again intersperses his own comments into the discussion. The Author]

By the 6th article, 'The United States promise to execute such treaties and articles as may have been agreed on between Spain and the tribes or nations of Indians'. This stipulation, Mr. Monroe observed, 'becomes us, though these people must be forever ignorant of the care that we take of their interests.'

This article prepared the good understanding that now exists between the Indians and the United States. They are treated with humanity: it is wished, it is true, to remove them from the settled parts of the country, a plan which is resisted by some of the tribes. The Cherokees have even given themselves a constitution [July 18, 1827], which appears to have been dictated by some whites settled among them. This phantom of a government has not seemed to deserve much attention. The intermixture with the whites has, however, introduced into the tribe the first element of civilization.

The 7th article contained a reserve which was them deemed important for the commerce of France and Spain, namely; 'the privilege of bringing in French or Spanish vessels from the ports of those two kingdoms or of their colonies, into the ports of Louisiana, the produce or manufactures of those countries or of their colonies, during the space of twelve years, without being subjected to any other or greater duties than those paid by the citizens of the United States.'

The commerce of the colony had been to that time almost exclusively carried on by the French under the Spanish flag. The 7th article would have preserved this advantage to France, if the peace of Amiens had not been broken at the same time that the treaty of cession was signed. The war lasted nearly twelve years, during which period this trade passed into the hands of the English and Americans: and the loss of St. Domingo [Haiti] put the seal to the separation. It is not believed that a single French ship profited by the provisions of this article.

The 8th article, which secures to French ships the treatment of the most favored nation, has given rise to discussions, the result of which we ought not to anticipate.

Such are the principal stipulations of the treaty of cession."

Source: Barbé-Marbois, François. *The History of Louisiana, Particularly of the Cession of That Colony to the United States of America.* (1829). Edited with an Introduction by E. Wilson Lyon. Baton Rouge: Published for the Louisiana American Revolution Bicentennial Commission by the Louisiana State University Press, 1977, 263–266, 281–286 and 292–298.

DOCUMENT 12

From the *Observations*
of James Pitot

James Pitot (1761–1831) immigrated to the United States from France, and before that Saint-Domingue where he had lived for ten years. He arrived in Philadelphia in 1793. He lived there for the next three years, and in the process became a naturalized citizen of the United States. After the Pinckney Treaty opened Louisiana to Americans in 1795, he went to New Orleans in 1796. He became part of the business community and active in city government. After the American occupation in 1803, he was appointed by Governor William C. C. Claiborne to the city council, which elected him mayor in 1804–1805. He retired from government, but was later appointed by Governor Claiborne as the first judge of the parish court of New Orleans in 1812, a position which he held until 1831.

Pitot's Observations provides a first-hand account of Spanish Louisiana during the last years of its administration, and although not a history per se, it goes into great depth on his understanding of the preceding years. Pitot is one of those writers who saw Spain's policy in Louisiana as being dictated by her priorities to protect Mexico and Central America from British, French and American influence. He saw and described the increasing expansion of the United States, and warned in 1802 that: "Perhaps Spain finally will know what she ought to have done for the happiness and prosperity of this colony only when her lack of concern and the mistakes of her administration will have caused her to lose it." Pitot discusses government and finances, judiciary and police, commerce, customs, agriculture, trade with the Indians, and the topography in Louisiana as chapters. Throughout his narrative, Pitot repeatedly warns of the impending takeover of Louisiana and aggressive actions of the United States. Yet, at no point does he admit that he had become a naturalized citizen in 1796! He provides valuable insights into colonial administration of Louisiana and the international scene during the years from 1796 to 1802. In 1802, he traveled to France with the idea of establishing further business connections for his firm, and to have his Observations published for presentation to French authorities. By the time he got there, the international scene had changed once again, and his work remained a collection of notes and chapters for future use.

The following selections are from James Pitot, Observations on the Colony of Louisiana *from 1796 to 1802. They are in two parts: Part One (pp.2–4), from his "Introduction" provides an overview as to his purpose in writing, and a general observations regarding Spanish Louisiana; Part 2, (pp.7–25.), examines the specifics of "Government and Finances." Pitot was a businessman, and therefore his comments give valuable insights into both Spanish administration and the economy of Louisiana on the eve of its transfer to the United States.*

PART ONE:

"I'm not writing these *Observations* for personal gain, but based upon rumors of the retrocession of Louisiana to France, I intend to present them respectfully to the government of its mother country as if it were indeed retroceded, or at least to make them known to businessmen who might be interested in commercial projects which I shall submit. I have done everything that was expected of me to know the truth. I have omitted those matters for which I have not obtained at least virtual certainty; and if by chance my criticism of the government seem to be exaggerated, I can only refer to the approval which, I believe, any impartial resident or traveler will give them. Be that as it may, let no one identify me with the preachers of insurrection; I would be ashamed to be compared to them.

The errors of the Spanish government in Louisiana are those that perpetuate the mediocrity of a country, but which individually do not bother its citizens. Such an administration restrains commerce, restricts population, and does not encourage agriculture; and, by this unchanging policy, as well as the mingling of Spanish families with French one, it has hardened an indifference in the colony that scarcely suspects the possibility of a better existence. Finally, the administration is, in fact, often arbitrary and corrupt, but most inhabitants are nevertheless, peaceful and perhaps content in their mediocrity. Several persons, probably no more concerned but certainly more discerning, have reflected, like me, on the causes that have retarded and still are retarding prosperity of this colony. And if it is likely that a true account of Louisiana's situation and resources can make the government owning it give closer attention to its needs, it is none the less certain that a revolutionary upheaval would cause its ruin.

When I arrived in Louisiana in August, 1796, all existing circumstances indicated to me that the colony was in a distressed state. Its languishing commerce was expiring under the weight of an exorbitant tax and from restraints which continually endangered its existence. Its debt-ridden planters and completely ruined agriculture—the result of either weather's uncertainty, destructive hurricanes, or the fury of a river which during five or six months every year threatens to swallow up all the inhabitants along its banks—foretold of total ruin. As much for the despair of the newcomer, as to curb the activities of the older resident and to hide from their view the wealth which the future promised them, political opinions which the government repressed or favored, guided by its self-interest, had in fact poisoned the populace who, through imitation, became in general either partisans of an obnoxious tyranny, or zealous adherent of Robespierre and the disrupting monsters who shared his crimes. The planter who was in comfortable circumstances through luck, or by savings from his previous crops, already shard the anxieties of those whose ruin was complete. The businessman, whose efforts in better times had been crowned with success, placed his capital in the sparse remnants of a commodity which the soil had almost refused to produce: indigo. And both of them, blinded by the situation in which France then found herself and surely by divine inspiration of what she is now experiencing, either looked toward their native land which they wished to see again at peace, or recalled to mind its government, hoping to obtain from it alleviation of their troubles. Such was the state of affairs which existed in Louisiana when I arrived there in August, 1796.

After this description, one will no doubt be surprised to find me attempting to write about a country whose condition has not yet undergone any improvement, and whose possession and tranquility, in most respects, have often been jeopardized by the policy of a government which should find, in its kindness and self-interest, reasons to have made it already enjoy the prosperity that the future in large part promises. It will be astonishing, I say, that I should rescue Louisiana from oblivion, and, I would dare say, from the kind of contempt in which it is held among the group of colonies which Europeans have established in the West Indies. That is, nevertheless, the objective I now set for myself in my "Observations." Written with both truthfulness and impartiality, they are the result of five years of reflection on this province; and, they are inspired by my wishes that colonial government by France will hasten to bring Louisiana out of the condition of nothingness to which it has long been condemned only by a conduct, all the more ill-advised, on the part of Spain which not, up to now, taken any of the necessary steps to maintain it. I do not pretend to give here the complete history of Louisiana. It would be tedious to repeat the particulars of its listless progress during the many years since its discovery; and although several other authors have written about in detail, the more renowned have, in their comprehensive surveys, refuted Louisiana's lack of productivity, which I myself should also like to prove.

Situated on a continent which generally appeared to the adventurers who discovered it as being one of a most savage nature, Louisiana provides very little of interest in the narration of its history. Similar in a way to Egypt, in its floods, climate, products, and fertility, in antiquity it was neither the cradle of the arts and sciences that have enlightened the world, nor the storehouse of a commerce as valuable ass it was rich, which exposed Egypt to so many revolutions, and which has recently made it of great importance in European affairs. Always civilized and listless in the past, the present begins to smile on Louisiana, and the future should make it a flourishing colony.

I shall not further distract the reader's attention by long recitations, or new stories, about the Indians who still occupy a part of these lands. In general ignorant and barbaric throughout America, they nearly all resemble one another in their morals and habits; and to arouse curiosity regarding them it would be necessary like so many others have done the expense of truth, to embellish some events about which even tradition gives no indication. A little more rational and more provident than the animals of the forests, less modest and generally filthier than they are, they had, and often still have, all of their ferocity. If among the viciousness of their customs, some fine examples of sensibility and courage are often observed, it is, nevertheless, true that someone like myself, who has visited several Indian tribes, or who has been to talk with reliable travelers about those thing of which he has no knowledge, finds everywhere the repulsive ridiculousness of their morals, the horror or futility of their religious ceremonies, the barbarism of their politics, and finally that veneer of bestiality which often make an Indian seem hardly better than part civilized and part tiger.

Thus, in writing these "Observations" I shall barely mention the past, as to which my comment is, I believe, incontestable. I shall be satisfied, ass to most recent events, to speak only about those which can throw some light on the present condition of Louisiana. Rarely, in touching on the different aspects of government, shall I refer to what preceded my arrival, and I shall end by offering my readers conjectures regarding the future.

PART TWO: CHAPTER ONE, GOVERNMENT AND FINANCES

Others before me have successfully demonstrated the influence that these first two divisions of administration have on those which are subordinate to them, and more particularly on commerce and agriculture. The observations that I shall present first on government and finances are not, so to speak, just exceptions to those that I shall have occasion to mention while referring later to all the other administrative branches of the colony. I shall, perhaps, even be so clumsy as to repeat myself sometimes, but I thought this preliminary outline necessary in order to give an idea at the outset of their moral influence and Louisiana's political situation.

Before beginning these "Observations," I think it necessary, in order to justify the kind of bitterness with which I shall express myself, to warn that I intend to speak only about the government in the province of Louisiana, and nothing I say in my "Observations" is written to reflect on the character of the Spanish nation. Never having traveled in any other Spanish possession, in general I want to speak only about what I know; and I seek, finally to permit myself to judge only by my own experience, and on the basis of reports sometimes basically true, but nearly always exaggerated or even embittered in their content.

The colony of Louisiana—either through contempt, distrust, or ignorance of its worth, or in fact through politics, as I am convinced— has been kept in unmistakable isolation in its relations with the mother country and other Spanish possessions. And I am inclined to believe that this colony's administration, in its vices and errors, has the same mark of isolation. After that expression of my views, I now go on to commence the *Observations*, which should result in my giving a statistical summary of the province of Louisiana. But it pains me to have more often only mistakes or corruption to criticize, and to be able to focus Europe's attention on it only by an almost continuous disapproval of a policy that reason and self-interest condemn, and abuses which make the results more pernicious.

The first reproach which one could make against the government, and which contrasts strangely with the opinion that one generally has of Spanish pride, is its lack of dignity, not only in the functions where law and authority call for it, but also, I would dare say, in the abuses which officials make of it. A governor general of Louisiana does not limit himself to the duties which, keeping him at a distance from most of the population, would maintain for him that dignity so necessary in the colonies. The minute details of police administration are carried on by him daily; in being present at the hearings he attends to a large number of people who should only be dealt with by police officers under his supervision. Moreover he devotes to unimportant local problems of his government the time and attention which he owes to a vast colony in need of so many improvements.

From this variety of duties performed by the principal head of a colony, arise many of the disadvantages harmful to his administration. Excessive arrogance provokes hatred among those governed; to much popularity often breeds contempt. A governor general should always know how to find a happy medium in order not to lose any of his dignity, yet by giving daily hearings to trivial or immoral police matters, which he should know about only from the reports of minor officials, how can he flatter himself as being to render equitable judgments in all cases? In such an event, he could he instill in the hearts of the punished or condemned a realization of their crimes? Indeed, half of the accused in this situation (being summoned before a governor general), thinking they have acquired the right to plead, show an attitude humiliating to the individual and harmful to authority. If, on the other hand, a chief of state knows how to govern in his own name by a strict and businesslike supervision, he has only the quarrels of his subordinates to answer for, the consequences of which will not reflect upon him. It is in his name that the victim of oppression has obtained justice. It is to him that the condemned person would have wished that his case had been submitted. It is to his tolerance that the guilty would have wanted to resort, and his authority is all the more respected, as he has less occasion to use it personally.

My second reproach, which an experience of five years justifies my making against the government of Louisiana, is that it is not understood in community life, at least in a manner to gain the respect of that portion of the population which, because of its customs, economic status, and education, is practically ignorant of the effects as well as the aims of the discussions concerning the police supervision of which I have referred above. One never sees around the governor that frequent and desirable gathering of a select group of estimable men which confidence would attract; instead, only those appear who are called there by duty despite themselves. Some flatterers among the residents, some adventurer among the foreigners, are mainly those constantly welcomed; and a governor general, who has become indifferent even to the military whose rank more closely approximates his, appears in the eyes of the entire colony only as a menacing lector armed with the fasces of authority, and not as the benevolent leader, dispenser of the king's bounties and patronage.

The third reproach to be made against the government of Louisiana is one that is unfortunately common to most: venality. I do not believe that there is a country in the world where duty to the sovereign is more shameless transgressed, and where there is hardly any secrecy in the selling of favors among those in a position to do so. Citizens of all classes buy for hard cash what equity, merit, or services rendered should enable them to enjoy freely. A privilege, a command, a permit to trade with the Indians, costs either a quadruple payment, or an allowance to the governor and the secretary, or the cancellation of a legitimately contracted debt. And, finally, to fill the cup to the brim, immoral establishments pay bribes to be protected from interference by minor police officers.

Although I do not believe that I can be accused of exaggeration, since at time a nobler spirit on the part of the governor could eradicate the vicious conduct spread throughout the colony, I do not say that there were no exceptions. Without either excusing or blaming those who governed the colony before my arrival, and allying myself with the tradition that does not spare them reproach, I shall specifically exclude M. de Carondelet, who was governing when I arrived in Louisiana, from the charge of venality. He is also worthy of being exonerated from the first reproach that I made against the government; his unruffled self-control when considering police matters, his person investigations and his efforts to be able to judge with full knowledge of the facts, surrounded him always with the respect that brought the reputable citizens closer to his presence. I should like to be able to exonerate him completely from the second reproach, as he should be from the charge of venality, but I am obliged to acknowledge that in the manner in which he arranged his private life, he sometimes gave an example that has only too often imitated and perhaps causes even today that kind of distrust and withdrawal by the citizens from contact with their leaders. This circumstance regenerates or perpetuates abuses to which Carondelet himself was a stranger, and which closer relations and contacts might perhaps have restrained. It was actually the weak side of his administration's routine, and in viewing the entire matter impartially, these faults should bed attributed to the critical circumstances under which he took over the government of the province. Because of wartimes and revolution, Carondelet was compelled to fear public disorders which he himself perhaps exaggerated, and to avoid men who were daily represented to him as seditious, and against whom he often thought that he was on the verge of having to take up arms.

The colony was barely emerging from these fears when I arrived. The treaty of peace between France and Spain removed any motives for distrust on the part of the government. The intended expedition for the conquest of Louisiana, led by the French representative to the United States, was more than ever imaginary, the citizens whom Carondelet had thought necessary to treat severely were back in their homes. But if the causes no longer existed, it was not so regarding the effects. People were still embittered. They could not forgive the measures which the government had thought necessary to adopt for its own protection. Through hatred, the majority of the population still spurned, or held aloof from, the few who had aligned themselves with the measures taken by Carondelet. They remembered an incident when the cannons of the forts were ready to be aimed at the city; they talked about the deportation and treatment of several French patriots; and, they did not forget the step that they had suspected the government of taking in preparing to reinforce itself against the whites with the help of the people of color. They cited the proofs, true or false, of the complicity of this very government in the insurrection of the Pointe Coupee Negroes. They thought themselves surrounded by treacherous spies who, through their activities, had compromised the serenity and wealth of many citizens. And, finally they saw in the treaty of alliance between Spain and France, only the necessity on the part of Spain to yield, for the time being, to the superior arms of France, and the formal and secret intention [by Spain] to seize the first opportunity for vengeance that would extend as far as the population of Louisiana.

In order to reach a reasonable conclusion regarding this quarrel between the government and its citizens, it would be necessary for an impartial observer to obtain from both parties admissions that might account for their mistakes and show them the error of their ways. Then also to find out from the citizen—forgetting that he was Spanish and not French—to what extent he has applauded in his public or secret assemblies, by his actions, and in his correspondence, a revolution that Spain opposed by force of arms. Finally, to ascertain to what point, manifesting his hopes for his former fatherland, he has justified the Spanish government's uneasiness and threats. If, on the other hand, it had been possible to obtain from Carondelet the orders that he had received from the court, the records verifying the plans of the French legation in the United States for the invasion by way of the Ohio River, and the reports of his spies on the collusion of the inhabitants with the enemy, to acquire evidence of their schemes concerning rebellion in favor of France, and, finally to submit to a truthful examination all the official papers of the government's secretariat relative to this alarming situation and the circumstances of the insurrection that took place among the Negroes, then a sentiment of reciprocal forbearance could possibly erase from all minds the bitter memories. A spirit of understanding might then have led to congratulating one's self on having had as governor as such a time a man of French origin who, in fulfilling his duties as a Spaniard, committed few errors where another might have resorted to violence.

Carondelet did a great deal for commerce, or wanted to do so, particularly when he was intendant or governor. I would venture to say that circumstances impeded his hopes for agriculture, he made some efforts to encourage it, either by granting concessions of land, or by reaching several decisions that could increase the population, or by seeking to procure seeds for the areas that were suitable for grain crops. The orders of the court, or his fears led him to employ money and labor for the building of imposing forts, money which colony could have put to much better use. But, if he was wrong on this score, or had a task to fulfill, one can hardly deny him the justice of admitting that, under the general subject of maintaining order in the colony and improving its waterways, he started some projects, or provided several models, that are today only in ruins or neglect. I shall nevertheless, not blame the indifference that the present government showed in maintaining the costly fortifications with which Carondelet needlessly surrounded New Orleans. I would decry, however, the neglect of the roads bridges, and levees; the relaxing of police regulations which he supervised more carefully, and the carelessness in failing to continue to maintain the work that Carondelet was hardly able to point out for drainage of the city's outlying sections, and for the development of navigation on the lakes.

Finally, I shall venture to render justice to Carondelet for the manner in which had looked upon the province of Louisiana. Its political value was, above all, perfectly well known to him, and if he foresaw the importance that western states of the United States would one day be to the commerce of New Orleans, he did not miss any occasion to influence them in favor of his mother country. The French Revolution that kept him from objecting to all of the measures initiated by many of his predecessors also largely favored the treaty which, reestablishing the former English territorial boundaries, frustrated his plans and projects for the moment. Soon recalled to a more lucrative government post, but perhaps less interesting politically speaking, Carondelet left Louisiana after having been able to outline some improvement there, and departing with none of those unanimous regrets which different times would have assured him.

A new governor [Manuel Gayoso de Lemos] finally took charge of the colony; and it was under him that the article of the treaty between Spain and the United States, which ceded to the latter the left bank of the Mississippi as far as the thirty-first parallel, was put into effect. Carondelet—as a clever politician and knowing the general value of the province of Louisiana to the court of Spain, perhaps even from the European powers who wanted to hold on longer to their colonies—eluded this cession as long as he could, well convinced, as his experience had shown him, that it was better to avoid compliance than to expose one's self to being eventually conquered. It is to be assumed that some very compelling circumstances forced the Spanish court to agree to boundaries that brought ambitious neighbors [Unite States] to the gates of New Orleans, and without any advantage for Spain, established their access to the mouth of the Mississippi. Those who gave some thought to this step foresaw all its consequences. Others saw in it an indifference on the part of the court towards this colony, confirming the already widespread rumor of a secret article in the treaty with France by which Louisiana was retroceded to its former rulers. Spain, in that case, was not making any real sacrifice, and the United States seemed to approve her conduct while awaiting full possession of Lower Louisiana, which they cannot fail to covet since it will keep their western states in submission. Lower Louisiana is the unique key and, consequently, the only obstacle to their ambitions in this part of the New World.

It was under this new governor [Gayoso] that many ill-advised or injurious steps were taken with respect to the routine of the former administration. Familiar with the needs of the colony and the character of its inhabitants as a result of the long period he had lived in Louisiana, one could expect from his knowledge a plan of development which the colony needed. But, poor and in debt, his needs often took precedence over his duties. His quarrels with the intendant brought about measures or compromises that benefited neither agriculture nor commerce, and his partiality for the United States, too strong not to be suspect, deprived him of all claims that he might have had to public confidence. The treaty with the United States had exacted a settlement in favor of commerce which broke several links in the Spanish government's chain of control in Louisiana, and it became a cover for the means that free access to the Mississippi gave the United States to ruin the local speculator by smuggling, and to deprive the intendant of customs duties. And a senseless act on the part of the intendant concurred in furthering the interests of the United States: their ships alone were allowed to enter the port by paying only the duties required of Spanish nationals, whereas this measure ought to have been extended to all neutral vessels in order to settle in New Orleans a population foreign to the United States, and not solely to attract neighbors whose number multiplies rapidly and becomes sort of taking over in advance. Spain would then have established there the foundations of a population that Europe could one day take under its protection, and they would not have sacrificed national interest to culpable exclusions, misconceived and harmful.

Without the circumstances [Convention of 1800] that have re-established peaceful relations between France and the United States, Spain would perhaps already regretted that she did not adopt to the fullest extent the means at her disposal to make of New Orleans a city as powerful through its resources as it is worthy of respect in its population. During the war it might have been a storehouse for the supplies of Mexico; Spain would have been more politic in that regard than she was in opening Vera Cruz and other ports to Anglo-American vessels, and perhaps she had lost sight of the fact that if there is a people on the globe today whom she should fear to admit into the ports of Mexico, it is indeed those of the United States.

The government was soon disturbed by the inevitable consequences of the cession to the United States of new boundaries on the Mississippi.

Menaced by a break in relations with the French that could not avoid causing one with Spain, the United States plotted to assure Lower Louisiana for themselves by a surprise attack. It was a political measure and necessary to avoid any further apprehension regarding their western states, whose vain efforts at rebellion in order to gain exclusive possession of the mouth of the Mississippi would thereby be frustrated. Under the pretext of uprising among the Indians and the landing of munitions and soldiers by the French on the Florida coast to help them, the United States recruited the little army in their eastern states which they rapidly moved into the Mississippi Territory [1798], and with which they destined to make Spain regret her culpable policies toward the province of Louisiana. In this manner they acted on expectations, all the more justified as perhaps I shall not exaggerate to much in saying, that the colony found itself half surrendered because of its situation to the person [James Wilkinson] whom Spain bribed several years before to condition favorably the sentiments of the Kentucky inhabitants, and governed by the man [Gayoso] who, when he held a lesser rank, disseminated the irresistible oratory and arguments of desertion.

By reciting these events, virtually proven in the eyes of all observers, I do not flatter myself that I have unimpeachable proofs in my possession; but in addition to agents and the eyewitnesses to many of these intrigues who have given me details confidentially, it is a fact that I was in the Natchez country in 1798, when the recruits and the general of the little army arrived. Many questions were put to me then on the state of affairs in New Orleans, and many inconsequential conversations took place in my presence among those who thought it richer than it really is. I traveled at the same time among Indian tribes who, far from rising up against the United States, were rather under that country's orders. In the western states, and especially in Kentucky, I heard discussed a hundred times the issue of the conquest of Louisiana, against which there was a majority in Kentucky, who, by preventing recruitments, made themselves suspect to the others. I visited Philadelphia, New York, and Baltimore under similar circumstances, where it was a crime to be a Frenchman. Finally, I read in the newspaper about the imaginary tale of the landing of French brigands on the Florida coast, and many other stories invented to serve as an answer to the responsible citizens of the United States who rightfully asked: Why then an army? Why so many useless expenditures by the government? Show us the enemy we must repulse. Apart from the fact that I saw and heard all that I described above, and many other things useless to report here, I shall say again that there is perhaps not an intelligent man in New Orleans who after what was taking place has not followed my example in repeatedly saying to his friends: There is talk about a United States army that is assembling in the Natchez district to come and seize Lower Louisiana. But do you not believe that in the absence of Louisiana's measures and preparations for resistance, the United States can regard it as its own property?

Fate decided otherwise. France and the United States not having engaged in open warfare, and thus having no pretext to justify a break in relations with Spain, the little army disbanded without having been able to undertake anything. And chance thus ordained that having been a witness to its formation during the course of my travels, I was present at its disbandment, for it was leaving the Spanish frontier, when I passed through Natchez on my return. Wilkinson, its general, came to New Orleans several months later in order to see his old friend, the governor general of the province. He was lodged and entertained at the governor's home, but the toasts to their joyful reunion were repeated so often that as soon as Wilkinson departed for the United States, a malignant fever ended Gayoso's career.

The political crisis which I have just described was not the only one that threatened Louisiana, for at the same time another was in preparation which did not escape the surveillance of Chevalier d'Urujo Spanish Ambassador in Philadelphia, and which finally failed, having involved only spies, couriers, and letter writing. Its center of activity was also in the United States, under the direction of Colonel or general Blount, but it was in the interest of the British government. The alleged armament of French brigands, who were supposed to furnish weapons, munitions, and soldiers to the Indians, was invented only to cover up those measures which the British themselves were preparing and which they entrusted, as the outcome would seem to indicate, to one of their fellow citizens living as an Indian for many years among the Creek Nation. This man named [William Augustus] Bowles had been deported to Europe by the Spanish government for having already caused trouble, and I shall have occasion to speak later about his arrival and his delayed and unsuccessful efforts.

A particular event might have favored either one of these plots, as a "cedula" or royal order, dated April 20, 1799—to which I shall refer in my observations on commerce—might have arrived thanks to the slowness or uncertainty of the European mail destined for the colonies, at the time of the attack upon Louisiana, if it had taken place. This order prohibited Louisiana from using the only means that its particular situation afforded to import supplies or exports its commodities. What kind of argument had justified the need for such an order? Would the Louisianians in a state of destitution and abandon, and for a fatherland that sustains this province only in a sort of precarious adoption, have preferred fighting to peace, misery to abundance, chains to freedom? And to assure themselves at that time of supplies as rich as they are abundant, and the exportation of all the colony's products, would not the farmers, businessmen, and citizens of all classes have joined with the enemy rather than expose themselves to the dangers of a decree, the success of which would have driven out of the province those [the Americans] who alone could have brought it to life and furnished it with supplies? Spain would have then begun to realize her failures and errors with respect to the means of retaining Louisiana, and England or the United States would soon have convinced her of its importance.

More than two years of interim government followed the death of the governor general, and that provided an example of the confusion into which the Spanish government falls. At the outset, and for several months, a number of commanding officers, of equal rank in the service of the province, made known their claims to take over temporarily the military affairs under the title of commandants. Civil government and police supervision was assumed by the military counselor who is normally only the governor general's consulting attorney. This arrangement, which the Spanish law ordained, created a third executive, the effect of which was to place shackles on the business of government by claiming to take advantage of, or usurping, certain rights and prerogatives. As a result, there is more arrogance in the intendant's office, dilatoriness in the courts, and more provocation in the military command where often an officer, who has spent his life in the service of the colony, cannot do the good which he knows is urgently needed, and who in strengthening the esteem and confidence of fellow citizens, would also merit for himself the gratitude of the court.

A governor [Marques de Casa-Calvo] then arrived whom the captain general of Havana commissioned as interim commander of the armed forces. I shall certainly have occasion to give an idea of his character in my observations on commerce; but, in several circumstances, the colony had to express its satisfaction that he took a more active role than the law accorded him—first of all in the protests regarding the royal "cedula" of April 20, 1799, which I have just mentioned, and then, as will be seen, with respect to the importation of Negro slaves, which the intendant nevertheless had the power to thwart.

It was during the military government of Casa-Calvo that Bowles—European by birth, Indian by profession, who had escaped from the pursuit of the Spaniards and was finally employed by England—arrived on the Florida coast with weapons, gifts, and munitions in order to induce his Indian brothers to declare war against the Spaniards. He had been up against delays and adversities which had led him on to Jamaica. There he had gathered together a kind of general staff. But much greater misfortunes awaited Bowles on the shore, and a shipwreck cast him on the beach with all his followers, after he had jettisoned the most essential items in his armament. Advance sentry of a British foray, he had a short-lived success in taking from the hands of a coward the fort of the Apalachee Indians, but soon repulsed by the forces that the Spanish military commander sent against him, he fled to haunts of the tribe to which he had been attached for so long. His secretary with one of his lieutenants—young men deceived by that adventurer whom England would have acknowledged only after some great victories—were only too glad to find refuge in the colony.

The arrival of a governor general finally ended the temporary appointments in the military and civil departments, and it is with the beginning of his official duties that I end my observations on the government, so as not to repeat myself too much on that which I shall have occasion to present later. The interim military commandant—whose fits of anger and partiality had made the colony apprehensive lest the king might have appointed him governor general, and who better informed than he had ben when he first arrived, may not have governed as badly as one might have feared—departed. Soon there was a renewal and even an expansion of the routine and venal ways of continually vicious administration. That commandant [Casa-Calvo] either through wealth or pride, or even principle, had not been corrupt; but an old man [Manuel de Salcedo] near the end of his life—infantile, poor, almost paralyzed, angered by family reverses—sought to profit in his old age from the advantages which his position gave him, and in combining frequent abuses of his military authority with maneuvers of financial pilferage, took advantage of all the circumstances to put an end, a bit late as matter of fact, to the adversities of fate in his regard. Privileges and commissions were confirmed; changes were made in the commercial auctions; and the prohibition of importing slaves maintained without any political, rural or commercial advantage. That government will go from bad to worse.

I come now to the question of finances, about which I cannot say very much without the risk of repeating myself, as the close connection between commerce and finances forces me to reveal later on the corruption and errors of its conduct in this regard. An intendant is the chief financial officer and from his tribunal rise up that swarm of extortionist tax collectors that Spain pays to become themselves the instigators of a contraband trade as culpable for them as it is degrading for the smuggler. Depraved by gold that they covet, they also spread corruption among the merchants, and becoming in turn informer of one and the accomplice of the other, they steal from the government or harass the citizen.

In addition to the proceeds from the sole duty of 6 percent on imports and exports, the king of Spain allocates to the province of Louisiana, for the total expenses of its administration, a sum of 650,000 *piastres gourdes* [$650,000], including funds for the army and navy, this amount, used with the good management, talents, and honesty of a governor who would indeed occupy himself with the prosperity of the colony, would long ago have presented some very considerable advantages and hastened the time when the grateful colony would have ceased to be a burden on the royal treasury, and would have covered its own expenses by collecting duties on its consumer goods and commodities. But it has always been quite different. The heads of the government and their assistants have squandered the colony's funds. One of them destroyed confidence in the paper money which he gave in payment of his obligations, and which he acquired with his own silver and sometimes even that of the king. Another has made some deals in which the contracting party gave back in the thousand and one ways of emptying the public treasury in order that, the use of the local paper money making it seem legal, the possible savings passed with impunity to their own profit.

In the customhouse it is even worse; there the employees, dependent on and absolute strangers to the workings of the intendant's office, were supposed to pay into the treasury the total amount of the duties collected. However, as annoyed as they are aware of the cake that they are not sharing, they know, as cautious individuals, how at least to take their own slice, while not even leaving to the one with whom they are dealing the need to bribe them. Individually and to the detriment of each other, or together, they dream up ways of depriving the treasury of part or all of what is due it. And by common consent, in agreement with the importer of *pacotilles* or cargoes, they grade as mediocre or damaged that which is of extra quality or undamaged; and they alter the weights to their own advantage and appropriate a fourth of the duties legitimately owed, while cutting them in half. The office of the intendant, which clothes itself with all the appearance of conforming to the regulations, opposes these arrangements as well as it can; arrangements which at the same time also diminish the part that falls to its lot in handling; but it is in vain. Pillage covers itself with another cloak in spite of what the intendant's office tries to do, and woe unto him who would not buy the right to cheat the sovereign! A strict enforcement of the entry procedure would then bring delay or harm to his business.

This is how the finances of the province are administered, and it is one of the truths about which I have less fear of contradiction for in my capacity as a merchant it was necessary for me to yield again and again to the flood of fiscal depravity. I shall not estimate to what extent the customs receipts have increased each ear, since in my summary of commerce, as well as agriculture, it will be easy to determine what they should have produced. Moreover, from what I have just said about finances, one would have an incorrect basis for calculations in using their statistics regarding the resources of the country. Be that as it may, I shall admit that some savings have escaped pillage. But alas! It is only for a moment, and how, with past experience, can one expect that in future these savings will be judiciously and equitably employed to the best advantage of the province?

It would be reasonable to suppose that, in a province whose mother country makes good the administrative expenses without any reciprocal business to provide compensation, the head of finances would convince himself of the direct profit in his favor if he furthered all the means of imports in order to encourage the planter, who, his needs being adequately supplied, would tend by his labors to increase the fees that enlarge the revenue in the treasury under the intendant's control. This action could not have any political inconvenience, unless it be considered that of binding the population more securely to the sovereign through the advantage of free trade which no other government could perhaps provide them. And, in addition, by the guarantee of an outlet for its commodities which, because of Spain's scorn or indifference, would otherwise rot in the planter's possession. Nevertheless, it would be a mistake to imagine this happening in the province of Louisiana. Convincing proofs of this statement will be given in the section of my observations and notes on commerce and agriculture, and a recent example supports what I shall have to say in that regard. The commodities which the New Orleans market provides for export having now opened up an extensive reciprocal business for it, a ship of the United States arrived from Jamaica, bringing a quantity of silver along with several other articles, of which they were the result of business transactions which had caused it to put into port. It is difficult to believe, but the intendant decided that this silver, brought into port to purchase commodities from the colony, should pay duty along with the rest of the cargo. Thus, as he was driving away hard money, the arrival of which seemed to predict happiness and wealth for the colony, it was necessary, in order to avoid the intendant's inept persecution, to enter this silver as foreign property. Except for that, it would not have been used to purchase commodities in the colony, but this merchant who in good faith did not want to resort to a subterfuge, has acquired by that the step the right to export to the United States, and without paying duties the same amount of specie. Such is the way the intendant's office knows how to provide obstructions even in the case of minor transactions. A trifle that in all other countries would seem unworthy of the attention of an ordinary customs man occupies the time of the chief administrator, not a matter hours, but entire days, and causes the authorities to be needlessly despised when they would have many means of being cultivated.

What I have just described regarding the two principal branches of the colony's administration should help to explain what I intend to say regarding their moral and political influence. One has the treasury in its grasp, and the other wields the bayonet, and both nearly always have an attitude of rage and envy. The quarrels between the two principal leaders of the colony have often increased the difficulties that caused its lethargy. Because she wanted to balance the powers of one against the other, Spain has given them a thousand ways of opposing each other, and in the general administration, as in finances, the best intentions for the prosperity of the country were nullified if the vices or incapacity of one of the leaders created obstacles to their fulfillment."

Source: James Pitot, *Observations on the Colony of Louisiana from 1796 to 1802*, translated from the French by Henry C. Pitot. Edited with a Foreword by Robert D. Bush. (Baton Rouge: Louisiana State University Press, 1978). Selections reprinted by permission of the Editor.

Official Report from Messrs. Livingston and Monroe, to Mr. Madison, Secretary of State of the United States, dated May 13, 1803

*I*n *this Report, Livingston and Monroe justify their acquiring the whole of Louisiana, rather than just New Orleans or lands "adjacent to the east" per their original instructions from Jefferson. Their reasons included: they had no choice but to negotiate for the whole as France would not sell just parts; if they did not acquire it for the United States, some other power might; that the possibility of having any European power adjacent to the lands possessed by the United States would lead to conflicts and war; and, that the revenues from these lands would ultimately not only pay for the purchase price, which they negotiated downward from France's original offer, but provide an eternal source of revenue.*

"We have the pleasure to transmit to you by M.D.'Erieux, a treaty which we have concluded with the French Republic for the purchase and cession of Louisiana. The negotiation of this important object was committed, on the part of France, to M. Marbois, minister of the treasury, whose conduct therein has already received the sanction of his government, as appears by the ratification of the first consul, which we have also the pleasure to forward to you.

Our acquisition of so great an extent was, we well know, not contemplated by our appointment; but we are persuaded that the circumstances and consideration which induced us to make it, will justify us in the measure of our government and country.

Before the negotiation commenced, we were apprized that the first consul had decided to offer to the United States, by sale, the whole of

Louisiana, not a part of it. We found in the outset that this information was correct; so that we had to decide as a previous question whether we would treat for the whole, or jeopardize, if not abandon the hope of acquiring any part. On that point, few did not long hesitate, but proceeded to treat for the whole. We were persuaded that, by so doing, it might be possible, if more desirable, to conclude eventually a treaty for apart, since being thus possessed of the subject, it might be easy, in discussion, at least to lead from a view of the whole to that of a part, and with some advantages peculiar to a negotiation on so great a scale. By treating for the whole, whereby we should be enabled to ascertain the idea which was entertained by this government of its value; we should also be able to form some estimate of that which was affixed to the value of its parts. It was, too, probable that a less sum would be asked for the whole, if sold entire to a single purchaser, a friendly power who was able to pay for it, and whom it might disposed to accommodate at the present juncture, than if it should be sold in parcels, either to several powers or company of individuals; it was equally so, if this government should be finally prevailed on to sell us a part, that some regard would be paid in the price asked for it, to that which was demanded for the whole; lastly, by treating for the whole, whereby the attention of this government would be drawn to the United States as the sole purchasers, we might prevent the interference of other powers, as also that of individuals, which might prove equally injurious in regard to the price asked for it, whether we acquired the whole or any part of the territory. We found, however, as we advanced in the negotiation, that M. Marbois was absolutely restricted to the disposition of the whole; that he would treat for no less portion, and of course that it was useless to urge it. On mature consideration, therefore, we finally concluded a treat on the best terms we could obtain for the whole.

By this measure, we have sought to carry into effect to the utmost of our power, the wise and benevolent policy of our government, on the principles laid down in our instructions. The possession of the left bank of the river, had it been attainable alone, would, it is true, have accomplished much in that respect; but it is equally true that it would have left much still to accomplish. Be it our people would have had an outlet to the ocean, in which no power would have a right to disturb them; but while the other bank remained in the possession of a foreign power, circumstances might occur to make the neighborhood of such power highly injurious to us in many of most important concerns. A divided jurisdiction over the river might beget jealousies, discontents, and dissensions, which the wisest policy on our part could not prevent or control. With a train of colonial government established along the western bank, from the entrance of the river, far into the interior, under the command of military men, it would be difficult to preserve that state of things which would be necessary to the peace and tranquility of four country. A single act of capricious, unfriendly, or unprincipled subaltern might would our best interests, violate our most unquestionable rights, and involve us in war. But, by this acquisition, which comprises without limits this great river and all the streams that empty into it, from their sources to the ocean, the apprehensions of these disasters is banished for ages from the United States. We adjust by it the only remaining known cause of variance with this very powerful nation: we anticipate the discontent of the great rival of France, who would probably have been wounded at any stipulation of a permanent nature which favored the latter, and which it would have been difficult to avoid, had she retained the right bank. We cease to have a motive of urgency, at least for inclining to one power, to avert the unjust pressure of another. We separate ourselves in a great measure from the European world and its concerns, especially its wars and intrigues; we make, in fine, a great stride to real and substantial independence, the good effect whereof will, we trust, be felt essentially and extensively in all our foreign and domestic relations. Without exciting the apprehensions of any power, we take a more imposing parity of interest which will communicate to the several parts which compose it.

In deliberating on this subject in a financial view, we were strongly impressed with the idea, that while we had only a right of deposit, or, indeed, while the right bank remained in the possession of a foreign power, it was always to be expected that we should, at some or another, be involved in a war on questions resulting from that cause. We were well satisfied that any would cost us more than hereby is stipulated to be given for this territory; that none could produce a more favorable result, while it might, especially in the present disturbed state of the world, prove the ruin of our affairs.

There were other considerations which, though of minor importance, had, nevertheless, their due weight in our decision on this great question. If France, or any other power holding the right bank of the river, imposed lighter duties than comport with the revenue system of the United States, supposing even that had acquired the left bank, all the supplies destined for our extensive populous settlement, on the other side, would be smuggled in through that channel, and our revenue thereby considerably diminished. Should such power open offices for the sale of lands on the western bank, our population might be drained to the advantage of that power, the price of our lands be diminished, and their sale prevented. By the possession of both banks, these evils are averted.

The terms on which we have made this acquisition, when compared with the objects obtained by, will, we flatter ourselves, be deemed advantageous to our country. We have stipulated, as you will see by the treaty and conventions, that the United States shall pay to the French government sixty millions of francs, in stock, bearing an interest of six percent, and a sum not exceeding twenty millions more to our citizens in discharge of the debts due to them by France, under the convention of 1800; and also to exempt the manufactures, productions, and vessels of France and Spain, in the direct trade from those countries, respectively in the ports of the ceded territory, from foreign duties for the term of twelve years. The stock is to be created irredeemable for fifteen years, and discharged afterwards in equal annual installments: the interest on it is to be paid in Europe, and the principal, in case this government thinks proper to sell it, disposed of in such manner as will be most conducive to the credit of American funds. The debts due to our citizens are to be discharged by drafts on our treasury. We omit a more minute view of the stipulations of these instruments, since, as you will possess them, it is unnecessary.

Louisiana was acquired of Spain by France in exchange for Tuscany, which latter is settled by treaty on the son-in-law of the king of Spain, with the title king of Etruria, and was estimated in the exchange, in consideration of its revenue, 100,000,000 francs. The first consul thought he had made an advantageous bargain in that exchange, as appears by the high idea which entertained of its value, as shown on many occasions. Louisiana was the territory which he promised in his proclamation at the peace as an asylum to those who had become unfortunate by the revolution, and which he spoke of as vast and fertile. When he made up his mid to offer the cession of it to the United States, it was contemplated to ask for it 100,000,000, francs exclusive of the debts they owed to our citizens, which they proposed we should also pay, with a perpetual exemption from foreign duties on the manufactures, productions, and vessels of France and Spain, in the ports of the ceded territory. From that demand, however, in respect to the sum, he receded, under the deliberation of his own cabinet, for the first proposition which M. Marbois made to us, was, that we should pay eight millions, sixty of which in cash, the balance to our citizens, the whole in one year in Paris, with a perpetual exemption from foreign duties as above. The modification in the mode of payment, that by stock, for from the quantum he never would depart, and the limitation of the term of the duties to twelve years, with the proviso annexed to it, which was introduced into the treaty every other change from his project, was the effect of negotiation and accommodation, in which we experienced on his part and that of his government, promptitude and candor which were highly grateful to us.

In estimating the real value of this country to the United States, a variety of considerations occur, all of which merit due attention. Of these, we have already noticed many of a general nature, to which, however, it may be difficult to fix a precise value. Others present themselves of a nature more definite, to which it will be more practicable to fix some standard. By possessing both banks, the whole revenue or duty on imports will accrue to the United States, which must be considerable. The value of the exports, we have understood, was last year four millions of dollars. If a portion only of the imports pass through that channel, as under our government we presume they will, the amount of the revenue will be considerable. This will annually increase in proportion as the population and productions in that quarter do. The value of the lands, in the province of Louisiana, amounting to some hundred millions of acres of the best quality, and in the best climate, is, perhaps, incalculable. From either of these sources, it is not doubted that the sum stipulated may be raised in time to discharge the debt."

Source: Appendix No. 18, cited in François Barbé-Marbois, *The History Of Louisiana Particularly Of The Cession Of That Colony To The United States Of America,* Published for the Louisiana American Revolution Bicentennial Commission, (Baton Rouge: Louisiana State University Press, 1977), Edited by E. Wilson Lyon, 449–453.

Notes

1 President Thomas Jefferson to Robert R. Livingston, "Letter of April 18, 1802," *From Revolution to Reconstruction, Presidents: Thomas Jefferson; Letters: The Affair of Louisiana*. www.let.rug.nl/usa/P/tj/writings/brf/jefl146 (accessed July 20, 2013). And, Philip S. Foner, (Ed.), *Basic Writings of Thomas Jefferson* (New York, 1944), 656–657.

2 *Ibid.*

3 A comprehensive survey of Spanish Louisiana is provided by John Francis McDermott (Ed.), *The Spanish in the Mississippi Valley 1762–1804* (Urbana, Ill., 1964). For the Spanish military exploits during the American Revolution, see: Robert D. Bush (General Editor). *Tribute To Don Bernardo De Galvez*. Translated from the Spanish and edited with an "Introduction" by Ralph Lee Woodward, Jr. (Baton Rouge, 1979). See also: William S. Coker and Robert Rea (Eds.), *Anglo-Spanish Confrontation On The Gulf Coast During The American Revolution*. Pensacola, Florida, 1982. Volume IX, in the series: "Proceedings Of The Gulf Coast History And Humanities Conference"; and, John Walton Caughey, *Bernardo de Galvez in Louisiana, 1776–1783* (Berkeley, CA, 1934).

4 Pierre F.X. de Charlevoix. *Charlevoix's Louisiana. Selections from the History and the Journal*. Edited by Charles E. O'Neill (Baton Rouge, 1977). Charlevoix's original was published in 1744 as: *Histoire et Description Générale de la Nouvelle France avec le Journal Historique d'un Voyage fait par ordre du Roi dans l'Amerique Septentrionale*.

5 Antoine Simon Le Page du Pratz. *The History of Louisiana*. Edited by Joseph G. Tregle, Jr. (Baton Rouge, 1974). Originally published in 1758 as *Histoire de la Louisiane*, three volumes, included observations on the colony, and the Natchez Indians.

6 *Ibid.*, "Introduction," xxxiv.

7 Manuel de Godoy. *Memorias del principe de la paz*. Translated from the Spanish by J.B. D'Esmenard. (Madrid, 1856), II, 52.

8 See: Georges Lefebvre, *The French Revolution* in two volumes; and, *Napoleon* in two volumes. Translated from the French by Henry F. Stockhold (New York, 1965–1969). See *Napoleon, from 18 Brumaire to Tilsit*, I, 136–139, 147, 162,167.

9 Noble E. Cunningham, Jr., *The Jeffersonian Republicans: The Formation of Party Organization, 1789–1801* (Chapel Hill, NC, 1967); and, by the same author,

The Jeffersonians in Power: Party Operations, 1801–1807 (Chapel Hill: University of North Carolina Press, 1963); *Jefferson vs. Hamilton: Confrontations that Shaped a Nation*, Boston & New York, 2000. See also: Samuel Flagg Bemis, *Jay's Treaty: A Study in Commerce and Diplomacy* (New Haven, 1923); E. Wilson Lyon, "The Directory and the United States," *American Historical Review*, XLIII (1938), 514–532; William A. Williams, *The Roots of Modern American Empire* (New York, 1969); and, James L. Roark, et. al., *The American Promise A History Of The United States*, Fourth Edition (Boston & New York, 2009), 306–311.

10   Lefebvre, *Napoleon, from 18 Brumaire to Tilsit, 1799–1807*. I, 136–139, 147, 162, 167.

11   Laurent Dubois and John D. Garrigus, *Slave Revolution in the Caribbean 1789–1804*. (Boston & New York, 2006), 34–35; Alexander DeConde, *This Affair of Louisiana* (New York, 1976), 99–101, 139; DeConde, *The Quasi-War—The Politics and Diplomacy of the Undeclared War with France, 1797–1801* (New York, 1966); and, Henry Blumenthal, *France and the United States Their Diplomatic Relations, 1789–1914* (New York, 1970), 15–17.

12   Jack D.L. Holmes, "Maps, Plans and Charts of Louisiana in Spanish and Cuban Archives: a Checklist," *Louisiana Studies* 2, No. 4 (Winter 1960), 183–203; and, Holmes, "Maps, Plans and Charts of Louisiana in Paris Archives: Checklist," *Louisiana Studies*, 4, No. 3 (Fall, 1965), 200–221.

13   Mary P. Adams. "Jefferson's Reaction to the Treaty of San Ildefonso," *The Journal of Southern History*, Vol. 21, No. 2 (May, 1955), 173–188.

14   Ethan Grant, "The Treaty Of San Ildefonso And Manifest Destiny," *Gulf Coast Historical Review*, Vol. 12, No. 2 (1997), 44–57. And, Jon Kukla. *A Wilderness So Immense: The Louisiana Purchase and the Destiny of America* (New York: Alfred A. Knopf, 2003).

15   Edward F. Haas. (Ed.), *Louisiana's Legal Heritage* (Pensacola, Fl., 1983), 3; and, John E. Harkins, "Legal and Judicial Aspects in Spanish Louisiana," in *Readings In Louisiana History* (New Orleans, 1978), 41–48.

16   President Jefferson to Robert R. Livingston, American Minister to France, 1801–1804, "Letter of April 18, 1802", hand delivered in Paris by Mr. Dupont de Nemours. And, Foner (Ed.), *Basic Writings of Thomas Jefferson*, 656–657.

17   *Ibid.*

18   John Francis McDermott (Ed.), *The Spanish in the Mississippi Valley 1762–1804* (Urbana, Ill., 1964).

19   John Preston Moore, "Anglo-Spanish Rivalry on the Louisiana Frontier, 1763–1804," in McDermott, *ibid.*, 72–86.

20   DeConde, *This Affair Of Louisiana*, 30–31.

21   John R. Kemp (Ed.), *New Orleans An Illustrated History* (Woodland Hills, CA, 1981), 37–39.

22   Charles E. Gayarré, *History of Louisiana*, four volumes (New Orleans, LA, 1965), II, 290.

23   *Ibid.*, 293–303. And, Joe Gray Taylor, *Louisiana A Bicentennial History*. (New York, 1976), 21–23.

24   Gilbert C. Din, "Spanish Immigration Policy in Louisiana and the American Penetration, 1792–1803," *Southwestern Historical Quarterly*. LXXVI. (1973), 255–276.

25   Gayarré, *History of Louisiana*, III, 407–408.

26   C. Richard Arena, "Land Settlement Policies and Practices in Spanish Louisiana,"
      McDermott (Ed.), *The Spanish in the Mississippi Valley, 1762–1804*, 51–60.

27   Taylor, *Louisiana A Bicentennial History*, 30–38.

28   Jack D.L. Holmes, "Some Economic Problems of Spanish Governors in Louisiana,"
      reprinted in *Readings in Louisiana History* (New Orleans, LA, 1978), 60.

29   Taylor, *A Bicentennial History*, 34–37; and, Bush (General Editor), *Tribute to Don
      Bernado De Galvez*, 99–114.

30   Jack D.L. Holmes, "French and Spanish Military Units in the 1781 Pensacola
      Campaign," in Coker (Ed.), *Anglo-Spanish Confrontation On The Gulf Coast During
      The American Revolution*, 145–157.

31   See "Table V" on the origins of arrivals at New Orleans, in John G. Clark, *New
      Orleans 1718–1812. An Economic History* (Baton Rouge, 1970), 288. Clark provides
      the following explanation which describes the situation in almost any year. He
      wrote: "The New Orleans-American trade, whether direct or via St. Domingue,
      was of critical importance to Louisiana, providing as it did a major portion of the
      flour and provisions consumed in the colony. Patently illegal in any of its various
      forms, the trade was so essential that it could not be prohibited." Clark, *New Orleans
      1718–1812. An Economic History*, 233. And, Robin F.A. Fabel, "Anglo-Spanish
      Commerce in New Orleans during the American Revolution," in Coker (Ed.),
      Anglo-Spanish Confrontation On The Gulf Coast During The American Revolution,
      25–53.

32   Taylor, *Louisiana A Bicentennial History*, 39–40.

33   Arthur P. Whitaker, "James Wilkinson's First Descent to New Orleans in 1787,"
      Hispanic American Historical Review, VIII, No. 1 (Feb., 1928), 82–97. And, for the
      Spanish "Conspiracy" in the West, see: Jack D.L. Holmes, *Gayoso, The Life of a
      Spanish Governor in the Mississippi Valley, 1789–1799* (Gloucester, MA, 1968),
      25–26, 39, 40, 139–141, 175–176, 221, 260–261. Also, Andro Linklater, *An Artist
      in Treason: The Extraordinary Life of General James Wilkinson* (New York, 2009).

34   A.P. Nasatir and Ernest P. Liljegren (Eds.), "Materials Relating to the History of
      the Mississippi Valley from the Minutes of the Supreme Councils of State,
      1787–1797," *Louisiana Historical Quarterly*, XXI, No. 1 (January, 1928), 5–75. Text
      of "Confidential Dispatch No. 13," from Governor Miro to Supreme Council of
      State in Spain (September 25, 1797), cited by Holmes, *Gayoso*, 26.

35   Joslin Isaac Cox (Ed.), "Documents on the Blount Conspiracy, 1795–1797,"
      American Historical Review X (1905), 574–606.

36   James Pitot, *Observations on the Colony of Louisiana from 1796 to 1802*. Edited with
      a Foreword by Robert D. Bush (Baton Rouge, 1978), 17. Originally prepared as
      a manuscript by Jacques-François Pitot in 1802, entitled "Observations sur la
      Colonie de la Louisiane de 1796 a 1802," the report was intended for French
      officials, whom Pitot assumed would welcome the information, and which would
      accordingly benefit his own business interests.

37   James Alton James, *The Life of George Rogers Clark* (Chicago, 1928), 359–360; for
      the activities of Citizen Edmond Genet and intrigue in the West, see also
      Blumenthal, *France and the United States*, 12, 13, 218.

38   Samuel Flagg Bemis, *Pinckney's Treaty: America's Advantage from Europe's Distress,
      1783–1800*. New Haven, 1921. And, Arthur Preston Whitaker, *The Mississippi
      Question A Study in Trade, Politics and Diplomacy* (Gloucester, MA, 1962).

39   Jack D.L. Holmes, "The Choctaws in 1795," *Alabama Historical Quarterly*, XXX, No.1 (Spring, 1968), 533–549. See an overview of Spanish Indian policy by the same author, in, *Gayoso*, 142–161.

40   Holmes, "Letter from Governor Governor Gayoso to Daniel Clark, Sr., (Natchez, June 17, 1796), quoted in *Gayoso*, 178–179. Commissioner Ellicott saw only persistent Spanish deception and an unwillingness to fulfill the terms of the treaty, see the accounts in Holmes, *ibid.*, 183–193.

41   The details of Ellicott's mission to Natchez in: Andrew Ellicott, *The Journal of Andrew Ellicott, Late Commissioner On Behalf Of The United States During The Year 1796, The Years 1797,1798,1799. And Part of the Year 1800: For Determining The Boundary Between The United States And The Possessions Of His Catholic Majesty In America. Containing Six Maps.* Philadelphia: William Fry, 1814.

42   John G. Clark, "New Orleans As An Entrepot," in Dolores Egger Labbe (Ed.), *The Louisiana Purchase Bicentennial Series in Louisiana History*, volume III (Lafayette, La., 1998), 387–409. And, Pitot, *Observations*, 15–16, 45–46.

43   Jack D.L. Holmes, "Some Economic Problems of Spanish Governors in Louisiana," in *Readings in Louisiana History*, 60.

44   Pitot, *Observations*, 35.

45   *Ibid.*, 2–3.

46   Manuel de Godoy, *Memorias del principe de la paz*, II, 53–54.

47   *Ibid.*

48   Robert Livingston to Rufus King, Paris, (December 30, 1801). Quoted in *The Original Letters of Robert R. Livingston*. Compiled by Edward Alexander Parsons (New Orleans, 1953), 77.

49   DeConde, *This Affair of Louisiana*, 99–102; and Blumenthal, *France and the United States*, 18–20.

50   *Correspondence de Napoleon 1er* 32 vols. (Paris, 1858–1870), VI, 617–618.

51   Letter from Rufus King to Robert Livingston, January 16, 1803, quoted in Parsons, *Original Letters of Robert R. Livingston*, 24.

52   Robert D. Bush, "Colonial Administration in French Louisiana: The Napoleonic Episode, 1802–1803," *Publications of the Louisiana Historical Society*, Series II, Volume II (1975), 38; Georges Lefebvre, *Napoleon*, I, 170. See also, Jon Kukla (Ed.), *A Guide to the Papers Of Pierre Clement Laussat Napoleon's Prefect for the Colony of Louisiana and of General Claude Perrin Victor*. New Orleans: The Historic New Orleans Collection, 1993. The *Guide* includes 599 items of Laussat, 38 items of General Victor, and 12 miscellany items.

53   Pierre Clement de Laussat, *Memoires Sur Ma Vie à Mon Fils, Pendant les Années 1803 Et Suivantes, Que j'ai Rempli des Fonctions Publiques, Savoir: à la Louisiàne, en Qualité de Commissaire du Gouvernment Francaise Pour la Reprise de Possession de Cette Colonie Et Pour la Remise Aux États-Unis* (Pau, 1831). Edited, with a Foreword, by Robert D. Bush, *Memoirs of My Life*. Translated from the French by Agnes Josephine Pastwa, O.S.F. (Baton Rouge, 2003). Hereafter cited as *Memoirs*. In addition to the *Memoirs*, quotations from the *Laussat Papers* at the Historic New Orleans Collection are cited throughout. See also: Andre Lafargue, "Pierre Clement de Laussat, Colonial Prefect and High Commissioner of France in Louisiana: His Memoires, Proclamations and Orders," *The Louisiana Historical Quarterly*, Vol. 20, No. 1 (1937), 159–182; and, Andre Lafargue, "Pierre Clement de Laussat: An

Intimate Portrait," *The Louisiana Historical Quarterly*, Vol. 24, No. 1 (1941), 5–8; and, Albert Krebs, "Laussat, Prefet de la Louisiane, 19 Aout 1802–21 Avril 1804," in *Bulletin de l'Institut Napoleon*, No. 48, (Juillet, 1953), 65–72.

54   Letter from Louis Alexandre Berthier, Minister of War, to General Claude Perrin Victor, Captain-General of Louisiana (August 28, 1802), *Victor Papers*. The troops assigned were: three battalions of the 54th regiment of infantry, one squad of 150 dragoons, two squads of artillery and one company of mobile artillery. The breakdown of troops requested by Victor, and submitted in a report of the same date by Laussat, included: 167 officers, 3,540 non-commissioned officers and troops, and 32 general staff officers for a total of 3,739. See also: Ronald D. Smith, "Napoleon and Louisiana: Failure of the Proposed Expedition to Occupy and Defend Louisiana, 1801–1803," *Louisiana History*. XII (Winter, 1971), 21–40. By comparison to the French forces assigned to the Louisiana Expedition, the entire regular army of the United States in 1800 numbered around 5,000 men, most of whom were deployed in the west to protect settlers from Indian attacks.

55   Troop deployments for the Louisiana Expedition sent by Napoleon to the war department are his "Ordre de Reunir à Dunkerque des Troupes Composant L'Expedition de la Louisiane," (24 Aout 1802), in *Correspondence de Napoleon 1ᵉʳ* (Paris, 1858–70), VII, 4; and, orders sent to the navy of the same date, *ibid.*, 4–5.

56   By late January, 1803, expenses for the Louisiana Expedition had already surpassed half a million francs, and the expenditure for the naval convoy to take troops to Louisiana was estimated to add another 486,235 francs, in Marc de Villiers du Terrage, *Les Dernieres Années de la Louisiane Francsise* (Paris, 1903), 378, 381.

57   "Instructions from Admiral Denis Dècres to Laussat," (December 7, 1802). In *Laussat Papers*.

58   Laussat's journey to Louisiana and then his first few weeks after arrival, March 26, 1803, are recounted in his *Memoirs*, Book One.

59   Laussat, *Memoirs*, 20. One of the financial policies which led Laussat to this conclusion was Spanish depreciation of paper money during the late 1790s. The corruption occurred because Spanish officials would take hard money, or specie which they acquired as part of the annual allotment from Cuba, from the treasury and use it to acquire for themselves depreciated local paper currency. Then, they could use the latter to repay their personal debts at a huge savings, and if the creditor objected, his only legal recourse was against the very government officials who were defrauding him. James Pitot decried this policy in his *Observations*; and so too did the English merchant Francis Bailey in his *Journal Of A Tour in Unsettled Parts Of North America in 1796 & 1797*. Edited with an Introduction by Jack D.L. Holmes. (Edwardsville, IL, 1969), 154–156.

60   Laussat, *Memoirs*, 24–25.

61   DeConde, *This Affair of Louisiana*, 92–94; Blumenthal, *France and the United States*, 15–17. Blumenthal wrote: "In June 1798, Congress suspended all commercial transactions with France. In July, it authorized the capture of armed French ships and declared the Franco–American treaties of 1778 null and void by virtue of the fact that the French government had already violated them." *Ibid.*

62   *Ibid.* 97–102. And, Laurent Dubois and John D. Garrigus, *Slave Revolution in the Caribbean 1789–1804 A Brief History with Documents*. (Boston & New York, 2006), 34–35.

63   Laussat, *Memoirs*, 8–9; see also, Dubois and Garrigus, *Slave Revolution in the Caribbean 1789–1804 A Brief History with Documents*, who concluded that: "The French general Charles-Victor Emmanuel Leclerc, who led Bonaparte's expedition to the colony in 1802, blamed U.S. merchants for making Louverture's war against the French possible." *Ibid.*, 35.

64   Letter from Jefferson to Robert Livingston (April 18, 1802), quoted in Parsons, *Original Letters of Robert Livingston*, 31.

65   Extract of letter dated, Natchez, April 13, 1803, quoted as Appendix 11, in François Barbé-Marbois, *The History Of Louisiana*. Edited by E. Wilson Lyon, (Baton Rouge, 1977), 420. Published as part of the Louisiana Bicentennial Reprint Series, this volume includes not only Barbé-Marbois's *The History of Louisiana*, but several documents, letters and reports relevant to the Louisiana Purchase as appendices. The specific Spanish suspension of the right of deposit was an "Order of Juan Ventura Morales, state's attorney and interim intendant of Louisiana and West Florida, ending trade with neutrals," (October 16, 1802), Ms. Item 57, *Laussat Papers*.

66   President Jefferson to Robert Livingston (February 3, 1803), quoted in Parsons, *Original Letters of Robert Livingston*, 40.

67   "Memorial of the Legislative Council and House of Representatives of the Mississippi Territory to the President, Senate, and House of Representatives of the United States," (January 5, 1803), Appendix 9, quoted in Barbé-Marbois, *The History of Louisiana*, 417–418.

68   "Memorial to the President, Senate, and House of Representatives of the United States," (January, 1803), Appendix 10, *ibid.*, 119; and again, "Extract of a Letter, dated Natchez, 13th April, 1803, which stated in part: "There is not a well-informed man in this territory who does not perceive that our country is ruined." Appendix 11, *ibid.*, 420.

69   President Jefferson to James Monroe (January 10, 1803), Paul Leicester Ford, (Ed.), *The Writings of Thomas Jefferson* (New York, 1896), IX, 416; and, letter of (January 13, 1803), *ibid.*, 419.

70   Speech and resolution offered by Senator James Ross (Federalist, Pennsylvania) of February 16, 1803, and amended resolution presented by Senator John C. Breckenridge (Democratic Republican, Kentucky), quoted from "Louisiana: European Explorations And The Louisiana Purchase A Special Presentation From The Geography And Map Division Of The Library Of Congress," *Library of Congress*, 59; and, DeConde, *This Affair of Louisiana*, 140.

71   Instructions from Secretary of State James Madison to Messrs. Livingston and Monroe (March 2, 1803), Appendix 18, quoted in Barbé-Marbois, *The History of Louisiana*, 429.

72   *Ibid.*, 428–445.

73   *Ibid.*, 445.

74   Quoted in Stephen E. Ambrose, *Undaunted Courage Meriwether Lewis, Thomas Jefferson, And The Opening Of The American West*, New York, 1996), 78–79; and, DeConde, *This Affair of Louisiana*, 137.

75   President Jefferson to Governor James Garrard, Kentucky, quoted: www. monticello.org/site/research-and-collections/james-monroe (accessed July 20, 2013), 8.

76 Comments from Napoleon Bonaparte to François Barbé-Marbois (April 10, 1803), quoted in Barbé-Marbois, *The History of Louisiana*, 264.

77 Letter from Robert Livingston to the French Minister of Foreign Affairs (December 11, 1802), Appendix 8, quoted in *ibid.*, 415.

78 Quoted in James Alexander Robertson, *Louisiana Under the Rule of Spain, France and the United States* (Cleveland, 1911), I, 368.

79 Laussat, "Letter to Denis Decrès, minister of the navy and colonies," Paris, "List of gifts for Indian Tribes," (September 27, 1802), manuscript V5, in *Victor Papers*, The Historic New Orleans Collection.

80 "Instructions" to Captain-General Victor, cited in Robertson, *Louisiana*, I, 361–374.

81 Laussat, *Memoirs*, 34.

82 Quoted in Robertson, *Louisiana*, II, 39–41.

83 Letter from President Jefferson to Pierre Samuel du Pont de Nemours (April 25, 1802), quoted: www.yamaguchy.com/library/jefferson/1802.html (accessed July 20, 2013).

84 Quoted by Barbé-Marbois, *The History of Louisiana*, 260. Napoleon then added: "The English aspire to dispose of all the riches of the world. I shall be useful to the whole universe, if I can prevent their ruling America as they rule Asia." *Ibid.*

85 The rhetoric is illustrated in the text of the resolution offered by Senator James Ross (Federalist, Pennsylvania) who stated (February 16, 1803) in part: "It is time to teach the world that the balance of America is in our hands, that we are as dominant in this part of the globe as other nations are in Europe, that we fear none of them, and that we are entering on the age of manhood and are prepared to make use of our strength." Senator Ross's resolution was defeated, but a second offered by Senator John C. Breckenridge (Democratic Republican, Kentucky) passed, which provided for authorization for the President to call up 80,000 militia and in addition for $5,000,000 with which to cover expenses if diplomatic initiatives failed. *Annals of Congress, 7th Congress, 2nd session*, 83–88.

86 Jefferson to Livingston, letter of February 3, 1803, quoted in Parsons, *Original Letters of Robert Livingston*, 40.

87 *Ibid.*

88 Letter from Secretary of State James Madison to Mssrs. Livingston and Monroe (April 18, 1803), quoted in Barbé-Marbois, *The History of Louisiana*, 448–449.

89 *Ibid.*

90 Letter from Jefferson to Livingston (February 3, 1803), quoted in Parsons, *Original Letters of Robert Livingston*, 40. In the last paragraph of this letter, Jefferson concluded: "The future destinies of our country hang on this negotiation, and I am sure they could not be placed in more able or zealous hands." *Ibid.*, 41.

91 DeConde, *This Affair of Louisiana*, 172–173.

92 Barbé-Marbois, *The History of Louisiana*, 280. In the first meeting of the American negotiators on April 12, Livingston, who had been continually rebuffed by Talleyrand, confessed to Monroe: "I wish that the resolution offered by Mr. Ross in the Senate had been adopted. Only force can give us New Orleans. We must employ force. Let us first get possession of the country and negotiate afterwards." Quoted in *Journal of the Mission* by Colonel John Mercer, and later cited in Mr. Monroe's *Memoir*, in Barbé-Marbois, *History of Louisiana*, 278.

93 *Ibid.*, 281.

94   *Ibid.*, 278–279.

95   *Ibid.*, 281.

96   *Ibid.*, 302–308.

97   Letter from Livingston to Secretary of State Madison (Paris, May 20, 1803), Appendix 19, *ibid.*, 454.

98   Thomas Jefferson, "The Kentucky Resolutions," (November 16, 1798), quoted: www.civil-liberties.com/cases/kentucky/html (accessed July 20, 2013).

99   In a letter to Daniel Clark, Sr., (June 17, 1796), Governor Gayoso, who opposed the Pinckney Treaty and wished to delay its implementation, along with Minister Godoy in Spain, wrote in part: "It is more than probable that a separation of several states will take place which will alter the political existence of a power that could influence on the balance of that of others; therefore Spain, being deprived of that assistance which could arise from her connection with the Union, will alter her views." Quoted in Holmes, *Gayoso*, 179.

100 Jefferson to John Breckenridge, Monticello (August 12, 1803), (Ford, ed.), *Writings of Thomas Jefferson*, X, 7.

101 Jefferson's decision to proceed absent a Constitutional amendment was based on his assessment of the situation if he did not proceed immediately. Reports from Europe advised him that Napoleon was having second thoughts, Spain was upset over her being left out of the negotiations, in fact she had still not officially transferred Louisiana to France, and Europe was again at war. The loophole through which the Louisiana Purchase might drop was the clause in the Treaty which provided for a six-month time period for U.S. ratification, and that window of opportunity would close at the end of October. Jefferson therefore rationalized his decision, adopted the counsel of his advisors, and called for the special session of Congress to convene on October 17. Cited in: Monroe, http://monticello.org/site/research-and-collections/james-monroe (accessed July 20, 2013), 9.

102 Speech of Roger Griswold (Federalist, Connecticut), John Keats, *Eminent Domain The Louisiana Purchase and the Making of America* (New York, 1973), 345.

103 Eighth United States Congress (March 4, 1803–March 3, 1805), membership based on the Second Census of the United States (1800), with representation identified by political parties, see *Wikipedia, the free encyclopedia*, 3–8.

104 Extract of a letter, dated Natchez, 13 April, 1803, Appendix 11, quoted in Barbé-Marbois, *The History of Louisiana*, 420.

105 President Jefferson, "Message To The Senate and House of Representatives of the United States," (October 17, 1803), *Proceedings, Senate*, 11–15. See also, Dumas Malone, *Jefferson The President, First Term, 1801–1805*. Vol. 4, Charlottesville, VA, 2005.

106 President George Washington, "Farewell Address to the People of the United States," (September 19, 1796), in Michael P. Johnson (Ed.), *Reading the American Past Selected Historical Documents*, Fourth Edition (New York, 2009), 188.

107 Representative Roger Griswold (Federalist, Connecticut), debate on "The Louisiana Treaty" (October 24, 1803), *Annals of Congress, A Century of Lawmaking for a New Nation: U.S. Congressional Documents and Debates*, 386. There was some concern among French officials as well regarding Spain's known displeasure at France's transfer of Louisiana to the United States. In a dispatch to Prefect Laussat (October 13, 1803) from French *Charge d'affairs* in Washington, Louis Andre

Pichon, stated. "It does not appear that these dispositions have been voiced by a formal opposition, otherwise I would have surely been informed of it. Nevertheless, the Spanish minister [Marquis de y Riujo] either because he is executing or exaggerating his instructions, has taken steps which leads one to fear that, while circumspect in Paris, the court in Madrid may have given to New Orleans orders contrary to those of the month of October [1802]—orders that produce a refusal to turn the colony over to you. Not only does the Marquis d'Yrujo protest against the acquisition by the United States but he even presses them not to accomplish the [terms of] treaty by the payment of stipulated compensations. And what is no less significant, he has refused to certify the copy of the documents, both Spanish and French, which will authorize you to require the return of Louisiana from the Spanish officials." Pichon to Laussat, Ms. 287, in *Laussat Papers*, 2–3. Then, on October 23, 1803, Pichon again wrote Prefect Laussat on the same subject. "If, on the contrary, Citizen, the Spanish authorities refuse to deliver the colony, it will be advisable perhaps to make a protest and wait for the time when the ratification of the United States being given, these latter shall send their commissioner. You shall then transfer the order for taking possession from the First Consul to that commissioner, and probably that would be the most regular manner of executing the treaty in favor of the United States against the opposition of Spanish officials." *Ibid.* The possible refusal of the Spanish to cede Louisiana, because of their opposition to the French sale, and Spain's acceptance of the transfer to the U.S. was addressed later (May 15, 1804) in a letter from the Marquis de Casa Yrujo, Spanish Minister to the United States, to Secretary of State James Madison. Yrujo wrote: "The explanations which the Government of France has given to His Catholic Majesty concerning the sale of Louisiana to the United States, and the amicable dispositions on the part of the King my master towards these States, have determined him to abandon the opposition which, at a prior period, and with the most substantial motives, he had manifested against that transaction. In consequence, and by special order of His Majesty, I have the pleasure to communicate to you his royal intentions on the affair so important; well persuaded that the American Government will see, in his conduct of the King my master, a new proof of his consideration for the United States, and that they will correspond, with a true reciprocity, with the sincere friendship of the King, of which he has given so many proofs." Quoted in *A Century of Lawmaking for a New Nation: U.S. Congressional documents and Debates* (1804), 583. Once again, Spain, at war with Britain, was very mindful about the possibility of an Anglo-American alliance, and the possibility of a joint military action against her possessions in Mexico or Cuba.

108 Representative John Randolph, Jr., (Democratic Republican, Virginia), "Speech of October 24, 1803," *Annals of Congress*, 390.

109 Representative John Smilie (Democratic Republican, Pennsylvania), "speech of October 24, 1803, in *ibid.*, 392. Representative Joseph H. Nicholson (Democratic Republican, Maryland) then rose to speak. In a tone reflective of American nationalism, he responded: "If the House is satisfied from the information laid on the table, that Spain had ceded Louisiana to France, and that France had since ceded it to the United States, what more do they require? Are we not an independent nation?" Then, he concluded: "The treaty itself . . . and the conventions attached to it, furnished all the necessary information . . . And if France

shall fail to put us into actual possession, the United States are not bound to pay a single dollar. So that the call for papers can be of no possible use." Quoted in *U.S. Congressional Documents and Debates* (October 24, 1803), 398.

110   Quoted in "Speech of Representative John Smilie," (October 24, 1803), *Annals of Congress*, 393.

111   Representative Roger Griswold, October 24, 1803, debate "On the Louisiana Treaty," *Annals of Congress*, 391.

112   Representative Joseph H. Nicolson (Democratic Republican, Maryland), "Speech on the Louisiana Treaty," (October 24, 1803), *Annals of Congress*, 398.

113   The official title of the engrossed bill (October 29, 1803) was: "An act making provision for the payment of claims of citizens of the United States on the Government of France, the payment of which has been assumed by the United States, by virtue of the Convention of the thirtieth of April, one thousand eight hundred and three, between the United States and the French Republic." See full text in Primary Document 8 (page 144).

114   Laussat, *Memoirs*, 56.

115   *Ibid.*, 78–79.

116   *Ibid.*, 87.

117   *Ibid.*, 88–89.

118   "Proclamation By His Excellency William C.C. Claiborne, Governor of the Mississippi Territory, exercising the powers of Governor General and Intendant of the province of Louisiana" (December 20, 1803), quoted in *Foreign Relations, A Century of Lawmaking for a New Nation: U.S. Congressional Documents and Debates*, 582–583.

119   Robert Livingston, quoted in Parsons, *Original Letters of Robert Livingston*, 65.

120   Thomas Jefferson, "Message to the Senate and House of Representatives of the United States," (Monday, January 16, 1804), *Journal of the Senate*, 889.

121   Laussat, *Memoirs*, 90.

122   *Ibid.*, 96.

123   *Ibid.*, 23.

124   *Ibid.*, 34–35.

125   "Letter from Secretary of State Madison to Mssrs. Livingston and Monroe, (March 2, 1803), quoted in Barbé-Marbois, *The History of Louisiana*, 431–432.

126   "Letter from Jefferson to Rufus King," (July 13, 1802), cited: www.yamguchy.com/library/jefferson/1802 (accessed July 20, 2013).

Suggestions for Further Reading

Books on the subject of the Louisiana Purchase generally fall into two categories: (1) overviews of the era designed as scholarly studies; and (2) biographies of the participants. Both of these categories include some documents, correspondence, and illustrations. However, there is no single sourcebook on the Louisiana Purchase currently on the market that focuses its presentation for the undergraduate student in American history survey courses, or on the American West, and/or in diplomatic history. The bulk of the historical literature on the Louisiana Purchase is of some vintage; most of the standard works on Louisiana prior to 1803 date from the 1960s and 1970s.

Among those scholarly works in category 1 are: Alexander de Conde, *This Affair Of Louisiana* (1976) which traces what he calls "an expansionist Anglo-American ethos" with analysis of the documents and historical writings of fellow scholars. E. Wilson Lyon, *Louisiana in French Diplomacy, 1759–1804* (1934) is classic overview, and, along with his other relevant source, *The Man Who Sold Louisiana (1942)*, a biography of François Barbé-Marbois, are both worthy studies in Franco-American relations and history. An excellent overview narrative with documents on Haiti is that by Laurent Dubois and John D. Garrigus, *Slave Revolution in the Caribbean 1789–1804* (2006). Jon Kukla, *A Wilderness So Immense: The Louisiana Purchase and the Destiny of America* (2003) is a recent comprehensive and well researched interpretation of American expansionism within the political context of the young republic, and the future impact of the Louisiana Purchase on American society. Noble E. Cunningham, Jr.'s scholarly studies of the Jeffersonian era are: *The Jeffersonian Republicans; 1789–1801* (1957); and, *The Jeffersonian Republicans in Power: Party Operations, 1801–1809* (1963), plus later works on the Jeffersonian era. A comprehensive study of Spanish Louisiana, with bibliography and chronology, is that by Jack D. L. Holmes, *A Guide To Spanish Louisiana, 1762–1806* (1970), which provides excellent sources, both original documents and published works. Arthur Preston Whitaker's study, *The Mississippi Question 1795–1803: A Study in Trade, Politics, and Diplomacy* (1934) traces the Spanish decline and eventual demise. Although published several years ago, *The Spanish in the Mississippi Valley, 1762–1804*

(1974) *and Frenchmen And French Ways In The Mississippi Valley* (1969), both edited by John Francis McDermott remain as lasting contributions to scholarship and excellent introductions to specific topics in each era by leading scholars.

In category 2 are: Dumas Malone, *Jefferson and His Time* (1948–1974), letters and papers, vols IV and V; E. Wilson Lyon, *The Man Who Sold Louisiana: The Career of François Barbé-Marbois* (1942) which includes extensive quotes; and, François Barbé-Marbois, *The History Of Louisiana Particularly Of The Cession Of That Colony To The United States.* (1829). Edited, with an Introduction, by E. Wilson Lyon. Baton Rouge: Louisiana State University Press, 1977. On the subject of French planning for the occupation and administration of Louisiana, see Pierre Clement Laussat, *Memoirs of My Life* (1831), edited by Robert D. Bush. And, for insight into last years of Spanish administration by a contemporary, see James Piot, *Observations On The Colony Of Louisiana, From 1796 To 1802* (1979), edited by Robert D. Bush. One of the best sources of interpretation through the biography of Spain's governor in Natchez and then for the colony of Louisiana is *Gayoso: The Life of a Spanish Governor in the Mississippi Valley, 1789–1799* (1965) by Jack D.L. Holmes. In addition, there are numerous biographies of Robert Livingston, James Madison, James Monroe, Napoleon Bonaparte, as well as William C.C. Claiborne and General James Wilkinson.

Bibliography

Articles

Adams, Mary P. "Jefferson's Reaction to the Treaty of San Ildefenso," *The Journal of Southern History*. XXI, No. 2 (May, 1955), 173–188.

Bush, Robert D. "Colonial Administration in French Louisiana: The Napoleonic Episode, 1802–1803," *Publications of the Louisiana Historical Society*. 2nd ser., II (1975), 45–58.

_____. "Documents on the Louisiana Purchase: The Laussat Papers," *Louisiana History*, XVIII (Winter, 1977), 104–107.

_____. "Guide pour l'étude de la administration napoleonienne en Louisiane à travers les document d'archives et les collections privées de la nouvelle-orleans," *Revue de l'institut napoleon* (Sorbonne), No. 135 (1979), 87–91.

_____. "Civilian Versus Military Leadership in Napoleonic Louisiana, 1803," *The Journal of America's Military Past*, XXIX, No. 3 (Spring, Summer, 2003), 31–47.

Cox, Isaac Joslin, Ed., "Documents on the Blount Conspiracy, 1795–1797," *American Historical Review*, X (1905), 574–606.

Din, Gilbert C. "Spanish Immigration Policy in Louisiana and the American Penetration, 1792–1803," *Southwestern Historical Quarterly*, LXXVI (1973), 255–276.

Douglas, Elisha P. "The Adventurer Bowles," *William And Mary Quarterly*. 2nd ser., VI (1949), 3–23.

Fletcher, Mildred S. "Louisiana as a Factor in French Diplomacy from 1763 to 1803," *Mississippi Valley Historical Review*, XVII (December, 1930), 367–376.

Grant, Ethan. "The Treaty Of San Lorenzo And Manifest Destiny," *Gulf Coast Historical Review*, XII, No. 2 (1997), 44–57.

Hamilton, J.G. de Roulhac. "The Pacifism of Thomas Jefferson," *Virginia Quarterly Review*, XXXI (Autumn, 1955), 607–620.

Harkins, John E. "Legal and Judicial Aspects in Spanish Louisiana," in *Readings In Louisiana History* (1978), 41–48.

Hatfield, Joseph T. "William C.C. Claiborne, Congress, and Republicanism, 1797–1804," *Tennessee Historical Quarterly*, XXIV, No. 2 (1965), 156–180.

Holmes, Jack D.L. "Some Economic Problems of Spanish Governors in Lousiana," *Readings In Louisiana History*, New Orleans: *The Louisiana Historical Association* (1978), 55–60.

———. "The Choctaws in 1795," *Alabama Historical Quarterly*, XXX, No. 1 (Spring, 1968), 533–549.

———. "Maps, Plans, and Charts of Louisiana in Spanish and Cuban Archives: A Checklist," *Louisiana Studies*, II, No. 4 (Winter, 1963), 183–203; and, Holmes, "Maps, Plans, and Charts of Louisiana in Paris Archives: A Checklist," *Louisiana Studies*, IV, No. 3 (Fall, 1965), 200–221.

Liljegren, Ernest R. "Jacobinism in Spanish Louisiana, 1792–1797," *Louisiana Historical Quarterly*, XXII (January, 1939), 47–97.

Knudson, Jerry W. "Newspaper Reactions to the Louisiana Purchase: 'This New, Immense Unbounded World,'" *Missouri Historical Review*, LXIII (January, 1969), 182–213.

Krebs, Albert. "Laussat prefet de la Louisiane (19 aout 1802–21 avril 1804)," *Bulletin de l'Institute Napoleon*, XLVIII (Juli, 1953), 65–72.

Lafargue, Andre. "Pierre Clement de Laussat, Colonial Prefect and High Commissioner of France: His Memoires, Proclamations, and Orders," *Louisiana Historical Quarterly*, XX (January, 1937), 159–182.

Lyon, E. Wilson. "The Directory and the United States," *American Historical Review*, XLIII (1938), 516–517.

Nasatir, A.P., and Ernest P. Liljegren, Eds., "Materials Relating to the History of the Mississippi Valley from the Minutes of the [Spanish] Supreme Councils of State, 1787–1797," *Louisiana Historical Quarterly*, XXI, No. 1 (January, 1938), 5–75.

Smith, Ronald D. "Napoleon and Louisiana: Failure of the Proposed Expedition to Occupy and Defend Louisiana, 1801–1803," *Louisiana History*, XII (Winter, 1971), 21–40.

Sprague, Stuart S. "Jefferson, Kentucky and the Closing of the Port of New Orleans, 1802–1803," *Register of the Kentucky Historical Society*, LXX (October, 1972), 312–317.

Whitaker, Arthur P. "The Retrocession of Louisiana in Spanish Policy," *American Historical Review*, XXXIX (April, 1934), 454–476.

———. "James Wilkinson's First Descent to New Orleans in 1787," *Hispanic American Historical Review*, VIII, No.1 (February, 1928), 82–97.

Books

Abernethy, Thomas P. *The Burr Conspiracy*. New York: Oxford University Press, 1970.

Ambrose, Stephen E. *Undaunted Courage. Meriwether Lewis, Thomas Jefferson, and the Opening of the American West*. New York: Simon and Schuster, 1996.

Bailey, Francis. *Journal of A Tour In Unsettled Parts Of North America in 1796 & 1797*. Edited by Jack D.L. Holmes. Carbondale: Southern Illinois University Press, 1969.

Barbé-Marbois, François. *The History of Louisiana, Particularly of the Cession of That Colony to the United States of America.* (1829). Edited with an Introduction by E. Wilson Lyon. Baton Rouge: Published for the Louisiana American Revolution Bicentennial Commission by the Louisiana State University Press, 1977.

Bemis, Samuel Flagg. *Jay's Treaty: A Study in Commerce and Diplomacy*, 1923.

——. *Pinckney's Treaty: America's Advantage from Europe's Distress, 1783–1800.* New Haven, CT: Yale University Press, 1965.

Blumenthal, Henry. *France and the United States Their Diplomatic Relations, 1789–1914.* New York: W.W. Norton, 1970.

Bolton, Herbert E. *The Spanish Borderlands: A Chronicle of Old Florida and the Southwest.* New Haven, CT: Yale University Press, 1921.

Brecher, Frank W. *Negotiating the Louisiana Purchase; Robert Livingston's Mission to France, 1801–1804.* Jefferson, NC: McFarland & Co., 2006.

Brown, Everett Somerville. *The Constitutional History of the Louisiana Purchase, 1803–1812.* Union, NJ: Lawbook Exchange, 2000.

Caughey, John Walton. *Bernardo de Galvez in Louisiana, 1776–1783.* Berkeley: University of California Press, 1934.

Charlevoix, Pierre François Xavier de. *Journal of a Voyage to North America.* Edited and translated by Louise Phelps Kellogg, 2 volumes. Chicago: The Caxton Club, 1923.

Chidsey, Donald B. *The Louisiana Purchase: The Story of the Biggest Real Estate Deal in History.* New York: Crown Publishers, 1972.

Clark, John G. *New Orleans 1718–1812. An Economic History.* Baton Rouge: Louisiana State University Press, 1970.

Clark, Thomas D. and Guice, John D.W. *Frontiers in Conflict: The Old Southwest, 1795–1830.* Albuquerque: University of New Mexico Press, 1989.

Coker, William S. and Rea, Robert R., Eds., *Anglo-Spanish Confrontation on the Gulf Coast During the American Revolution.* Pensacola, FL: Gulf Coast History and Humanities Conference, 1982.

Conrad, Glenn R., Ed., *Readings in Louisiana History.* New Orleans: Louisiana Historical Association, 1978.

Cox, Isaac Joslin. *The West Florida Controversy, 1798–1813.* Baltimore: John Hopkins University Press, 1918.

Cunningham, Noble E., Jr. *The Jeffersonians in Power: Party Operations, 1801–1807.* Chapel Hill: University of North Carolina Press, 1963.

——. *The Jeffersonian Republicans: The Formation of Party Organization, 1789–1801.* Chapel Hill: University of North Carolina Press, 1967.

——. *Jefferson vs. Hamilton: Confrontations that Shaped a Nation.* Bedford Series in History and Culture. Boston & New York: Bedford St. Martins Publishing Co, 2000.

Dargo, George. *Jefferson's Louisiana: Politics and the Clash of Legal Traditions.* Cambridge, MA: Harvard University Press, 1975.

DeConde, Alexander. *Entangling Alliance—Politics and Diplomacy under George Washington.* Durham, NC: Duke University Press, 1958.

——. *This Affair of Louisiana*. New York: Charles Scribner's Sons, 1976.

——. *The Quasi-War—The Politics and Diplomacy of the Undeclared War with France, 1797–1801*. New York: Charles Scribner's Sons, 1966.

Dubois, Laurent and Garrigus, John D. *Slave Revolution in the Caribbean, 1789–1804. A Brief History with Documents*. Boston: Bedford/St. Martin's, 2006.

Ellicott, Andrew. *The Journal of Andrew Ellicott, Late Commissioner On Behalf of the United States During the Year 1796, the Years 1797, 1798, 1799 And Part of the Year 1800: For Determining The Boundary Between The United States And The Possessions Of His Catholic Majesty In America. Containing Six Maps*. Philadelphia: William Fry, 1814.

Fleming, Thomas J. *The Louisiana Purchase*. Hoboken, NJ: John Wiley & Sons, 2003.

Foner, Philip S., Ed., *Basic Writings of Thomas Jefferson*. New York: Wiley Book Company, 1944.

Frank, Lawrence Owsley, Jr. and Smith, Gene A. *Filibusters and Expansionists: Jeffersonian Manifest Destiny, 1800–1821*. Tuscaloosa: University of Alabama Press, 1997.

Garrigus, John D. *Before Haiti: Race and Citizenship in French Saint-Domingue*. New York: Palgrave MacMillan, 2006.

Gayarré, Charles E. *History Of Louisiana*, 4 volumes. New Orleans: Pelican Publishing Company, 1965.

Geggus, David P., Ed., *The Impact of the Haitian Revolution in the Atlantic World*. Columbia: University of South Carolina Press, 2001.

Godoy, Manuel de. *Memorias del principe de la paz*, 2 volumes. Madrid, De. I Sandia, 1856.

Haas, Edward F., Ed., *Louisiana's Legal Heritage*. Pensacola, FL: Perdido Bay Press, 1983.

Hatfield, Joseph T. *William Claiborne: Jeffesonian Centurian in the American Southwest*. Louisiana History Series. Lafayette: University of Southwestern Louisiana Press, 1976.

Holmes, Jack D.L. *A Guide to Spanish Louisiana, 1762–1804*. New Orleans: A.F. Laborde & Sons, 1970.

——. *Gayoso, The Life of a Spanish Governor in the Mississippi Valley 1789–1799*. Gloucester, MA: Peter Smith, 1968.

Kaplan, Lawrence S. *Jefferson and France: An Essay on Politics and Political Ideas*. New Haven, CT: Yale University Press, 1967.

Kastor, Peter J., Ed., *The Louisiana Purchase: Emergence of an American Nation*. Washington, DC: CQ Press, 2002.

——. *The Nation's Crucible: The Louisiana Purchase and the Creation of America*. New Haven, CT: Yale University Press, 2004.

Kemp, John R. *New Orleans: An Illustrated History*. Woodland Hills, CA: Windsor Publications, 1981.

Kennedy, Roger G. *Mr. Jefferson's Lost Cause: Land, Farmers, Slavery and the Louisiana Purchase*. Oxford and New York: Oxford University Press, 2003.

Kukla, Jon, Ed., *A Guide to the Papers of Pierre Clement Laussat*. New Orleans: Historic New Orleans Collection, 1993.

——. *A Wilderness So Immense: The Louisiana Purchase and the Destiny of America.* New York: Alfred A. Knopf, 2003.

Labbe, Delores Egger, Ed., *The Louisiana Purchase Bicentennial Series in Louisiana History*, volume III. Lafayette: Center for Louisiana Studies, 1998.

Laussat, Pierre Clement. *Memoires of My Life to My Son During the Years 1803 and After, Which I Spend in Public Service in Louisiana in That Colony and for Its Transfer to the United States.* (1831). Edited with a Foreword by Robert D. Bush. Translated from the French by Agnes Josephine Pastwa, O.S.F. Louisiana Paperback Edition. Baton Rouge: Louisiana State University Press, 2003.

Lefebvre, George. *Napoleon, from 18 Brumaire to Tilsit. 1799–1807.* Translated by Henry E. Stockhold. New York: Columbia University Press, 1969.

Le Page du Pratz, Antoine Simone. *The History of Louisiana.* (1758), 3 volumes. Edited by Joseph G. Tregle, Jr. Published for the Louisiana American Bicentennial Commission from the 1774 English Edition. Baton Rouge: Louisiana State University Press, 1975.

Lewis, James E., Jr. *Louisiana Purchase: A Noble Bargain.* Charlottesville, VA: Thomas Jefferson Foundation, 2003.

Linklater, Andro. *An Artist in Treason: The Extraordinary Double Life of General James Wilkinson.* New York: Walker Publishing Company, 2009.

Lyon, E. Wilson. *Bonaparte's Proposed Louisiana Expedition.* Chicago: University of Chicago Libraries, 1934.

——. *Louisiana in French Diplomacy, 1759–1804.* Norman: University of Oklahoma Press, 1934.

——. *The Man Who Sold Louisiana: The Career of François Barbé-Marbois.* Norman: University of Oklahoma Press, 1942.

McDermott, John Francis, Ed., *Frenchmen and French Ways in the Mississippi Valley.* Urbana: University of Illinois Press, 1969.

——. *The French in the Mississippi Valley.* Urbana: University of Illinois Press, 1963.

——, Ed., *The Spanish in the Mississippi Valley 1762–1804.* Urbana: University of Illinois Press, 1974.

Malone, Dumas. *Thomas Jefferson*, 6 volumes. Charlottesville: University of Virginia Press, 2005.

Owsley, Frank Jr., and Smith, Gene A. *Filibusters and Expansionists: Jeffersonian Manifest Destiny, 1800–1821.* Tuscaloosa: University of Alabama Press, 1997.

Parsons, Edward Alexander. (Comp). *The Original Letters of Robert R. Livingston, 1801–1803, Written During his Negotiations of the Purchase of Louisiana. To Which is Prefixed: A Brief History of the Louisiana Purchase from Original Documents.* New Orleans: Louisiana Historical Society, 1953.

Peck, Renee, Ed., *Degrees of Discovery from New World to New Orleans.* Exhibition and Catalog. New Orleans, LA: Harvey Press, 1976.

Peterson, Merrill D. *Thomas Jefferson and the New Nation. A Biography.* New York: Oxford University Press, 1970.

Pitot, James. *Observations on the Colony of Louisiana from 1796 to 1802.* Translated from the French by Henry C. Pitot. Edited with a Foreword by Robert D. Bush. Baton Rouge: Louisiana State University Press, 1979.

Robertson, James Alexander. *Louisiana Under the Rule of Spain, France and the United States*, 2 volumes. Cleveland, OH: Arthur H. Clark, 1911.

Rodriguez, Junius P., Ed., *The Louisiana Purchase: A Historical and Geographical Encyclopedia*. Santa Barbara, CA: ABC-CLIO, 2002.

Saricks, Ambrose. *Pierre Samuel du Pont de Nemours*. Lawrence: University of Kansas Press, 1965.

Taylor, Joe Gray. *Louisiana: A Bicentennial History*. New York: W.W. Norton & Company, 1976.

Terrage, Marc de Villiers. *Les dernieres Années de la louisianae francaise*. Paris: Librairie Orientale et Americaine, 1903.

Whitakaer, Arthur Preston. *The Mississippi Question: A Study in Trade, Politics and Diplomacy*. Gloucester, MA: Peter Smith, 1962.

Wilkinson, James. *Memoirs of My Own Times*, 3 volumes. Philadelphia: Abraham Small, 1816.

Woodward, Ralph Lee Jr., Ed., *Tribute to Don Bernardo De Galvez*. (translated from the Spanish by Ralph Lee Woodward, Jr.,) Baton Rouge: Moran Industries, 1979.

Index